Noises fr  ...oom

One of the most urgent challenges of our times is to formulate a vision of the human being that unites the rigour of scentific understanding with the moral and spiritual depth of religious experience. Written with clarity and humour, Guy Claxton's *Noises From The Darkroom* is a major contribution to this endeavour.

Stephen Batchelor, author of
The Awakening of the West

Noises From The Darkroom leads the reader through many of the intricacies of contemporary biological and psychological science in language that is direct, witty, and masterfully alive to the importance of personal experience. By means of some skilful interweaving of this scientific material with insights drawn from various mystical traditions, Claxton conveys a powerful and timely message about the human predicament which rightly challenges many long-cherished notions about self and mind.

Brian Lancaster, author of Mind, Brain
and Human Potential

The most urgent questions for the twenty-first century concern the nature of the mind. Without such an understanding, human kind is heading for disaster. This lucid, wide-ranging and informative book offers many sensitive insights into the relationship between human consciousness and the physical and spiritual forces that underpin it. Trained in both psychology and meditation, there is no-one better suited to lead us on this essential voyage of discovery than Guy Claxton.

Dr Peter Fenwick
Chairman of the Scientific and Medical Network
Consultant Neuropsychiatrist,
The Maudsley Hospital, London

Noises from the Darkroom

The Science and Mystery of the Mind

GUY CLAXTON

Mystery, clarity, wisdom and compassion are fundamental characteristics of the biological system that we human beings consist of; characteristics that happen to have been obscured by a few bad habits that the mind has acquired on its evolutionary journey.

Aquarian
An Imprint of HarperCollinsPublishers

Aquarian
An Imprint of HarperCollins*Publishers*
77–85 Fulham Palace Road
Hammersmith, London W6 8JB

First published by Aquarian 1994

10 9 8 7 6 5 4 3 2 1

A catalogue record for this book
is available from the British Library

ISBN 1 85538 381 0

Printed in Great Britain by Mackays of Chatham PLC.

Our minds lie in us like fish in the pond of a man who cannot fish.

Ted Hughes

It is the impossible job of the mystic, if he wishes to try to teach what he knows, to scrute the inscrutable, speak the unspeakable, and eff the ineffable.

Alan Watts

Contents

PART IV: UNCONSCIOUSNESS REGAINED

Foreword

The human mind is mysterious in two fundamentally different ways. It is mysterious in the sense that we do not yet have a clear understanding of how it works. Penetrating this mystery is the job of science, and there is, currently, a flurry of very fruitful and exciting activity going on in laboratories and seminar rooms around the world. One of the aims of this book is to provide a reader-friendly synthesis of, and some novel contributions to, this research. The approach of 'cognitive science', as it is called, sees the mystery of the mind as a temporary fog of incomprehension which precise experimentation and smart theorizing will eventually dispel.

But the mind is mysterious in a much more profound and indelible sense—and this meaning of mystery is not scientific but religious. The great spiritual traditions of the world agree that a brush with God is a close encounter of an essentially mysterious kind. The more clearly we see, the more obvious it becomes that at the very heart of human experience there is an ineffable Something, greater by far than the human mind could ever, in principle, encompass. 'The peace of God passeth all understanding', and 'God moves in a mysterious way', not because we don't yet have enough data about the Almighty, but because He/She/It/They are fundamentally, intrinsically enigmatic. And that enigma, so the mystical explorers tell us, is not remote but present, accessible in every moment of mundane human experience. Thus the larger aim of this book is to bring these two meanings of 'mystery' into conjunction, and to show how science, by clarifying what it is to be a living human being, demands that we remember the invisible bedrock on which we are built. For our modern intuitive understanding of our own psychology leaves it out. And this oversight is not a matter of academic interest, but of vital personal and even global significance.

Not to put too fine a point on it, the world is in a mess because the human mind is in a mess. The problems we face are not at root

ix

technological, political or economic; they are psychological and spiritual. And the mind is in a mess because it misunderstands itself. We pollute the skies and ruin the earth because we are confused about who and what we are. It is because of our improper and unjust relationship with our own psychology that some of us plough up fields of good wheat while others of us are starving; some of us confess to murders that others of us have committed. Every culture lives within an invisible myth; and a central part of that myth, the most invisible of all, concerns human nature. Our culture has developed a particularly disastrous mind-myth, and while that myth remains unconscious and unexamined, we will continue to wreck the nest and hurt each other.

One of the symptoms of the mind's disease is that it will go to great lengths to examine every conceivable option except the right one. It will think endless new thoughts, but has extreme difficulty in scrutinizing that-which-thinks. The fundamental strategic problem of our time, therefore, is how to get individual minds, in sufficient quantities and with sufficient speed, to embark enthusiastically on the requisite process of demythologization—brain-washing, in the sense of laundering away our misconceptions, you might say. If cognitive science can demonstrate to rational minds how and why they have expurgated their own mystery, and what it has cost them to do so; if it can open our ears to the noises from the darkroom and make us wonder about them, then it will have proved itself valuable as well as merely interesting.

The science on which we have to draw is biological and psychological. Twenty years ago, the dialogue between science and religion was revitalized by the appearance of Fritjof Capra's classic *The Tao of Physics*, and since then there have been many attempts to account for the basic mysteries of human spirit and consciousness in terms of the fascinating concepts of cosmological and particle physics. But these accounts, it has turned out, while they offer intriguing metaphors and allegories, are not real explanations at all. Heisenberg's 'uncertainty principle', however powerful in the world of the atomic nucleus, tells us nothing of interest about the emergent properties of brains and minds—just as the study of liver disease in principle cannot explain the Nuremberg rallies.[1] Spirituality is a phenomenon of whole human beings embedded in their biological and social worlds, and it is therefore from the shores of brain science, evolutionary biology, and transpersonal psychology that we have to build out towards the far bank of mystery.

It is a pleasure to acknowledge some of the major bridge-builders in this area, whose masterly construction work has enabled me to reach out as far as I have. Not all of them will approve of the uses to which I have put their work, but without them it would not have been possible. There are the founders of systems theory, such as Ludwig von Bertalanffy, and Gregory Bateson with his famous search for 'the pattern which connects'. There are those who have forged links between religion (a word whose root meaning is itself 'to bind back together')—especially the Eastern traditions of Taoism, Hinduism and Buddhism—and forms of Western psychology: most notably Alan Watts and his 'dharma heir' Ken Wilber. More recently there are the pioneers of 'ecopsychology' such as Warwick Fox and Theodore Roszak. And then there are psychologists such as Nicholas Humphrey and Robert Ornstein, whose informed speculations about the evolution of mind and consciousness have contributed much to the development of my own thought. The fact that I have come to the conclusion that the origins of the unconscious are much more important than those of consciousness in no way detracts from my debts to them. Finally there are the cognitive scientists, whose bold ideas about the nature of brain, mind and self have contributed per-haps most of all to the story that I want to tell. I am thinking espe-cially of philosopher Daniel Dennett, and neuroscientists Gerald Edelman and Michael Gazzaniga. To all of these, and many others, my thanks for their building materials.

On a more personal note, I am most grateful to Jenny Edwards and Liz Puttick, my editor, both of whom read drafts of the book and made suggestions for improvement, the wisdom of which I could not deny. Thanks to Stephen Batchelor for sharing on many occasions his profound understanding of Buddhism. Though Buddhism as such hardly appears in this book, its insights permeate Parts II, III and IV.

Finally, a note on style. Because the web of ideas in this book is spun within a context of practical concern, I have endeavoured to write in an evocative, sometimes even jaunty, manner that will, I hope, engage both the general reader and the experts in the various fields on which I touch. Where this has meant throwing my more natural scholarly caution to the winds, I have done so. One of my draft-readers wrote to me: 'I can't remember ever having read another science book that made me laugh aloud!' I admit that comment pleased me almost as much as any learned approbation. In keeping with this attempt to treat weighty matters with a light touch, the referencing is minimal and illustrative rather than comprehensive—though if you wrote to me I could give you chapter and verse— and in the interests of good story-telling I have written as if I were propounding the absolute truth, rather than constructing a flexible, equivocal span of ideas.

Guy Claxton
Dartington, October 1993

1

Evolution of the Mind

ONE

Science and Mystery

The mind is far too narrow to contain itself. But where can that part of it be which it does not contain? Is it outside and not in itself? How can it be, then, that the mind cannot grasp itself? A great marvel rises in me; astonishment seizes me. Men go forth to marvel at the height of mountains and the huge waves of the sea, the broad flow of the rivers, the vastness of the ocean, the orbit of the stars, and yet they neglect to marvel at themselves.

St Augustine

Mind, *n.* A mysterious form of matter secreted by the brain. Its chief activity consists in the endeavour to ascertain its own nature, the futility of the attempt being due to the fact that it has nothing but itself to know itself with.

Ambrose Bierce

Pooh got up and began to look for himself.

A.A. Milne

The Overestimation of Consciousness

When people talk about something being 'second nature', they are referring to what seems natural, obvious, or habitual—common sense. It is the business of both scientific and religious enquiry (in their very different ways) to keep showing us how far this second nature misrepresents and oversimplifies '*first* nature': the reality of Nature and—more importantly in this book—Human Nature. We take our view of ourselves for granted. Yet what is second nature to us about ourselves is at least as suspect as our flawed intuitions about the natural world outside.

The two most vital ingredients of human nature, to which our 'second nature' does not do justice, are its mystery and its history. Instead of a core apprehension of the mystery we truly are, we have unwittingly constructed a bogus sense of self, full of hubris, that is closely identified with consciousness: so closely that we are no longer sensitive to the underlying, inaccessible layers and motions of mind, brain and body that form the moment-to-moment swell from which the breakers of consciousness emerge. It is as if we imagined that the drama of our lives were being played out on a brightly lit stage, oblivious to the wings, the dressing-rooms, the technicians, and all the invisible paraphernalia without which there could be no play.

We do not need to go back-stage, to know every detail of what goes on behind the scenes, in order to enjoy the production. But if we do not know, at some level, that there *is* a 'behind-the-scenes', then we confuse playing and reality. We become busy and anxious, forced to duck down in our seat when the villain pulls a gun, and to clamber on to the stage to rescue the heroine. When the mystery of the mind is unappreciated, people become compulsively drawn into the drama, as campaigners, insurers, money-makers and busybodies. When the dark surround is acknowledged, and the attempt to *control* everything is put in perspective, play is possible. God—or 'enlightenment', or the Tao—is essentially a sense of mystery; a mystery that is impenetrable, but entirely understandable. When Nietzsche wrote 'God is dead', he was declaring that humankind had lost its sense of mystery.

By identifying ourselves with a mobile pinprick of self-awareness, we overestimate the importance and the trustworthiness of the conscious mind, and we become out of touch with the invisible layers of brain and body on which it rests. This is unfortunate because while the modern conscious self is solitary, a candle in the night, the earlier evolutionary strata that continue to comprise the bulk of our being are ecological, connected, 'at home'. The surface of our skin and the end of our driveway are not the limits of our personal terrain; they form our connection, our joints, the points at which each 'member' of the human race is connected to the wider body of nature and society. If we do not 're-member' ourselves, we must continually strive to forge links of love (or, in desperation, domination) that are caricatures of what, in the mystery, is already, still, in place.

In the last three centuries, we have completed a complicated process of evolution, each individual step of which has helped us to survive, but which eventually has led us to lose our understanding of mystery, and with it our sense of wholeness, belonging and reverence. Consciousness has become the adopted seat of our identity. People nowadays do not just think a lot; they think that who they are is someone who is doing a lot of thinking. *Cogito, ergo sum.* We think that, if we do not notice something, it has no effect on us. We think that our deepest interests are served by pursuing those things that we are aware of wanting. We think that, if only we could figure things out carefully enough, most of life's difficulties could be smoothed out. We take our perceptions for granted, and think that what we think matters frightfully.

We have been taught by Descartes and his heirs to be ignorant of those aspects of human life that are not easily available to conscious inspection. We inhabit a world made up of consciousness, and what cannot enter into that world is None of My Business. How the blood gets round the body, by what alchemy a cauliflower is transmuted into human flesh and bone: these may be miracles—they can intrigue me, as a Black Hole or a Desert Orchid may intrigue me—but I feel a bystander, not a participant. I do not, except rarely (on occasions such as this), even become aware of *not* being aware of the millions of processes that sustain me and comprise me. We do not even bother to think of such things as unconscious.

And when we *do* think of 'the unconscious' we have been taught by Freud to associate it with the murky bits of the mind; those aspects of emotion and personality from which we shy away in fright or revulsion. The unconscious is 'The Little Shop of Horrors'; it is 'Where the Wild Things Are'. It is the cellar in which we put everything about ourselves that we have (or had) good reason to forget. It is selfish, infantile and embarrassing. It wants to shout 'I'M BORED', 'LET'S FUCK' or 'DON'T HURT ME'. If 'I', the conscious censor, were to let it, it might even erupt with hate or lust or sheer energy that would make me, the conscious me, think I was mad.

Creatures of Belief

Because we are creatures of belief, what we believe—without know-ing that we believe it—about our minds determines the reality we inhabit. It determines what we allow ourselves to see. It determines the goals we must pursue. It determines the laws we pass and the motorways we build and the forests we fell and the restaurants we frequent. Even the countryside, throughout vast areas of the world, is a monument to mind: a representation not only of what genera-tions have believed in and lived for, but of the view they have had of themselves—of their emotions, memories, thoughts and identities. Our 'folk psychology', woven out of landscape, language and a mil-lion subliminal events, forms the invisible filter through which we have to look as we look inward.

We do not see this filter because we see *through* it. It is the unac-knowledged background against which our mental life stands out in relief. We say 'You make me mad', without ever pausing to inspect the theory of emotion which this dubious claim demands. We say 'I'm sorry—I wasn't myself', without noticing what a curious view of personality is being implied. We say 'I changed my mind', without wondering who exactly it is that changed what (or what it was that changed whom). We try in our courts to decide whether a mass mur-derer is mad, only rarely doubting the sanity of the question itself.

The See-Through Mind

The cornerstone of contemporary folk psychology is the assumption that the mind is see-through: that when we look inward, through the window of introspection, we see what is there. We imagine the mind to be like a clock in a glass case, with all its important workings available for inspection by its one privileged owner. We think we know ourselves already, or could know ourselves if we chose, if not completely, then at least intimately and directly. This is the cardinal misconception, and its appreciation forms the starting point for the exposé with which this book is concerned.

Contrary to popular opinion, the human mind is a closed book. The room behind the eyes is forever dark. No access is possible, either by thinking or via the senses—for thoughts and experiences are the produce of this obscure factory, not glimpses of its operation. As with the manufacture of Cointreau or Tabasco, what goes on behind the scenes is a jealously guarded trade secret. All we get to do is taste the concoction; to the world of the concocter we are not privy at all. In the mind feelings are fabricated, thoughts are marshalled, perceptual pictures are painted. But of the painter and the engineer we have no idea.

Or rather, we can *only* have ideas. We think we are looking at ourselves through transparent windows. We think that consciousness gives us privileged access to our process and our nature: that the dark-room of the mind is light and airy, and our natural home. We think that the stories it tells about itself are true. Yet we are not looking through clear glass. We are looking at a screen on which some rather special products of the mind's activity are back-projected. Behind the screen there is a director producing a constant stream of interwoven films, one of which—one recurring theme—concerns the work of a director making a constant stream of interwoven films. As in Frederico Fellini's masterpiece 8½, we are not seeing the director at work, but only the director's partial and fictionalized view of a hypothetical director at work. We are invited to believe that the fictional and factual Fellinis are one and the same. But we have no right to do so, and we can never know the degree to which they really correspond—for the real Fellini remains always beyond the filmgoers' ken.

If the images that the mind created of itself were truthful—if the pictures projected onto the blind showed what we would actually see if the blind were raised—then nothing would be lost by mistaking one for the other. If appearance matches reality, the distinction becomes unimportant, indeed loses its meaning. But if the mind dissembles, then the consequences of *buying* its pronouncements may be more interesting, perhaps more serious. If the mind tells you that you are 5 feet 3 inches tall, and take a 14 inch collar, when you are really 6 foot and a 16, then you are going to bang your head on a lot of lintels, and buy a lot of clothes that leave you with cold ankles and restricted breathing. Like the man suffering from a perpetual headache, the only doctor who is going to be able to help you is the one who persuades you to buy bigger shirts.

Inside the dark-room, inscrutable though it is, are collected all the data and beliefs that give life its meaning and construct its purpose.

Buried there are the files that tell us how to be happy, who and what to care about, when to react and when to keep still; the programs that enable us to understand language, to record the past, to spin fantasies, and to tell the 'real' from the 'imaginary'. Manifesting indirectly, in attractions and expectations, spontaneous allegiances and solitary dreams, there are the casts of mind that tell us how to recognize a human being who will take care of us, or give us sexual pleasure; how to feel when Arsenal lose the Cup ('Ecstatic', 'Destroyed', 'What's "arsenal"? What "cup"?') And somewhere right at the centre of operations is the unarticulated specification of what it means to be a person: what kind of a being is a *human* being. From the frisson of an impulse buy, to the image of a Good Death, all is fashioned by the back-room boys and girls of the human mind.

Reasonable Doubt

There are three potential sources of information which could give us cause to doubt this picture: everyday experience, the reports of the mystics, and science. What about the many occasions on which we have suddenly 'come to', and realized that we have been carrying out complicated tasks requiring accurate perception, subtle action, and intelligent judgement—driving, say, or even walking along a crowded pavement—without any conscious knowledge or memory? While consciousness has been occupied with important affairs unconsciousness seems to have been coping very nicely on its own. What about the times when we have reacted instantaneously to a sudden event—a dog runs under the wheels, a fierce backhand from an opponent comes hurtling at your face—and before the conscious mind has even taken in what is happening the brakes are applied, or a winning volley is played? The excitement may be all over before consciousness comes puffing along with its self-centred commentary and its *post hoc* efforts to take the credit or shift the blame.

For 2,500 years at least there has been another source of evidence for the power of the unconscious: the writings of the mystics. As we shall see, they have couched their experiences in very different terms, drawing on whatever images were provided by their diverse cultures in their attempts to convey what they have seen. But time and again they describe their experience in terms of an abrupt shift in their relationship to the unconscious. Using theistic imagery, as most of them in the Western world were bound to do, they claim a direct encounter with a God who is, paradoxically, absolutely unknowable; whose being is to be found not in some remote heaven, but at a person's innermost core, prior to any form of knowing or conceptualization. From 'The Cloud of Unknowing' to Rilke's 'no matter how deeply I go into myself my God is dark', they agree that the most profound experience of truth is to be found by diving into the silent spring, the well-head, from which all consciousness arises. If you can but let yourself be sucked into the Black Hole at the centre of your being—if you can walk boldly into the darkroom—then an enormous weight of anxious, self-centred concern will drop away, and a light and kindly wisdom will immediately emerge to take its place.

Science

The third and most recent source of information about the nature of mind comes from science; not the questionable analogies that have been drawn between mysticism and the speculative world of sub-atomic physics, but the emerging, biologically based investigations of systems theory, human evolution and the new hybrid discipline, comprising psychology, neuroscience, philosophy and artificial intelligence, known as 'cognitive science'. What is emerging from this joint enterprise requires a startling reappraisal of the human mind; one which leads us to see the experiences of the mystics as no more and no less than a spontaneous 'correction' of the working of the brain.

Science is much revered, and equally maligned, at the present time, being seen as both villain of the ecological piece, and the only possible contender for the role of Saviour. Neither of these extreme reactions is justified, though each is true in part. It is true that the scientific world-view, by installing itself in our culture as the Only (Worthwhile) Epistemological Game in Town, has squeezed out of our minds other less explicit or articulate ways of knowing that are actually vital (as I shall argue in a moment) if we are to recover our 'basic sanity'. And it is true that science has fathered the most unspeakable inventions of all time. But it is also true that science has provided us with a most powerful and elegant set of ways of thinking about the physical and biological worlds, and that this framework has made possible the development of technologies (of housing, transportation, medicine, communication...you name it) that have genuinely improved the quality of life for millions of people.

And science, however prone to witting or unwitting abuse, offers a powerful method for 'sailing straight'; for getting our theories and assumptions to reveal their logical and practical conclusions, *whether they suit us, whether we like them, or not.* Common sense can happily and unwittingly sail round and round in circles, while convincing itself it is on a voyage of discovery. Rational thought by itself (contrary to its own Public Relations literature) is bound to follow the tracks laid down by our unconscious presuppositions, and being the servant of hidden dictates, its claims to objectivity are disingenuous. Science, for all its faults, though it zig-zags and falters, has the potential to help us to escape from the self-serving mental world of 'common sense'. The inexorable power of its method can force us to think what had previously been unthinkable: what we had been prevented from even considering by the unconscious habits of thought on which we had been relying.

One of the contemporary misunderstandings of science is that it will relentlessly sweep away religion, spirituality and mysticism, like a bulldozer in a rain-forest, leaving only the flat and open land of Pure Reason. Nothing could be further from the truth. The value of science is in its ability to expose the shortcomings of 'common sense', and thereby to enable cultures to *see*, and to improve, their own myths. (Philosophers, shamans, poets and mystics are the traditional 'scientists of the mind' in this sense.) And having drawn attention to a limiting assumption, science can offer in its place not the 'truth' (for science can only ever deliver theories) but a more workable myth: a better model of some aspect of life. A scientist may be led by her theories to ask a question that 'common sense' would never have thought of, and if it had, would have written off as ridiculous. And every so often, the reply to such a question will challenge received wisdom, and make us think.

For example, take the simple word 'see'. What could be more straightforward than the process of noticing what there is around, and acting in a way that takes account of what has been seen? Our common sense does not make a distinction between the conscious *experience* of seeing, and the more functional idea of 'registering' what is there, and incorporating that knowledge into our plans. It hardly makes sense to suppose that we could register anything if we could not 'see' it. Yet that is exactly what has been shown, by careful tests, to happen to patients who have suffered a certain kind of brain damage. They cannot 'see' anything in one part of their visual field, yet they can respond to questions in a way that they only could if they 'knew' what was there. They must be able to 'see', because they can act appropriately; yet they have absolutely no visual experience, and strongly deny that they 'saw'.

We can either mutter 'weird', and write this phenomenon off as another piece of psychological trivia; or we can ask what this does to our common sense, to our 'obvious' relationship to our own consciousness. Just how much interpreting and decision-making actually goes on *without* the intervention, or even the knowledge, of the Chief Executive? Is where 'I' am sitting really the seat of power, or am I just a puppet, fed not with high-grade intelligence but with a thoroughly expurgated version of events, and handing down edicts to which the unconscious company turns a collectively deaf ear?

The Miracle of Mindfulness

Scientific knowledge will not of itself correct the underlying faults in our inner-vision, any more than reading a textbook on optics will improve your eyesight. But it may well help us to understand and accept the diagnosis, and increase our willingness to seek a more powerful cure. For this we need more than rational understanding of the problem. We need methods for cleansing the 'doors of perception', and for these we shall have to turn back to the advice of the mystics again. They offer a bewildering variety of practices, but all share the view that wisdom arises not from more and more understanding, only through a personal programme of 'perceptual re-education'. Scientific demonstrations, and reasonable argument, may take us to the brink of this process, but it cannot take us any further.

All these varied 'technologies of transformation', if they are to have a lasting effect, rely on a single potentiality: mindfulness.[2] It is fortunate indeed that evolution has equipped us with a tool to effect this perceptual cleansing, for it would have been quite possible for humankind to have painted itself into a psychological corner from which there was no escape. At the end of every episode Batman used to appear to have got himself into a hopeless position...only for some trick or gadget to save him at the start of the next programme. Luckily we have up our sleeves a particular reflexive use of consciousness that can help us too to escape. In our case the traps are of our own devising, and consist of assumptions and beliefs, dissolved in the very way we see the world, which create apparent problems, and prevent us both from solving them, and from seeing that they are of our own making. Mindfulness involves cultivating the knack of making them visible, and of freeing ourselves from the power they exert to make us 'shrink to fit'.

In this 'cleansing of the doors of perception', as William Blake called it, the presence and the power of the unconscious is revealed. We cease being so *eccentric*, so displaced from our natural centre of gravity, and can relax into the unknowable heart. This, finally, is the revelation of divine truth: not a glimpse of any conceivable God, but a close encounter of an essentially mysterious kind. So spirituality, it turns out, resides in a simple correction of the brain—or perhaps we should say the 'world-body-brain-mind', as it becomes increasingly clear, as the story unfolds, that we cannot legitimately separate them from each other. Neuroscience, the scientific study of the brain and the nervous system, is now able to give us a working picture of the brain that can explain how mystical experience occurs, and why it takes the forms it does.

The mystics have talked of peacefulness and belonging, of wisdom and clarity, of an indiscriminate, impersonal love, of naturalness and simplicity, of *knowing*, without knowing what it is one knows, of a vivid and fiery quality to perception. Yet why just these qualities should appear together has itself been a mystery. Why should the body course with energy, and vision become luminous and penetrating, at the same time as one is suffused with tranquillity, understanding and compassion? The answer is to be found in the way the brain is built to work, and in the way its processes are corrupted by a small coterie of unrecognized beliefs (principally about the mind itself). When the 'Self System' is sidelined or short-circuited, the brain *instantaneously* reverts to a more basic *modus operandi*, of which what we call 'Buddha mind', or 'the grace of God', is the natural efflorescence.

Evolutionary Beginnings

But let us start at the beginning, with a résumé of the evolutionary history of humankind—a fuller version of which comprises the first part of this book—to orientate you. The twists and turns of our long evolution have bequeathed us a mind that, below the surface, is a curious tangle of abilities and limitations, strengths and weaknesses. It is not an instrument of elegant design, but a ramshackled raft, constructed out of a hodge-podge of materials, each of which happened to float by at a time then they could be used. If we could put the human mind in dry dock, take it to bits, and start again from scratch, we would never come up with the Heath Robinson contraption that has been handed down to us.

The vast majority of this mental raft—and the vast majority of its *intelligence*—lies below the surface. Conscious awareness arrived, in the course of evolution, probably with the evolution of active *hunting* as a method of catching food, and probably earlier and more clearly in species that were prey than those that were predators. And it emerged as a corollary of a particular kind of 'alarm reaction'. But with the development of social living, of language, and of the technology that could make life stable and relatively affluent, consciousness got appropriated by a variety of other systems within the mind, until today it has almost (but not quite) lost its original nature and purpose. In the detailed unravelling of this story, we can find an adequately complicated diagnosis of where and how the mind missed its way.

The mind is a specialized development of the brain, which is a specialized development of the body. The current myth of the body as a mobile pillar of meat piloted by an individual blip of conscious intelligence is false and harmful. Biology is telling us clearly that the body, with all its physical and psychological accoutrements, is a *system*, an intricate dance of processes and interactions that depends for its existence on continual penetration and perturbation by wider systems of which it is an inextricable part. The body 'knows' this; the brain 'knows' it; the mind 'knows' it. Only the self-conscious 'I', sitting atop this mountain of interdependency, denies and ignores it. When 'I' is switched off, the brain-mind immediately recalls what it had affected to forget. 'Ah yes,' it whispers to itself; 'I remember. I *belong*.'

If the essential mystery at the heart of human experience has somehow been squeezed out of the myths by which we are living, then science—twentieth-century empirical science—can re-mind us of this, just as powerfully as Mozart or meditation. 'The mind's new science', as Harvard psychologist Howard Gardner has dubbed it, is doing just that. It shows us that mysticism is necessary, and mystery is logical.

TWO

Body-Building:
The Origins of Life

Evolution is a change from a no-howish untalkaboutable all-alikeness to a somehowish and in general talkaboutable not-all-alikeness by continuous sticktogetherations and something-elseifications.

William James

We Do Not Compute

The pickle in which humankind currently finds (and loses) itself is due to the mind, and the mind is due to evolution. The conscious human mind cannot be understood just by looking at the way it is now. It is the tip of a vast evolutionary iceberg that has taken millions of years to form. As in all evolution, the later builds on the earlier; it can modify what went before, but it can never replace it. We have become so preoccupied with consciousness that we have forgotten the unconscious bulk below the surface. Minds are merely the software of the intricate biocomputers we call brains. And brains are the central organizing systems, the communications rooms, of high-tech bodily communities that have multiple goals and needs, and which live in environments that afford almost limitless opportunities. And all *this* is in aid of smart, tenacious, replicating molecules, who have it in their nature to persist and to breed. The abilities to solve crossword puzzles, to bungee-jump, and to have rows with our children are recent curiosities, balanced precariously atop a tower of earlier discoveries and developments.

Already, in this very first paragraph, I have slipped into using the most widely used metaphor for the brain-mind—the computer. And while in the most general sense 'computing' *is* what the brain-mind does, the analogy can be terribly misleading. Computers have no

15

intrinsic goals. The programs that tell the machinery what to do, and what to 'want' to do, arise not from an evolutionary source, but from the mind of the programmer. In the case of we human beings, however, the brain and its mind developed over millennia as tools for helping bodies, and the genes that designed them, to survive. Bodies are made of a kind of stuff that needs to keep trading, in a whole variety of different ways, with the world around it, if it is to persist. Computers can be left switched off for years and (all being well) will leap into action again, as if no time had passed at all, when they are next turned on.

Human beings and other animals grow and evolve. Computers get redesigned, sometimes from scratch. People need to eat to live. No computer has yet been discovered taking a bite out of its desk. There has been a film called *The Cars that Ate Paris*, but not yet one called *The Laptops that Ate IBM*. You can understand everything important about a computer by looking at it 'now'. You can understand very little about the human mind without investigating how it came to be. Computers can be built out of a variety of different materials, and they may end up doing very similar kinds of things. The operation of brains and minds is entirely dependent on the stuff of which they are made, and the worlds they and their ancestors grew up in.

Yet the conscious mind's view of itself downplays its evolutionary history, and its unconscious substratum, shamelessly. Part of the problem with the human brain-mind is that it has come to see itself as a kind of computer—without embodiment, without any history other than its own experience, without ecology. It has even come to identify only with what comes up on the screen of consciousness, and to ignore its own circuit boards and microchips. To straighten the mind out, it is necessary to remind it of its relationship to its brain, its body, its world and its 'unconscious'. That is where we have to start.

A Brief History of Slime

Let us briefly go back right to the beginning of life: to the primaeval ooze.[3] A very long time ago—4 billion years or so—there was no life; only an atmosphere containing simple molecules such as methane, ammonia, carbon dioxide, nitrogen and water vapour. There was no free oxygen, no ozone layer between the Earth and the sun, so powerful ultraviolet rays could enter the atmosphere unfiltered. Since Stanley Lloyd Miller's classic experiment in the early 1950s, it has been known that some at least of the basic molecular building blocks of life—the amino acids—can be produced by subjecting mixtures of these gases to the levels of ultraviolet radiation and the types of electrical discharge that would have been around in those early days. Simple chemical processes would have enriched the prehistoric broth to the point where it contained several of the necessary chemical ingredients of life.[4]

It is a long way, though, from simple proteins and sugars to the molecules and structures that are characteristic of all living systems, from amoebas to Buddhas. There are 200 or so of these essential 'molecules of life', and they collaborate with each other in such intricate and self-supporting ways that the whole structure of relationships on which life depends seems to hang together like a multi-dimensional archway—remove one piece and the whole thing collapses. And while some of them can be found in different brands of primordial soup, many of them, in order to be synthesized, seem to need exactly the kind of environment provided by the living cell—whose origins we are eventually trying to account for. We are faced with a classic 'Chicken and Egg' situation: in order to explain how cells were made, we seem to need to postulate the existence of cells!

There are a number of ingenious theories about how the bridge between simple molecules, and life, was built. Graham Cairns-Smith of the University of Glasgow has suggested that, just as an archway needs a temporary support while it is under construction, which can then be taken away when the arch is finished, so the first molecules of life were able to be synthesized and concentrated within the tiny cell-like cavities that are present in certain types of clay. Once these carbon-based molecules had formed their mutually supportive society, they were then able to kiss the clay goodbye.[5] However it happened, there emerged, amongst these molecules of life, the ones that were to serve as the powerhouse for the whole of evolution: the self-replicating molecule known as DNA. Each DNA molecule is like a long message, an instruction manual for making all the different constituents of living matter, written in an alphabet comprising only four letters. A simple bacterium needs a manual equivalent to about 1000 book pages to make it and keep it going. The 'library' needed to construct and run a human being, contained within the 46 chromosomes of every cell in the body, is equivalent to about a million pages. And, of course, each of these chromosomes is able to photocopy itself with incredible accuracy and elegance, whenever its parent cell divides.

Under the conditions that might have been expected 3,500 million years ago, amino acids have been shown to form into primitive cell-like structures. By 3,000 million years ago, cells had developed which were able to generate energy from light: they were capable of photosynthesis. As this process consumes carbon dioxide, and liberates oxygen gas, the composition of the atmosphere was slowly but radically changed. The development of the ozone layer meant further reductions in the amount of ultraviolet radiation penetrating through to the Earth's surface, and increasingly hard times for the original bacterial or *prokaryotic* cells. In order to take advantage of the changing conditions, much more complex kinds of cells developed— the *eukaryotic* cells, from which all multicellular species are derived. These basic building blocks of animal tissue are themselves comprised of collections of different kinds of simpler prokaryotes.[6] Each of our human cells, for example, contains *mitochondria*, which were originally completely independent little creatures. They still have their own DNA which is quite different from that contained within the nucleus of their adopted parent cells, yet have chosen to settle down and work as the energy factories of the cell in return for board, lodging and protection.

The first multi-cellular organisms began to appear on the Earth about 700 million years ago. The basic design of the animal body has over millions of years ramified into the galaxy of different species of which television nature programmes constantly remind us. But the fundamental specification has remained surprisingly constant. Just as city society has evolved in strikingly similar ways all over the world, so the body has come to delegate its necessary functions to a familiar repertoire of subsystems. Like a colony of ants, but more compact and sticky, cells cling together, throwing their lot in with each other, and contributing their specialized talents to the overall good of society, in the hope that 'All for One and One for All' will turn out to be a successful strategy.

For example, all bodies develop subsystems whose job it is to turn food into a usable form, transport it round the far-flung part of the empire, and deal with waste disposal. Some citizens roll themselves into a tube, the walls of which learn to weep lubricants that soften

the food and start the process of converting raw antelope or sun-
flower seeds into a usable nutritious juice. To make use of a greater
variety of raw materials, some of them quite tough, other brave citizens build themselves into hard white rocks at the entrance to the
tunnel, and crush the ore that passes between them. Constant supplies of fresh water are needed by the food processors, and the
development of a flappy pink proboscis helps to flip moisture into
the front end of the tunnel. While at the other end, sewage operatives divide the waste products into liquids and solids, and develop
short-term holding capacities, so that the garbage can be dumped
when it is safe, and smart, to do so. If you are evolving into a fish, it
does not matter too much if you leak as you go; but if you are on
your way to becoming a bird, you are at an evolutionary advantage
if you can learn the trick of not fouling the nest.

To work properly cells, like cars, need not only suitable liquid fuel
but air, so another subsystem evolves to extract the vital ingredients
of air and deliver them. The body grows an internal complex of
beaches, a vast coastline along which the air can continually lap,
and where chemicals can trap the precious oxygen. In order to maxi-
mize the vigour and intimacy of this contact, the enfolded coastline
develops into an internally-regulated bellows that constantly
exchanges used air with fresh. While inside the body there develops
an intricate network of canals that make Venice look like the Sahara
desert, again with a central pumping station that keeps the currents
flowing, and ensures that supplies reach every nook and cranny.

Ingestion is a crude process, and sometimes things get sucked in
at the front end of the tube that interfere with or threaten the
smooth workings of the community. Gradually some residents are
delegated to lookout duty, their task to discover, through evolutionary trial and error, how to predict by sight or smell or taste what is
wholesome and what it is better to avoid or spit out. But mistakes
are still made, and so other members of the commune are bred for
fighting, forming a territorial army that constantly patrols the system, riding shotgun on the precious supplies, detecting and over-
powering intruders and dissidents before they can throw a spanner
in the works. And this immune system has to develop the ability to
tell, with great accuracy, friend from foe, so that it does not inadvertently submit innocent but unrecognized members of its own family
to 'friendly fire'. Chilean neuroscientist Francisco Varela has shown
that these internal defenders of the community must possess, like the

Freemasons, an increasingly sophisticated repertoire of secret hand-shakes which will unmask the imposters—increasing because the ranks of the potential invaders are always changing, and their powers of penetration and impersonation are always growing.[7]

Unless the whole body is fortunate enough to find itself rooted in the Promised Land, where abundant supplies of milk and honey naturally and continually drift into the open end of its tube, it may well discover the advantages of arms and legs. With arms (and especially with hands on the ends of them) that are hooked up to your lookouts, you are able to reach out and grab passing morsels that would not otherwise have fallen into the top of your tube. (A long sticky tongue that you can aim and flick does the same trick.) Legs expand your hunting ground even further, as well as enabling you to take some evasive action when you find that you have unwittingly strayed into someone else's. Both attack and escape are hit and miss affairs, of course, and it will have taken hundreds of generations, and many of its great uncles starved or eaten, to get to the point where any animal is as skilled as it is. And each species is of course never a finished product, but just one snap-shot of the continually unfolding evolutionary drama.

What is Evolution?

It will be obvious that I am assuming the general validity of an enlightened neo-Darwinian view of evolution. There may have been a few amino acids or simple proteins that arrived on the earth via meteorites, and these may even have helped to kick-start the evolution of self-replicating molecules. But within a scientific context we are not yet obliged to take seriously such imaginative fancies as the arrival of fully-fledged life-forms from other planets, or the guiding hand of a Cosmic Architect in whose eyes humanity is the highest pinnacle of Creation. To a shark, a beaver, a cockroach or a bacterium, it must also look as if *they* are the target towards which evolution has been unerringly aimed, and the species for whom the world has been designed.

The increasing complexity of the living world is real enough, but any 'intention', any overall 'design' or 'purpose', can only be conceived, and projected backwards into history, with the benefit of hindsight. We can say, in general, that it is in the nature of a world that contains self-replicating entities subject to the developmental constraints of natural selection, that things are going to diversify, become more intricate, colonize more inhospitable habitats, and develop greater flexibility in the face of environmental change; but how that is going to pan out would be in (if there were any) the laps of the Gods. As Graham Cairns-Smith puts it: 'What does happen in evolution depends so much on particular circumstances that the course of evolution over the long term is about as predictable as the meandering form of a river or the exact shape of tomorrow's clouds: one can only illustrate possibilities and indicate general expectations.'[8]

The course of true love between species and habitat never runs smooth for very long, however, because the incumbents themselves are changing the environment—using up resources, creating waste, building nests or commuter towns. And other tribes or other species are learning new tricks that will keep you on your evolutionary toes. Gradual changes of cooling or warming are happening on a local or a planetary scale. Huge lumps of flying rock—meteorites, or more likely, comet showers—occasionally land in your back garden. And so on. As Cairns-Smith goes on to say: 'Any theory that is to explain the variety and complexity of living things must also take into account the varied and varying challenges sat up by a varied and varying environment. Nature, as breeder and show judge, is continually changing her mind about which types should be awarded first prize.'[9]

Another vital constraint on evolution is its inability to subtract. It is never possible for evolution to reconsider an earlier 'decision' in the light of subsequent experience. Each step can only modify the existing gene-pool; it can never rub it out and start again. A favourite example of Stephen Jay Gould's is the giant panda, a beast that is evolved from carnivorous stock, yet now has a vegetarian lifestyle. The carnivore's paw comprises five equivalent fingers or toes, and has no 'thumb', as the primates do, which can move independently of the fingers to provide a powerful grasp or a precise grip. Yet this is just what the panda now needs; its diet requires it constantly to strip the leaves from young bamboo shoots—a job for which an opposable thumb would have been ideal. Trapped by its pre-set evolutionary trajectory, the best the panda can do is develop a clumsy pseudo-thumb out of one of its fingers. As Gould says: 'If

God had started from scratch to construct a panda to eat bamboo he would have built it differently...The world is full of these imperfections, and they record the path of history'.[10]

Just as the path of evolution is littered with these awkwardnesses, so is it full of serendipity. Structures, faculties and behaviours arise as an 'answer' to a local 'question', and then may turn out to have more potential than met the original eye—or, to take a different sense, the tongue. This may have originally evolved as part of the drinking mechanism, as a device for moving food around in the mouth, as the prime site of the taste buds, or as part of the apparatus for making sure that the intake of food and air do not get muddled up. It probably did *not* originally develop as part of the Fur Insulation System of the ancestors of the cat family. Yet, once in existence, it came, opportunistically, to play an important role in keeping the fur clean. Dirty, matted fur insulated much less well, and the job of keeping it clean may well have stimulated the tongue to become rougher, in order to make a better brush. But such a development would have only have been 'allowed' to the extent that it enabled the tongue to continue to play its role as part of the Food Processing System.[11]

Other species have capitalized on the tongue in different ways. Dogs use it to help reduce body heat by panting, while human beings, in certain cultures, use it for exactly the reverse purpose—as an essential component of the Sexual Arousal System. Not to mention the fact that without it we would all be speaking in sign language, and there would be no singing. As I shall argue later, we can only understand the evolution of *consciousness* if we look at it in the same way. What it is and what it does *now* have to preserve the function for which it was first evolved. But there have been so many twists and turns to the evolutionary tale since then that this original function has become quite obscured by later developments.

Contrary to popular belief, natural selection does not pit every individual against each other in a 'Nature red in tooth and claw' kind of way. If cooperation helps individuals to stay alive long enough to breed, and to increase the chances of their genes, through their offspring, surviving, well and good. Neo-Darwinism is quite at home with the principle of *enlightened* self-interest; in fact cooperation and collaboration both within and between species are turning out to be the rule rather than the exception. Sophisticated flowers make nectar for the bees, but they also make sure that their visitors leave with a good blob of pollen on their backsides. Big fish allow little fish to clear up their leftovers (without the tiddlers fearing that they themselves are on the menu) provided they floss their host's teeth while they are about it.

The balance between 'selfish' and 'altruistic' behaviour emerges as a pragmatic issue of genetic survival long before it surfaces as a moral question or a cultural concern. Indeed there may still be within human beings a biological morality which we have, in our enchantment with consciousness and spoken language, forgotten; which our explicit ethical codes are a poor substitute for; and which it might be possible, if we were to relocate our personal centres of gravity, to re-experience. At the very least the neo-Darwinian theory of evolution advises us to keep this an open question.

THREE

The Plastic Brain

Every civilised human being, whatever his conscious development, is still an archaic man at the deepest levels of his psyche.
Just as the human body connects us with the mammals and
displays numerous relics of earlier evolutionary stages going
back even to the reptilian age, so the human psyche is likewise
a product of evolution which, when followed up to its origins,
shows countless archaic traits.

C.G. Jung

'Organism'...means a self-regulating system of processes tend-
ing to maintain themselves, i.e. to maintain the life of the individual or species. But the processes of the organism do not of
themselves maintain life; without the continuous influence of
the environment the internal organic processes cannot sustain
life for more than a moment, their tendency being to break
down organic material towards more stable states.

Lancelot Law Whyte[12]

Bodies as Systems

One of the most remarkable and pervasive characteristics of the
genetically designed body, throughout the animal kingdom, is the
extent to which it retains its form despite the continual interactions
with a changing world. This property has recently been highlighted
by Chilean scientists Humberto Maturana and Francisco Varela, who
refer to it as 'autopoiesis', or 'self-organisation', though it was
remarked upon as long ago as 1937 by Sir Charles Sherrington in his

Gifford Lectures *Man on His Nature.*[13]

> Life is an example of the way an energy-system, in its give-and-take with the energy-system around it, can continue to maintain itself for a period as a self-centred, so to say, self-balancing unity. Perhaps the most striking feature of it is that it acts as though it 'desired' to maintain itself. But we do not say of the spinning of a heavy top which resists being upset that it 'desires' to go on spinning. The very constitution of the living-system may compel it to...[14]

And it follows that:

> Life as an energy-system is so woven into the fabric of the Earth's surface that to suppose a life isolated from the rest of that terrestrial world even briefly gives an image too distorted to resemble life. All is dove-tailed together.[15]

Animals do not exist by 'being'; they exist by *happening*. An animal is not like a coffee mug, which was once made and now can be full or empty, warm or cold, sitting on the table or hanging from its hook, but basically the same 'thing', constituted of the same stuff, and continuing to be so until it breaks. An animal is like a whirlpool; it derives its relative stability, and even its form, from its *motion*, and it is only kept moving through its interactions with the wider system of which it is part. Try to take the vortex home in a bucket and you will be disappointed. Disconnect an animal from its 'life support systems' and it too begins to lose its form and fall apart into constituents that are simpler, more independent of one another, more *dead*.

There is nothing very mysterious about this view. It only needs stressing in the context of a lopsided scientific tradition which has taught us that the *only* way to know something properly is to take it to pieces, and study those exhaustively. This analytic, reductionistic approach works well in some areas of enquiry, most notably in the inorganic worlds of physics, chemistry and geology. But if you pull an animal to bits, whether literally or conceptually, it dies. It loses the integrity, the interwovenness that is its central defining characteristic. And it loses the form that only emerges as a result of this interwovenness.

The Inner Web

To understand the body, and all the complicated psychological harmonies that have been overlaid on this basic physical melody by evolution, we have to remember its essential embeddedness in the wider system of the world. But we also have to pay attention to the fine details of its internal make-up. An animal is composed of inner systems that are interlaced so finely that they too cannot exist, or be comprehended, simply as a collection of parts. No subsystem of an animal stands alone; the heart, the lungs, the stomach and the kidneys only make sense in terms of each other. You can look at their tissues separately under a microscope, and describe their structure. But if you want to get very far in explaining what they *are*, you will find that the boundaries between them rapidly dissolve.[16]

The same applies to the way animals behave. We have to see them as much in terms of inner co-ordination as of differentiation. Even a very small and simple creature has to keep track of three crucial aspects of its world: what, at the moment, it *needs*, or needs most; what opportunities the world is currently affording (as revealed by its stock of *sensibilities*); and what it is capable of doing, its repertoire of possible *responses* to differing combinations of desires and opportunities.

If your powers of perception are extremely limited—say to the concentrations of one or two nutrients in the stream you live in—and your needs are mercifully few—for example, that the levels of concentration of these nutrients are neither too weak nor too strong, and your actions are limited to orienting yourself in one direction rather than another (so that you can keep facing upstream), and opening and closing your pores...if you are as simple as that, then it makes sense for the connections between need, opportunity and capability to be clearly and unambiguously specified, so you do not have to worry about what to do next. You are a simple little soft machine, with reflexes that work to keep you alive, as long as your food keeps coming and your pores do not clog up. You are well adapted to a world that varies only within the limits that you are capable of responding to, and when it gets too hot or too cold, too dry or too salty, or when a family moves in next door that has things like you on its menu, then you have not got a clue what to do, and you and your kind are in trouble.

But our animal forebears rapidly grew to be more complicated than this, in almost every possible way. First, their physical structure is larger, and certainly more differentiated. They have specialized organs, each of which confers a range of new perceptual and behavioural abilities, and they found ways of moving about: using fins or wings or tails or legs. Their world comprises more needs (as each internal organ requires particular conditions to be able to work), and certainly more sensibilities and more capabilities. If you can see and smell and run around, life gets more interesting.

Now the perennial problem of *prioritization*, the question 'What do I do next?', is no longer a trivial one, and simple reflexes will not do. There are too many shifting contingencies for that to work. You need some sort of information system that will provide a way of letting the eye and the legs know what the stomach needs, and of letting the stomach know what is on the menu, so that it can lay the table with the right kinds of cutlery and condiments. You will be handicapped, in other words, if you are not able to co-ordinate the different aspects of your insides with each other, and to co-ordinate your system as a whole with the shifting kaleidoscope of threats and opportunities that are round about you. The price that any society pays for specialization is the need for internal communication—and the more complex the community, the more sophisticated its communication, both internally and externally, needs to be.

Walkie-Talkie

In simple multicellular creatures, a nervous system that keeps the different subsystems directly in touch with one another will do well enough. They can talk to each other by CB radio, without having to invest in any central administration. The Portuguese man-of-war, for example, is technically speaking not a single creature but a large sticky conglomerate of interdependent organisms who have decided to throw in their evolutionary lot with each other. Some of these are specialized for floating and providing buoyancy. Others engage in collecting and digesting of food, or in sensing different forms of incoming energy (who can tell by the stimulation of the water whether there is anything interesting in the vicinity, and if so whether it is likely to be a meal or an enemy). Others specialize in mounting guard and manufacturing ammunition for the poisonous tentacles. And others in planning and preparing for reproduction. This colony manages to co-ordinate its complicated set of senses, activities and needs without any central information point, or sophisticated nervous system, simply by enabling various sensory and response subsystems to talk directly to each other.[17]

Beyond a certain degree of complexity, however, this point-to-point form of communication begins to become cumbersome and inadequate. The system as a whole needs to be able to hold 'conference calls', as well as allowing each department to talk directly with one another. So evolutionarily there is a move towards greater 'networking' between the different systems, and eventually towards some kind of centralization—an office, like that which controls a fleet of taxicabs, which can keep an overview of what is going on, and co-ordinate the different activities. And at this point the distributed nervous system begins to develop into a 'central nervous system', the CNS. Not that there has to be any controller who sits in the 'head office', deciding what is best. The design of the animal CNS, and ultimately of its brain, as we shall see, is such that this kind of centralized decision-making about what is best for 'all-of-me', can be conducted very well by a communication system that is wired up in clever ways, so that the wiring itself determines how choices are made. No ghost in the machine is required.

Getting Around

One of the evolutionary moves that must have stimulated the development of the first brains was mobility: the discovery of the advantages of being able to get about. Couple mobility with a sensory system, and you are able not just to close your mouth and hold your breath when something nasty comes along, but to get out of the way. You are not dependent on what the stream happens to be serving that day; if you don't like it you can go and see what is available at the restaurant across the road. But there are also inherent questions and problems associated with being mobile. Do you become nomadic, of no fixed abode, or do you have a home that you return to each evening after a hard day running about chasing things? Either way there are pros and cons.

If you were a tunicate—a sea squirt—for example, you would have opted for an interim solution. The young sea squirt is a tadpole-like larva that possesses a primitive brain, which can be informed about what is going on by an organ of balance (such as we humans have in the middle ear), and a simple eye. It is equipped to navigate its way through changing aquatic conditions whilst engaged in a process of once-and-for-all house-hunting. When it finds its ideal home, the sea squirt gratefully settles down for life, and turns itself back into a plant by the simple expedient of eating its now redundant brain. (It has been suggested that this behaviour parallels that of university academics on finally obtaining a tenured appointment.)[18] We might also note, to anticipate later discussions, that the issue of what to do with a brain that has evolved to a level of power that is out of all proportion to the current survival demands—when a species finds that, for a while, it has 'got it made'—is one that bears on the contemporary situation of *homo sapiens*. Eating a good chunk of the brain seems a solution to the problem that it might pay us to consider.

Sophistication and The Proliferation of Needs, Part 1

The major components of the mammalian survival kit are sometimes (rather coarsely) referred to as the Four F's—flight, fight, feed and mate—in approximately that order of urgency.[19] If a predator appears, make yourself scarce. If you are cornered, or are trapped by the over-riding need to defend territory or young, stand your ground and see them off. When it is safe enough to do so, turn your energies back to the perennial search for sustenance. And if these other claims are assuaged for the moment, and the time is ripe, let your fancy lightly turn to thoughts of procreation. Each of these general departments ramified into elaborate rituals, and intricate signalling systems evolved to get these survival jobs done with the minimum of risk and inconvenience.

As the nervous system, and the body that it serves, grows in complexity, so the behavioural repertoire gets broader and subtler, and the sophistication with which different actions can be selected for different contingencies gets higher and higher. But at the same time, the vulnerability of the creature also increases. Sophistication aids survival, but it also calls into being new *threats* to survival. The more intricate a machine, the more ways there are in which it can break down. Choosing the evolutionary path of becoming high-tech means that the basic drive to survive and reproduce fragments into dozens of secondary and tertiary priorities.

For example, the more delicate your constitution, the more things there are that might upset you, or even kill you, if you ingest them by mistake. So your appetites, and sense of taste and smell, need to develop to provide an adequate level of protection. (And if you live in an environment that teems with chemicals that have not co-evolved with you, and so there has not been the evolutionary time for knowledge of their risks and benefits to be incorporated into your preferences and aversions, you will be at risk, especially from those chemicals that are harmful in the long term—which decrease your fertility, for example—but which produce no short-term effect for you to learn from.)

If you have evolved a skeleton to support a big body, you are at risk from breaking bones. The more delicate your bits, the more carefully wrapped they have to be. If you developed a circulation system to carry oxygen to all those cells who work deep in the liver-mines, then they, and all the other underground workers, are at risk from any passing cloud of molecules that happen to bond more strongly to haemoglobin than oxygen does. If you grew lungs to get the oxygen into the right sort of contact with the blood, you can be beaten at your own game by a virus that makes the lung surface weep thick mucus, so that, like fish who drown when oil is spilt on the surface of their pond, you are disconnected from your vital power source.

If you have developed fast legs that enable you to outrun preda-tors (rather than sharp teeth to see them off, and thick skin to mini-mize the danger of being punctured in a fight), you have to be able to see them coming, and are therefore vulnerable to twilight and cataracts. And if you have evolved an immunological secret police, who recognize and execute any enemies who have infiltrated the palace, you become all the more vulnerable when they go on strike, or worse, when they run amok and start attacking honest citizens (or each other).

Each new threat constitutes another priority that the system as a whole has to take into account in planning its next move. Any course of action is liable to disruption before it is complete. A snake may suddenly appear, or the urge to defecate slowly grow, and the response to each has to take into account the other priorities, the opportunities currently afforded by the world, and the range of available options for action. Should I stop chasing that gazelle and pay attention to the pain in my foot? Can I safely take a nap here, or should I wait till I get home? Am I likely to find a familiar snack on the way, or should I eat these berries now, even though they taste a bit funny? The more diverse your portfolio of requirements, the more you need a brain to keep track of them all; to register the competing claims for attention and action, and come up with a good guess as to what the system as a whole is best advised to do next.

Neural Webs

The brain is a focus for the co-ordinating aspect of the body, just as the intestines are the main centre for digestion, or the legs of loco-motion. But if you want to understand digestion or locomotion fully, you will have to take a systems view, and understand the role of the jaws, and of exercise, in digestion; or of the lungs and the spine in mobility. Just so, the brain plays a central part in integrating processes *but the processes are themselves essentially bodily.* 'Mind' is an aspect of an animal that is distributed throughout the body— even though some facets of 'mind' are most closely associated with the nervous system. The unit of intelligence of an animal is its body, not its brain, just as the unit of 'music-making' is the orchestra, not the conductor. If the orchestra is big, and the music intricate, the conductor's role is all the more important. But he never transcends his role as a valued member and servant of the musical collective. He never becomes a dictator.[20]

For example the immune system is usually discussed in relative isolation from the CNS. However, some interesting recent research has revealed how 'brain-like' the immune system actually is, and has explored the ways in which CNS and immune system continually talk to each other. A class of messenger molecules from the peptide family has been shown by Candace Pert and others to mediate between the neural and immune systems, and thereby to co-ordinate, and effectively integrate, them. She goes so far as to say that: 'White blood cells are bits of brain floating around the body.'[21] Francisco Varela has referred to the immune system in a recent paper as 'the second brain', and has argued that the secret handshakes that enable the antibodies to recognize 'friend' from 'foe' also act as the basis for the body's overall sense of identity. The immune system, like the CNS, is primarily a communication system, he argues; one which subserves the vital bodily feeling of 'family'.[22]

By taking an evolutionary perspective, we are forcibly reminded of the extent to which intelligence is a bodily, not purely (or even mainly) a mental, phenomenon. And just as most of the workings of the body are 'dark' to us, beyond the reach of conscious introspection, so we may begin to open up the question of how much of what we have thought of as our 'intelligence', our 'cognition', is also inaccessible to the conscious mind. Perhaps intelligence does not reside in consciousness. Perhaps consciousness no more shows us the workings of the mind than a television picture shows us the workings of the television.

Plastic Brains

No amount of genetic adaptation can prepare you for the unpredictable. The world is always liable to change in unprecedented ways, and the animal that is not completely pre-set, but which comes with the facility to tune itself to new environmental frequencies as they come on air, has a head start over one that was built on the assumption that its world would last for ever. The ability of an individual to learn a new pattern, and a new trick to cope with it, is one of the most amazing discoveries of evolution, but it needs, if it is to work, adequate resourcing.

This is the second good reason for having a brain. A nervous system intricate enough to co-ordinate a wide range of pressures and resources makes a good basis for the next great evolutionary jump: incorporating a degree of flexibility into these interconnections, so that the way they are wired up can (within limits) respond to the success of the system in promoting the individual's (and her children's) survival. If it is useful to be born knowing what to do when you see a snake, it is even more useful to be able to record the kinds of situations in which you personally have met snakes before, and to be able recognize a fresh trail, and the distinctive way the grass moves. From the point of view of this book, the brain will be the most interesting of the body's intelligent subsystems precisely because it is the one that is tuned so comprehensively by experience—and therefore by culture. Muscles and antibodies too are affected by what happens to them, but to nothing like the same extraordinary extent.

The Brain's Priorities

The brain is the centre where information gathered by the rest of the nervous system, about the state of things both inside and outside the body, is collated and integrated. It is the 'General Communications Head-Quarters' of the body. Information continually arrives along all the neural pathways, coded as patterns of electrical impulses. The eyes, ears, tongue and nose bring news of what is happening off-shore. Internal monitoring stations tell of the level of blood sugar, the fullness of the bladder, the oxygen/carbon dioxide balance in the lungs, the acidity of the gastric juices...and a hundred other indices of the well-being, or the imminence of required action, in different parts of town. The lookouts have just sighted something—is it the long-awaited supply of fresh meat, or is it that marauding pirate? The miller has more corn to grind than he can cope with: is the store-house full or not? The garbage disposal operatives say it is time to take a dump. The power-station workers are complaining because they have missed their tea-break....All these different 'interests' make claims on the attention and orientation of the community as a whole. Cases must be heard, priorities decided, less urgent needs postponed, plans of action prepared.

For example, receptors in the skin, the joints and the muscles tell of aches and pains, pricks and tickles, and update the story about where the limbs are, so that when you need to move, perhaps in an emergency, you already have information about where 'here' is, and can therefore compute the arm movement required to get from 'here' to 'there'. A baby reaching for a toy makes a 'ballistic swipe': it throws out the hand like a harpoon fired from a ship. If the toy is moved after the movement is started, there is nothing she can do to correct the movement in mid-air. But an older child, whose monitoring of body states and dynamics is more develo[ ]d, can change the direction of reach immediately. Her hand is now not a simple projectile but a toy-seeking missile, locked on to the target in a much more subtle and responsive fashion. She has learnt how to link the sight of the toy, the sight of her arm, the feel of the arm as it is moving, and the muscular commands that control the arm movement, in a flexible way.

In this chapter I have explained the evolutionary value of plastic brains, and illustrated some of the different jobs that they may be called upon to do. And we have seen how the design function of a brain gets more complicated as the sophistication and differentiation of its body increases. We have developed an overview of what the brain *does*. But in order to understand it in more detail, we need also to be able to talk about what it *is*: what it is like, and *how* it does what it needs to do in order to fulfil its role. This is the subject of the next chapter.

FOUR

The Self-Organizing Organizer

The cardinal background principle for the theorist is that there are no homunculi. There is no little person in the brain who 'sees' an inner television screen, 'hears' an inner voice, 'reads' the topographical maps, weighs reasons, decides actions and so forth. There are just neurons and their connections. When a person sees, it is because neurons, individually blind and individually stupid neurons, are collectively orchestrated in the appropriate manner...In a relaxed mood we still understand perceiving, thinking, control and so forth, on the model of a self—a clever self—that does the perceiving, thinking and controlling. It takes effort to remember that the cleverness of the brain is explained not by the cleverness of a *self* but by the functioning of the neuronal machine that is the brain...In one's own case, of course, it seems quite shocking that one's cleverness should be the outcome of well-orchestrated stupidity.

Patricia Churchland[23]

Since man is above all future-making, he is, above all, a swarm of hopes and fears.

J. Ortega y Gasset

Brain-Mind Language

If we talk about the workings of minds in the language of common-sense, we can consider the kinds of important, human things that we want to consider—hopes, fears, aspirations, experience. But in doing

35

so we have to take the concepts of everyday language on trust. If there is something *wrong* with the assumptions about the mind that are built in to these categories and idioms, no amount of vernacular talk will reveal it. Our familiar 'mind-language' is too suspect; if we rely on it we may be inadvertently begging the most crucial questions.

On the other hand 'brain-language', the neuroscientists' vocabulary of neurons and synapses, enzymes and axons, is not up to the job either. It may be 'sounder' in some ways, but it is simply too low level, too fine-grain, to enable us to discuss the issues we need to discuss. Human beings are *systems*, and one of the things this means is that they have properties at 'higher' levels of organization that are not predictable or explicable in terms of the properties of 'lower' levels. At each level of discourse one needs a new language for talking about 'wholes', a language which builds on the language of 'parts', but which can say things that the language of parts cannot.

(This incidentally is the reason why currently fashionable attempts to talk about, or worse to 'explain', *consciousness* in terms of the language and phenomena of quantum physics—or any other kind of physics, come to that—are nothing short of ridiculous. While claiming to be based in 'new paradigm' thinking, they are in fact reductionism *ad absurdum*. The parallel between the (presumed) 'free will' of human beings and the 'indeterminacy' of fundamental particles is of no more interest or significance than a pun like Thomas Grey's 'They went and told the sexton, and the sexton toll'd the bell'. It is the basis of a cheap joke, not of a serious intellectual conversation. The sciences of nuclear physics, chemistry, biochemistry, genetics, neurophysiology, cognitive psychology, sociology, anthropology and cosmology are distinct, and hierarchically arranged, for very good reasons. Each attempts to find the best language for talking about a particular level of organization within the cosmic system as a whole, and to do so it must pay attention to what the people working in the next layer up and the next layer down are also saying. But to jumble up the language of quarks and the language of consciousness is just conceptual vandalism.)

To talk of the brain is to talk in a dialect that is vital to builders—brick-laying and plumbing, foundations and joists—but which is quite unequal to the needs and interests of an interior designer, who uses a vocabulary of spaces, functions, aesthetics and style; a language of human purpose and desire. 'Brain' is builder language for one specialized part of the body. 'Mind' is designer language for the functions that the brain carries out.

An architect needs to be bi-lingual: she has to be able to talk to both electricians *and* designers in the language that is appropriate to the concerns and problems of each. One of the main assumptions on which this book rests is that we need to be architects in order to stand a chance of getting an adequate overview—let alone a comprehensive understanding—of how human beings work. We need at times to be able to talk the language of human beings' fears and aspirations; at others to see what understandings are offered by the construction of the brain; and at times to be able to explore the traditional concerns of one in the language of the other. Just as new materials make possible creative solutions to old design problems, so cognitive science is making available ideas that give a new purchase on the perennial issues of 'la condition humaine'. We have reached the point in our discussion where we begin to need to introduce 'brain-mind language'.

There are about 100 billion neurons in the average brain, so densely interconnected that there is a potential pathway that can be found between any two. Our intermediate-level brain-mind language has to respect what we know about the brain, but reduce this massive complexity into an image or a model that we can use to talk about the actions, needs and experiences of sophisticated animals. Over the last fifteen years or so brain researchers have revived a level of modelling first developed by Canadian neuropsychologist Donald Hebb back in 1949, in his classic book *The Organisation of Behaviour.*[24] Hebb's achievement was to devise a way of thinking about the brain that was faithful to what was then known about its real biological nature, but which was easier to visualize. The revival of this approach, known as 'neo-connectionism', has drawn heavily on work in Artificial Intelligence, the science (or perhaps the art) of writing computer programs that simulate aspects of what people do, and the ways they do them.

Let me give you a rather fanciful metaphor that captures the main ideas behind this kind of thinking. As you will see, even this simple image rapidly becomes quite intricate: the next few pages are the most 'technical' (despite the picturesque language) of the whole book. But bear with me. I shall not give you more detail than is necessary to follow the rest of the story as it unfolds. Without this overview of the brain-mind, and the way it does what it does, it will be difficult to understand how it is that the developing science of the mind offers us a radically new way of interpreting religion and religious experience.

The Octopus Discotheque

Imagine a small tropical island, perhaps a few hundred metres across, that has been colonized by a large troop of unusual octopuses who have turned it into a 24-hour-a-day discotheque. At an octopus disco you do not move around much. You all pile up in a big heap, and you extend your tentacles in all directions until you make contact with another octopus's head. In fact we should really call these particular creatures 'centipuses', because they have not eight legs, but hundreds. These legs vary in length considerably, so that some of those whose heads you are touching are beside you, while others can be right across the other side of the dance-floor.

Octopuses, who need their rest as much as anyone, cannot stay awake the whole time. In fact, at any moment, only a small proportion of the total clientele is actively awake. You can tell when an octopus is awake because its skin turns from a dull grey colour to a bright lobsterish pink—as if it has been boiled. When it is awake and 'dancing', all it does is make small movements of the tips of its tentacles, thereby making their presence felt by all those other octopuses it is touching. Each octopus can affect its contacts in one of two quite different ways. If it *tickles*, the octopus on the receiving end is irritated and stimulated, and becomes more likely to wake up itself. But if the first octopus *caresses*, the other is relaxed and calmed, and is inclined to fall asleep (or more deeply asleep, if it is already asleep). Strangely, these caresses mean that if octopus A has been giving octopus B a gentle, tranquillizing massage, B will become *more* responsive to other sources of stimulation as soon as A falls asleep.

Each octopus wakes up when the total amount of tickling it is receiving from all the others who have their tentacles on its head, exceeds a certain amount. Like human beings, some octopuses are generally very sensitive, and will wake up and start squirming with only a couple of tickles. Others are heavy sleepers, and it takes the concerted tickling of dozens of tentacles before they come to and join the dance. And others are choosy: they will respond to tickles from certain other octopuses of whom they are fond, but will be more resistant to the approaches of those they care for less.

There are actually three kinds of octopus: those that live on the windward side of the island; those that live on the leewards; and those that live in the middle. Those on the windward have some of their tentacles resting in the sea, and they can be woken up, as well as by tickles on their heads, by particular patterns of waves. These are called the Lookout Squad. It is their job to detect the ripples that are caused by approaching ships, or impending bad weather, or other influences that might disturb the fun. On the other side, the leeward, are the Bottle Squad, whose job it is, if tickled in various ways, to stuff messages in bottles asking for help, or more music tapes, or whatever. In the middle are those who simply pass the tickles around.

The combined effect of this curious collection of stimulating and tranquillizing influences is to *ensure* that only a small proportion of the assembled company is awake at any moment. And it also ensures that the group of awake octopuses keeps changing. A couple of tentacles start tickling you, you wake up and start swishing your own tentacle-tips; but soon you start to get tired and drowsy, or to succumb to the relaxing massage. So if an observer were hovering over the island on a clear night, she would see these patterns of pink octopus bodies continually shifting around; and she would see a general increase in activity if the wind got up, or if a boat was sighted; and sometimes she would see a flurry of activity on the leeward shore as a bunch of messages were scribbled, stuffed into their bottles, and hurled out to sea. And the observer would notice that the pattern of activity at any moment was likely to be quite widespread throughout the network, not bunched up. She would be more likely to see an irregular pink ring extending across the whole island, rather than a concentrated pink blob.

The observer would also see, if she hovered long enough, gradual changes in the way the patterns of activity moved through the total octopus population, and this is because each time one of octopus A's tentacles is successfully involved in waking up octopus B, the spot on B's head where A's tentacle is resting develops a little bit of extra long-term sensitivity. Now the next time A tickles B, the net effect on B is greater, and fewer other contributing tickles are needed to make B wake up. So the more often A and B are awake at the same time, the better A becomes at wakening B on its own. And the more likely it is, when A is awake and tickling, that it will be B that is roused, as opposed to Z, who A is also tickling, but with whom it has a less successful track record. What is more, if a number of octopuses are regularly involved in each others' awakenings, then they will develop into a 'gang'—what Hebb called a 'cell assembly'—who will tend to turn on or turn off as a unit.[25]

Priming

One very important feature of the octopus colony is that, even though an individual or a gang may be asleep, they may be sleeping more *lightly* or more *heavily* as a result of stimulation which is not yet strong enough to wake them up fully. So if an octopus or a gang of octopuses, A, can sometimes awaken gang B and sometimes gang C, which one *actually* wakes up—i.e. which direction within the octopus colony the flow of 'wakefulness', or activity takes—will depend on the relative level of this 'priming' of B and C, as well as on the long-term state of their connections to A.

In fact this phenomenon of priming can operate more generally than between single octopuses, or individual gangs. We could suppose that buried in the tangled heap are groups of octopuses with different musical tastes. For one group Miles Davis tends to make them sleep more lightly, while Madonna lulls them into an even deeper slumber; for another group, Madonna gingers them up, while Mozart makes them insensitive to almost anything. Thus the 'path' that the area of wakefulness takes through the colony depends on what music happens to be playing. The difference might be sufficient to make A wake up B when the background music is jazz, but C when it is Country and Western. In other words the behaviour of the whole community is highly context-dependent and situation-specific. The effect of any particular stimulus depends on the state of the whole system—its priming, its state of sedation, its tiredness—as well as on its whole idiosyncratic history of who has woken up whom in the past. And conversely an individual input can 'set' whole areas of the community to be either more or less sensitive to what happens next.

Resources and Attention

Another important feature of this model is that the total wakefulness of the community—the overall 'amount' of activation available to the system at any moment—is finite. If there were no sources of inhibition as well as activation, the octopuses could wake each other up until they were all wide awake at once. Clearly such an eventuality has to be prevented: it would put us in a state of cortical meltdown—a condition of total perceptual and behavioural freak-out. Everything would be 'On', but we would be incapable of being *appropriate*. The beauty of the system of checks and balances built in to the fabric of the octopus colony is that it becomes, of its very nature, selective and integrative. The colony as a whole has to choose and moderate amongst what is going on.

This is not to say that the total level of activation is always fixed. If you looked down from your helicopter and counted the pink bodies, there would not always be exactly the same number. Sometimes the total might be a bit greater, sometimes a bit less, but the important point is that the total is *relatively* fixed, and is certainly finite. It cannot explode, though it may vary somewhat as a reflection of the overall state of 'alertness' of the system.

In fact, though, there is a very important source of variability in the *effective* amount of energy that the system has at its disposal, independent of variations in the total energy available. Imagine that, when a particular gang of octopuses, A, is awake, one of its 'jobs' is to send a constant low-level tickle (or massage) to a variety of other gangs or individuals, B, C and so on. In addition, suppose that A is able to stay awake for long periods of time. These continuous 'trickles' of excitation and inhibition will make a network with one set of connections respond as if it were a network with a different pattern of strengths. The crucial difference, however, between the effect of priming, and the long-term change in the strengths of the connections, is that, in the former case, it is possible for the priming overlay to be removed. If A were turned off, even for just a few moments, there would be an instantaneous, apparently 'magical' reorganization, perhaps a re-prioritization, of the brain system as a whole. What had always been 'at the back of one's mind', or 'on the tip of one's tongue', now would no longer be there, or would stand out with unfamiliar clarity.

And in this hypothetical situation there would be another interesting effect as well. While unit A has been 'on', it has not only been keeping particular other units or groups of units on a hair trigger; it has in so doing been keeping tied up some proportion, perhaps a significant proportion, of the total activation permitted in the brain. If there is only so much energy available at any time, then if 10 per cent of it has to be dedicated to certain locations to keep them primed, there is less available—less *free* energy', we might say—to underwrite the activity of the rest of the system. And the less free energy there is, the more crude or stereotyped we might imagine the response of the system to be. Only those octopuses with the lowest thresholds, and the biggest and most numerous inputs, get woken up. (This option, for the brain to change its way of operating by tying up some of its total pool of activity, will become very important later when we try to explain the phenomena of mystical experience.)

The Brain with No Self

In the octopus colony there is no privileged group with special status or special powers. Just as the brain as a whole has to be seen as a subsystem of the whole body, so each octopus gang must be seen as a member of a participative democracy. What happens in the brain, and the momentary conjunction of priorities, interpretations and actions that it is involved in computing, arise naturally and uniquely from the state of the system as a whole—brain, body and world.

Many of those who have been working in the area of neuroscience have made it very clear that their object is to see just how much of human functioning can be accounted for *without* recourse to any 'ghost in the machine'. How far can we get before we have to call upon 'the self'? Could it be that we can even get all the way: that the hypothetical ring-master or engine-driver, the personal 'I', is not actually in control; that the biology, when it comes down to it, does the lot? Donald Hebb, the Godfather of neuroscience, was in no doubt:

This discussion...represents my attempt to be rid once and for all of the little man inside the skull who *approves* of some sensory events relayed to him by the nervous system, *disapproves* of others, and guides behaviour accordingly....By some such approach as the one suggested, it may be possible to understand the directedness and order in behaviour, and the variability of motivation, as produced by neural functioning alone.[26]

And Francisco Varela of the Ecole Polytechnique in Paris is of the same mind:

Each component operates only in its local environment...but because of the system's network constitution, there is a global cooperation which spontaneously emerges....In such a system...there is no need for a central processing unit to guide the entire operation.[27]

As Patricia Churchland points out (in the quotation at the beginning of this chapter), however, this leaves us with some explaining to do when we come to consider the prevalent sense that we all have that there *is* some instigator behind the eyes, with whom we are rather closely identified, who can override what is going on and impose its 'will' on the rest of the brain/body system.

One latent misunderstanding that the octopus analogy might induce needs to be scotched straight away. The ideas of 'awake' and 'asleep' simple translate in brain terms as 'switched on' or 'activated', and 'unactivated', or 'dormant'. An awake octopus is one whose connections and characteristics are currently instrumental in determining where the activation or the 'energy' in the network flows next. A dormant octopus is one who is not currently involved. There are no implications in this model about consciousness. The pattern of awake octopuses has nothing (so far) to do with what is conscious. As we shall see later, what enters consciousness is often only very distantly related to what is going on 'behind the scenes' in the octopus disco-land of the brain-mind.

The Continuum of Attention

As well as the *location* of the activation varying, we might also notice changes in its *concentration*. At some times, and in some areas, the pattern of pink bodies might be very tight and clear-cut. At others, it might be much more diffuse. And at some times the *flow* of energy is likely to be quick, clear and unambiguous; at others, where the trails are less well defined, or when a mistake might prove costly, then the kaleidoscope of patterns may shift more slowly, and there is more time for activation to accumulate in a particular area, and for different by-ways or shades of meaning to be 'explored'. Not that there is anyone or anything which is 'deciding' to explore. It is simply in the nature of the network sometimes to run fast and deep, and at other times to behave like a stream which comes to a hollow and 'waits' for the bowl to fill into a small pool before it can overflow and run on again.

We might contrast two extreme modes of attention; one focused, sharp and 'serial', with each thought or sensation following another in clear order; the second broad, diffuse and 'parallel' or 'holistic'. The first would be like a spotlight with a narrow beam; the second like a floodlight or a candle. Each, we might note, has its uses. There are situations in which we would prefer the candle: finding our way around a pitch-black cave, for example. The candle, casting a broad light, would enable us to get our bearings much more effectively than the spotlight, whose beam, illuminating only one tiny part of the whole cave at a time, would tell us, at this stage, too much about too little. But if the candle-light enabled us to pick out an object of interest—a carved stone, say, or a parchment scroll—then we might find its all-round light too dim for close inspection, and we would thankfully switch on the intense, tight beam of the torch, to investigate in detail.

So it is with these two extremes of activation in the brain. Sometimes it serves us best to take it slowly, to allow the shadows and ambiguity to remain while a 'felt sense' (an idea borrowed from psychotherapy) of the situation as a whole is allowed to form. If the need for action is not urgent, we can, so to speak, prevent a 'solution' from crystallizing quickly, raise the thresholds of the 'action units', and allow the pool of activation to build up in one area of the network. By doing so, new options and connections may become apparent whose discovery had been prevented by the normal fast run-off of activity down the first familiar trail. The brain, in other words, has it in its constitution to offer *reflection*, a kind of leisurely exploration of latent possibilities, unhassled and undirected by the need to find an answer to a pressing predicament.

And the brain can also operate at the other extreme. When the demands of the situation are saying: 'Don't just stand there, do something', the brain can usually oblige. It can compute very quickly the tongue-flick required to catch the fly, or the top-spin lob that might win the point. When the front tyre of your bicycle hits a slippery man-hole cover as you are going round a corner, lightning calculation and correction may, if you are lucky, keep you in the saddle—again without the help, or even the presence, of the normal conscious commentary, which may be paralysed with fear while the brain/body is fighting for its life.

We might guess that the more complex and delicate the computations, and the more long-term rather than immediate the goals to which they relate, the more useful, the more frequently appropriate the diffuse, reflective mode would be. Yet we might also ponder on the plight of an animal, awash with goals, projects, interests and desires, in an intricate environment replete with opportunities but also dangers, who has become locked in to the quick-sharp way of operating; who finds itself in a blacked-out cavern, full of tantalizing smells, unfamiliar protuberances and ominous noises, equipped only with a torch that gives a light spot the size of a pea. I shall argue later that people in modern industrialized societies are in precisely that position.

One salient difference between the diffuse/holistic and the focused/analytic modes of processing is in the picture they give of the world. The focused mode shows you objects only one, or maybe only one piece or aspect, at a time. Individual figures stand starkly out from the ground. It is like having to do a 1000 piece jigsaw puzzle without having access to the picture on the lid of the box. Small details or objects seem to be self-existent; if they have a life it is a life of their own, and any overall sense of relationship, of the ecology of the situation, has to be painstakingly constructed with the help of memory, rather than, as with the candle, apprehended as a whole. Diffuse processing, on the other hand, gives an ecological view; it leaves out detail, but conveys a sense of the relationship between 'figure' and 'ground', to use Gestalt psychologists' terms.

How the Brain Behaves

Some of the most general features of human psychology arise simply from the nature of the brain-mind system—without our having to add any other assumptions. It is obvious, for example, that such brains are built to generalize and categorize in the same way that humans do. Experience wears metaphorical 'grooves' in the brain, as a river gradually wears a V-shaped valley through the landscape. And just as rain falling on the sides of the valley tends to run down into the river, so experiences that share most, but not all, of the features of a very common category will tend to be treated as if they were typical members of the category.[28] If it has got soft fur, likes fish, mews and rubs itself along my legs at supper time—well, that's good enough for me: it's a cat. It may only have three legs, be at least six inches longer than any other cat I've ever seen, and have fur the colour of the sky...OK, it's a lame, gross, exotic cat—but still, basically, a cat.

Psychological research since the turn of the century has been full of demonstrations—if we needed them—that we see what we know; we look at the world through the categories and concepts of our minds. In one of the most famous demonstrations, people were flashed very brief exposures of playing cards which they were asked to try and identify. Unbeknownst to them, some of the cards were tricky ones: they crossed the colour with the suit, so every-so-often there would be a red six of clubs, or a black ten of hearts. People found it impossible to see what was there, insisting, until the cards were actually put into their hands, that they were regular cards—'but a bit fancy'—would be about as far as they were prepared to go.[29] We have noted before that it is effectively part of the design characteristics of a tuneable brain that it should lead you to see what is familiar, and consequently have trouble, especially if time or attention is short, with the unprecedented.

The basic features of *memory*, too, are already laid down in the octopus model. If you take a familiar concept, memory or scenario—a gang of octopuses—then the more details of this group you subsequently activate, the more likely it is that the rest of the gang will also wake up. Memory works by part of a group *recruiting* the rest. That is why, if you have got a word on the tip of your tongue that will not come to you, the best strategy is not to keep straining for the word, but to let yourself free associate to it. In this way you can aim to build up sufficient 'active' ingredients of the memory trace for the whole thing to fire off, and the word or name pop into your head. And this is also why, if I asked you to think of the names of the other children in your class when you were seven, few if any would pop up. But if I took you back to your old classroom, or even sat you down and asked you to recreate in your mind a vivid picture of the room, then lots of previously hidden details would 'miraculously' start to come back to you.

In this chapter I have developed, with the help of the octopus model, the view of the brain-mind, and its basic *modus operandi*, which is emerging from the sophisticated labours of cognitive science. It is a brain without a control centre; a brain composed of thousands of simple constituents linked together in such a way that, collectively, they can perform complicated life-saving and life-enhancing computations. And they can, by altering the way different units are primed, make decisions either as quick as lightning, or in a slower, more reflective manner. So far, so good. As we shall see in the next chapter, however, even such a brain becomes clumsy as it gets bigger, and the next twist in the evolutionary tale has to occur.

FIVE

Mosaic Mind

I am large; there is a multitude within.

Walt Whitman

Brain Clumsiness:
The Proliferation of Needs, Part II

As we look back along the evolutionary trajectory that was, eventually, to lead to *homo sapiens*, we can see the intricacy of our animal forbears becoming ever greater; and as it did so, the complexity of the operations required of their brains grew enormously. As the range of needs, the repertoire of deeds, and the sophistication of the information they can pick up got bigger and bigger, so the problem of keeping track of all the different operations became more formidable.

The brain began, in evolutionary terms, to adopt the solution that is typical of almost any system of increasing complexity. Just as the body had differentiated itself into subsystems (one of these subsystems being the nervous system itself), so the brain sought a way of managing its increasingly unwieldy complexity by the same strategy. Indeed the noted American cognitive scientist Herb Simon argued in an important essay published in 1962, called 'the Architecture of Complexity',[30] that it is part of the internal 'logic' of complexity that an evolving system has, at some point, to adopt a hierarchical structure, with the whole breaking into intermediate parts (what the writer Arthur Koestler called 'holons'[31]), which themselves may also comprise further sub-assemblies.[32]

Effectiveness is Not Necessarily Tidy

The form of internal organization that the brain-mind develops does not need to look very logical from the outside. One of the mistakes that brain researchers have sometimes made is to assume that the brain is designed on the basis of elegance and economy. But evolution, as we have seen several times already, does not, indeed cannot, work like that. Natural selection has to build on what is already there, it has to work with the kinds of mutations that just happen to occur, and it can only take account of the particular local conditions that happen to obtain. It can never say: 'Hold on a minute; this brain is getting untidy. Let's go back to the drawing board and start again.' Paul Churchland talks in his book *Matter and Consciousness* of a car he used to have when he was a student. One of his friends insisted that it was not so much a car as 'a squadron of nuts and bolts flying in loose formation'. So it is with the brain. We can ask how it has solved the problem of making sure you can quickly find the right 'book' in a rapidly expanding 'library'. But we should not expect to find anything as neat as the Dewey Decimal System. We would be well advised to expect to find something that behaves like a patchwork of linked components, rather than something with a clean overall design.

There are of course many ways of sub-dividing the work of the brain, just as there are many ways of effectively organizing one's own kitchen. A kitchenologist could no doubt come along to each of our homes and convince us that it is irrational, or uneconomical, to keep the paper napkins in the same drawer as the bagels, and she may well be right. But the much more important consideration is: does the way I have it organized work for me? If I'm having a phase of Italian cooking, why should I not keep the tagliatelle, the tinned tomatoes, the cookbook and the oregano all together? And if I've gone off Italian, and am now wild about Thai, why should I not *continue* to keep the Italian ingredients together, if I have got used to the arrangement, and make space for the coconut cream and the freeze-dried coriander alongside them? The organization of the brain is likely to be a record of our evolving preferences and strategies for feeding, housing, protecting and perpetuating ourselves, in just the same way.

So instead of one big 'theory' about how the world works, and how to shove it around to my own advantage, the brain begins to divide—functionally, not structurally—into a library of 'minitheories'.[33] Each of these sub-minds is designed to tie together a package of knowledge, skill and experience that can be brought to bear on a particular domain of life. This package specifies what it is *for*—the purposes to which it can be appropriately put; in what *conditions* it can be used—what environment it is likely to work in; and what it can *do*—what abilities, mental and physical, it makes available.

Two points about these minitheories. First, nothing is needed, in the brain, to play the role of the 'librarian', of course. The currently active priorities make themselves known by priming their relevant minitheories to different extents (depending on the urgency of the need or desire); and the sensory receptors feed activation into those minitheories that seem to match what is going on outside. The network quite effortlessly performs its job of selecting a course of action, by waiting to see which 'gang' awakens first, and thereby activates its associated bundle of dispositions and expectations. And secondly, the concept of a 'minitheory' (or a 'module') is one that bridges the domains of 'brain-language' and 'mind-language'. As you zoom in on a minitheory, so you can start to see its fine structure, and describe it in the language of octopus gangs and ultimately in terms of individual neurons and their properties. As you pan back from any particular minitheory (as we are in the process of doing), so you are able to see more clearly the whole mosaic mind-scape of which it is just one part.

Keeping the Brain on Track

One of the major technical problems which the evolving brain had to solve was that of keeping its activities precise. When an impulse was sent from A to B, it had to be sure of arriving at the right place and not being side-tracked. Marcel Kinsbourne has suggested that this problem of 'functional insulation' of higher level packages of capabilities, in the absence of any structural walls, is solved by the strategic use of the brain's powers of *inhibition*.[34] Each area of the brain that is active may, almost as a matter of course, tend to create a halo of inhibition around itself. Members of an 'awake' octopus gang will be strongly activated enough, by mutual stimulation from each other, to resist the soporific effects of the inhibition. But other nearby units, even though they may have some connections with the active network (but which are not at the time being stimulated directly) will have insufficient 'strength' to prevent themselves succumbing to the inhibition. As we know, this strategy for keeping the system 'on the rails' is by no means foolproof. There are many occasions when our minds slide off the point, and the train of thought finds itself chugging off down some apparently irrelevant siding. But no mechanism is perfect, not even in the brain.

Mini-Worlds

The evolution of predation, and especially of active stalking and hunting down of prey, would have acted as a stimulant for the evolution of minitheories. The hunter needs keen eyesight, hearing and sense of smell; powerful muscles for running, pouncing and killing; and greater abilities to predict the behaviour of its prey under various conditions. When the prey goes to ground, or disappears behind a clump of rocks, the more successful hunter will not immediately give up the chase and wander off, puzzled at the sudden dematerialization of its lunch.

To keep concentrating on something you cannot see, but which you presume is still there, demands a brain that is able to keep active a representation of some bit of the world that is not, at that moment, being stimulated from outside. The minitheory for Hunting, the subroutine for Rabbit, and the running memory of The Story So Far, must be able to be stay activated, and the minitheories that relate to alternative goals must stay inhibited, at least until you have satisfied yourself that the rabbit has truly retreated to a safe place, or that it might just have been a few leaves stirred by the wind in the first place. The activity of the brain, in other words, has to become ever more capable of proceeding in an inner-directed, self-organized fashion, of 'ignoring' some environmental changes and fleeting body sensations, and of pursuing 'plans' and 'intentions'.

So each minitheory develops the capacity to represent one of the sub-worlds which the animal regularly inhabits. A minitheory is a functional map of the recurrent patterns which the sub-world has been found to contain. It provides a manual that enables you to 'diagnose' the different options that are likely (on past experience) to occur, and to know instinctively how to 'treat' them. The ideal minitheory is one that so comprehensively covers all the angles that it is no longer possible for this sub-world to surprise you.

A minitheory keeps tabs on a domain—'mating', 'hunting', 'parenting', whatever—in two senses. First it distils different experiences and encounters into a general set of expectations and capabilities. But secondly it also provides a continually updated record of how any particular encounter is going. As each episode unfolds, so the general expectations are continually being modified to take into account gambles that paid off and discrepancies from what was predicted. In brain-language, the levels of priming and inhibition are constantly being adjusted, on the basis of present experience, to shift the balance of priorities and dispositions that the network represents. Each bit of the brain-mind system is energized or sedated so that the system as a whole is ready to respond to whatever (on the basis of both long-term and recent influences) is the most likely and/or the most significant thing to happen next.

Note again that, though I have used words like 'plan', 'intention' and 'believe', I have put them in quotes to mark the fact that these words refer to capabilities that we can infer from the way an animal behaves, without implying any role for consciousness whatsoever.

Overcoming Internal Isolation

Marvin Minsky has pointed out an additional benefit of a brain that is designed to keep some of its resources and processes separate. A knowledge store that is *not* subdivided is not capable of being very *creative*. The flow of activity in an undifferentiated brain-mind can only follow the grooves laid down by genetics and experience. Different areas of the colony that are functionally far apart are never going to be able to meet up. If such a network 'tries' to get two distant areas to be simultaneously alive by allowing its area of activation to get bigger and bigger, any possible benefit of *having* opposite edges 'awake' at the same time will be lost in the general clamour of activity. It would be like match-making by holding an enormous cocktail party in a confined space: even if the candidate lovers meet one another, the din will be so great they will not be able to hear what they are saying. But if two circumscribed, special-purpose areas can be activated side-by-side, then their tête-à-tête might well be more fruitful. A network that is divided up into sub-areas has the potential to put those areas in touch with one another more specifically.

But how is this potential asset to be realized? In the octopus model there is no way of getting different gangs to 'talk' to each other, unless they have already been put in touch by direct experience. What is needed is some kind of alternative access system; a way of enabling cross-talk between these different little capsules of intelligence. It is this need to expand the flexibility of *internal* communication within the brain-mind, and thereby to enable speedier and more precise access, as well as greater creativity, that posed the next major evolutionary problem.

SIX

The Pressures of Society

Individuals buy in to (their) community...by eternal psychological vigilance. They may spend time apparently doing nothing, passing time in idle gossip. But this time spent socialising is as crucial to their survival as any time spent hunting or gathering in the field. For it is round the campfire or lying out in the sun that the social backbone of...society is laid down and, if necessary, repaired: friendships are established, problems talked out, plans hatched, love affairs commented on.

Nicholas Humphrey[35]

It is hardly an exaggeration to say that a chimpanzee kept in solitude is not a real chimpanzee at all.

Wolfgang Kohler

The brain-mind's retrieval problems obviously get more acute the more different scenarios you have to keep tabs on. A solitary animal has only a few different types of situation that it has to take part in. Sociable animals such as fish and birds may also have only a limited number of roles to play as they do not make many distinctions between other members of the group. Animals such as the large cats that hunt in packs have to be rather more concerned about their roles and relationships.

But it is when we get to the social primates, and our own human ancestors, the early hominids, that the number of different scenarios which each individual has to keep track of begins to mushroom. The nature of each encounter becomes increasingly dependent on the particular individual you are dealing with. And if you have to have a separate minitheory for every member of your community, the larger and more complex that community becomes, the more the fragmentation of the brain-mind is likely to become a problem. (When we get on to the complexities of modern industrialized human society, the extent of the problem becomes staggering.) If each of our familiar scenarios were stored separately, there would be an enormous duplication of effort, and an incredible waste of usable information.

The Mixed Blessing of Community

Before we embark on the story of how the brain-mind solved the problem of scenario-overload, we need to say something about why it was that social living—and the development of individual 'character'—came about.

Living together in groups is a survival strategy that bodies can adopt, in just the same way as living together in bodies is, as we have seen, a survival strategy that cells can adopt (and living together in cells is a survival strategy that even more primitive little creatures can adopt). Gambling on community is not, at any of these levels, the only way to go. Solitary multicellular animals abound in the modern world, just as there are unicellular organisms and bacteria of many different sorts. But human genes opted for the corporate life, so it is that path that I shall focus on here.

The basic advantage of community is, of course, that there is safety in numbers. A cooperative group of animals can defend their young, collectively, against the unwanted interest of a predator, more successfully than a single mother can on her own. A pride of lions can hunt together more subtly and reliably than any one of them alone. And if the kill is big enough to feed them all, then the strategy has paid off well. Furthermore, living in herds—of antelope, let us say—increases the likelihood that those of the extended family who *are* caught by predators will be the older or weaker members. As the herd wheels in confusion, or turns and flees from the approaching lions, and as the mothers do their best to ensure that their offspring are concealed and surrounded in the middle of the herd, it will be the slowest or the most confused, and not necessarily the youngest, that will become exposed, and the most likely target of the lions' attentions. Thus, even though the creation of a herd may not save you from the periodic loss, it acts as another mechanism for strengthening the gene pool, by increasing the chances that it is indeed the fittest that survive.

But collaboration demands its price, and poses its problems. When the catch is good, everyone is happy; but when food is scarce, who is it who has to go short? Must there be equal hardship all round, or will some kind of pecking order emerge? When 'we' are under threat, where exactly do the fundamental loyalties of any individual lie? When such choices have to be made, the demands on the group to develop some form of social organization, even of hierarchy, becomes stronger. And this in its turn requires the development of more elaborate forms of social intelligence and social communication.

At its most fundamental, communal living continually poses the dilemma of how selfish, and how self-less, to be. Living in society, there are benefits to be gained from individualism and entrepreneurship but there are also costs, in terms of social cohesiveness, collective trust and goodwill. When a society starts to be dominated by a few conspicuously successful bandits, a wave of imitation may be stimulated that is not only bound to fail, as more and more people try their hand at outwitting each other, but sooner or later undermines the very rationale for social living. Anarchy is a useful call-to-arms in a passive and oppressed culture, but a hopeless game plan for any species that is indelibly, genetically sociable. (The individualistic consumerism of the 1980s, and the short-lived financial bean-feast to which its 'Greed is Good' philosophy gave rise, is of course the most recent case in point.)

In a complementary fashion, altruism is a valid strategy, especially if directed towards kin whose genes are very similar to one's own, or towards those who can protect you and promote your status or interests. But it can clearly be to an individual's disadvantage to give away everything, or always to direct any passer-by to your precious store of winter food, if your altruism is not, at some level, reciprocated. It is also possible for a whole society to be too caring or trusting, and to lose a competitive edge when it comes to dealing with a rogue member of the tribe, or a stranger. 'Third world' societies, such as Ladakh in Northern India for instance, have proven to be tragically easy prey for silver-tongued purveyors of 'development', and have happily abandoned a thousand years of ecological and social wisdom for the promise of a pair of denim jeans, and the reality of urban poverty.[36]

'Enlightened self-interest' would be the ideal compromise, but the practical definition of enlightened depends on who your neighbours are, and on a whole host of ever-shifting considerations. In many species, kinship turns out to be the medium through which 'enlightenment' is manifest, and unrepentant nepotism is rife. A group who share genes will share more in the way of resources, labour and defence with each other than with other members of society—with the possible exception of the very important category of 'potential mates'. If the clan's preference for its own members extended also to each member's choice of sexual partners, then the gene pool would be at risk, so this is the one area in which it pays to look outside the immediate family circle. In human societies, of course, the clan itself, or its 'elders', have often reserved the right to define who is a 'potential mate', and not to leave it up to individual caprice.

The Machiavellian Primate

Other than in human societies, the tension between cooperation and competition shows up nowhere more clearly than in the primates—not surprisingly, as it is only six million years or so since our common ancestors were on the Earth. There are now many observations, especially on chimpanzees, which demonstrate the dilemma, and show how it is resolved in different ways in different situations. In one lovely example,[37] chimpanzee A observes a keeper hang up a bunch of bananas in an inconspicuous place. Chimp B, however, is in the vicinity, and for as long as he remains, A potters about with a nonchalant air, completely ignoring the bananas. After a while, B leaves, apparently 'taken in' by A's performance...but only apparently. He must have sensed that something was up, because he immediately finds a hiding place from which he can observe A without being seen. Sure enough, as soon as A 'believes' himself to be unobserved, he runs off and retrieves the bananas—only to be rapidly dispossessed by the larger B, whose patience and perceptiveness are finally rewarded.

A second example, worth quoting in full, comes from research by Frans de Waal.

Yeroen hurt his hand during a fight with Nikkie. Although it is not a deep wound, we originally think it is troubling him quite

57

a bit, because he is limping. The next day a student, Dirk Fokkema, reports that in his opinion Yeroen limps only when Nikkie is in the vicinity. I know that Dirk is a keen observer, but this time I find it hard to believe that he is correct. We go to watch and it turns out that he is indeed right: Yeroen walks past the sitting Nikkie from a point in front of him to a point behind him and the whole time Yeroen is in Nikkie's field of vision he hobbles pitifully; but once he has passed Nikkie his behaviour changes and he walks normally again. For nearly a week Yeroen's movement is affected in this way whenever he knows that Nikkie can see him.

Interpretation. Yeroen was playacting. He wanted to make Nikkie believe that he had been badly hurt in their fight. The fact that Yeroen acted in an exaggeratedly pitiful way only when he was in Nikkie's field of vision suggests that he knew that his signals would only have an effect if they were seen; Yeroen kept an eye on Nikkie to see whether he was being watched. He may have learnt from incidents in the past in which he has been seriously wounded that his rival was less hard on him during the period when he was (of necessity) limping.[38]

Such examples, of which there are now many, demonstrate the chimpanzees' impressive ability to manipulate each other's feelings, control their actions, and direct their attention—and to do so in ways that depend subtly on who they are dealing with. And the engine for this remarkable skill is their ability to observe each other closely, and to build the resulting brain-mind patterns into accurate working models of each other *as individuals.*[39] When you live in a society where there are fine gradations of social status, and in which individuals whom you meet day after day have quite intricate 'personalities' and preferences, it pays you to develop a very sharp eye for behaviour, and to learn the non-verbal language of the culture, so that you too can play the games.

Nicholas Humphrey, the Cambridge parapsychologist, was one of the first to argue that the extraordinary developments in the mental abilities of human beings, over the other species (even the primates), was stimulated by just this need to be a skilled player of social games; and that, as each 'move' could potentially be met with a counter-move—as in the first example, where chimp B pretended to be fooled by chimp A's attempt to put him off the scent of the bananas—so society became involved in an accelerating 'arms race' of social sophistication. 'The formative years for human intellect were the years when man lived as a social savage on the plains of Africa' says Humphrey.[40] And:

> It was...the circumstances of primitive man's *social* life—his membership of a complexly interacting human community, his need to do well himself while at the same time sustaining others—which did more than anything to make man, as a species, the subtle and insightful creature we know today....If men were to negotiate the maze of social interaction, it was essential that they should become...capable of looking ahead to as yet unrealised possibilities, of plotting, counter-plotting and pitting their wits against group companions no less subtle than themselves.[41]

Even before the appearance of verbal language, the business of reading other people's intentions—and broadcasting or concealing your own—via subtle variations in posture, behaviour and the direction of gaze was well developed. Indeed, many of these signals, and their responses, developed long enough ago to have become embodied in the genetic code.[42] But genetics cannot prepare you for all the idiosyncrasies of the other members of your primate colony: for this learning is required, and preferably not just occasional observations and encounters, but sustained, close-quarters 'getting to know you' sessions. What better medium for these prolonged 'conversations' than mutual grooming? Chimpanzees and baboons, who live in groups of 50 or so, spend up to 20 per cent of their day in this activity, not only establishing 'goodwill' between each other, but inevitably, through spending so much time at close quarters, building up quite a detailed minitheory of each other's preferences and dispositions. In groups of this size, and with a primate lifestyle, this amount of time can be devoted to fostering relationships without encroaching on other necessary activities.

However, as social groups get larger, and society even more intricate, so the amount of time required for physical grooming becomes a luxury that can no longer be afforded. Robin Dunbar of the University of London has suggested, on the basis of contemporary hunter-gatherer and simple horticultural societies, as well as archaeological evidence, that early human societies settled into groups of 120–150 people: considerably larger than the primate groups.[43] To give the same amount of time to one-to-one grooming, in such a group, would require not 20 per cent but nearer 40 per cent of daily activity, a proportion that would jeopardize food-gathering and all the other jobs needed to service the community. Grooming becomes inefficient as a social adhesive because it is necessarily an activity between only two (or occasionally three or four) animals at a time, and you cannot get on with much else simultaneously. What is more, a three-fold increase in group size greatly increases the amount of social learning there is to do.

So Dunbar argues that there would have been an evolutionary pressure to devise an alternative form of communication that would enable individuals to get detailed information about each other rapidly, while preferably leaving your hands and feet free to get on with other tasks. Enter, finally, the spoken word, as the ideal solution to the 'grooming' problem.

It would of course make social learning very much quicker if people were able to tell each other, not just how they were feeling at the time—which their observers then had to distil inductively into tentative images of 'character'—but what *kind* of person they were. If people were able to gossip, as it were, about themselves, social cement would accumulate much faster. And if they were able to communicate generalized information about 'third parties', then individuals would be prepared (not always accurately or adequately, of course) to get along with characters whom they had not met before.

It is a commonplace that when a more sophisticated, but more recent (developmentally or evolutionarily) strategy is proving inadequate, an animal or a person frequently reverts to an earlier or more primitive way of operating—even when that too may patently fail to meet the needs of the situation. As the evolutionary precursor of gossip was grooming, it would not be surprising to note this 'need' for physical contact reasserting itself, either in the face of loneliness or confusion, or in those special cases where words can never be enough. As Dunbar notes: 'when it comes to really intense relationships that are especially important to us, we invariably abandon language and revert to that old-fashioned form of primate interaction—mutual mauling'. But what form, in the modern world, with our smooth bodies, should this 'mauling' take? Should we be busy shampooing each other's hair, or gently cleaning out the wax from our loved ones' ears? Perhaps the closest analogue is to be found in massage, cuddling and non-erotic stroking. Perhaps the contemporary fascination with sex represents a mishearing, a perversion of this faint, evolutionary, call to arms—to embrace and be embraced.

Modern Times

If Dunbar's speculations are anywhere near the mark, it would mean that our genes are still equipping us to master living in communities of 150 people. Yet in our industrialized, urbanized, televised society we rarely operate in groups of such a size. On the one hand, the nuclear family (with all its current variations), plus an individual's active friendships, may number only a dozen or less. From this point of view, once we have developed our intimate relationships and observed each other about as much as we can, we are left with unfulfilled gossiping-inclinations, and unused gossiping-capacity. What do we do? We read the tabloids and become addicted to TV soaps. They will provide us with instant 'Neighbours' to get to know, and to have feelings and opinions about. Even though we will probably never meet Princess Diana or Michael Jackson, we add them to our list of 'virtual acquaintances', and prepare ourselves rigorously for encounters that are never going to take place. The spare capacity of the social brain gladly seizes on the next salacious revelation of 'what Prince Charles is *really* like'.

On the other hand, the social institutions of which we are part—the schools and corporations in which we study or work—frequently contain a thousand or more people. And the media daily introduce us to dozens more. The modern teenager flails about in a maelstrom of faces—different classmates and teachers, 'real' heroines and 'fictional' characters whose reality status is hardly distinguishable—and almost always escapes into a restricted world of 'brightness', 'naughtiness' or fanatical devotion to some sports team or rock star.

While the smaller groups leave us with spare capacity, the larger groups are too hard to handle; our brains, big though they are, cannot enable us to develop a relationship with every shop assistant or taxi driver we meet. (The central humour of the Crocodile Dundee character, you may remember, lay in his attempts to apply his 'small group' social habits to New York, by, for example, endeavouring to pass the time of day with every cab driver and policeman he ran into.) The global village has grown far too big, while the local community is far too small; so we top ourselves up with celebrities.

These are truly the days of the 'fragmented mind', and the problems that such a culture poses for the brain-mind are formidable. How are the separate files to be kept apart, so that you instinctively know how to *be* with different people; and yet integrated in such a way that your developing array of social skills distils out into a general purpose savoir faire? This is the problem to which we return, after the brief excursion of this chapter, in Chapter 7.

Just before we do so, however, we should pause to note one vital conclusion. Humankind is indelibly sociable. Just as it is etched into our bones that we are biological systems, both greater than the sum of our internal parts, and inextricably entwined, moment to moment, with larger systems, so it is also written on our hearts that we are meant to *belong*. The sociability of humankind is not something that needs further explanation. It is genetically inscribed in our marrow. And it is therefore not the fact that humanity congregates that should puzzle us, but the occasional hermetic exceptions. It is round-the-world solo yachtswomen, and monks on five-year solitary retreats, who have some explaining to do. For almost all of us, almost all of the time, it is belonging that we crave.[44]

SEVEN

Languaging the Brain

We speak, not only to tell others what we think, but to tell ourselves what we think.

J. Hughlings Jackson

The most significant moment in the course of intellectual development, which gives birth to the purely human forms of practical and abstract intelligence, occurs when speech and practical activity, two previously completely independent lines of development, converge.

L.S. Vygotsky[45]

The Enquiring Mind

Primates, as we have seen, struggle in their communication between keeping quiet, telling it like it is, and being 'economical' with the truth. Sometimes, at least, it pays to share what you know. So when you find yourself chatting with another member of the community, especially one who has proved generous with her information in the past, it would naturally be useful to be able to *ask questions*. If your current project hit a snag, and if no-one happened to be in the vicinity doing the same thing with greater success who could act as a model, then a polite enquiry might just elicit the clue that you need in order to proceed. Questions like 'What's that?', 'How do you get into this?', and 'What is Emma like?' would be useful tools—by no means invariably effective, but helpful additions to the range of learning strategies, nonetheless.

Sometimes the audience would communicate something back that would provide the missing link in the problem-solving chain. But sometimes their offering would not so much tell you something new as remind you of something that you 'knew' already, but which, by virtue of being registered and stored within a different sub-compartment of the brain, was not currently functioning. At the end of Chapter 5 we saw that one of the problems with the mosaic mind is that individual minitheories might well possess information that would be potentially useful in a different context, but the system as a whole had no way of 'knowing' this. It would help enormously if different sub-minds were able to talk to each other.

Asking questions, and receiving answers, therefore, has the power to bring together—to make concurrently active—different minitheories, so that they are able to share their *internal* resources. If it turns out that this collaboration is fruitful, then some sort of functional alliance could be forged between them. You could leave a little message in 'file' X saying 'If you are having trouble of such-and-such a sort, go and look up file Y'. So the net effect of a helpful respondent could be to build bridges *within* the existing brain-mind system.

However, as Daniel Dennett has pointed out, the audience in this scenario could sometimes be redundant.[46] Suppose I ask a question of someone who is unable, or disinclined, to help me; or even, originally as a mistake, I ask my question out loud when there is nobody around. Of what possible value could this be? How, asks Dennett, could asking myself questions be any less futile than tipping myself for making myself a drink? Because the question itself might contain a 'word' or an action that is, of itself, able to wake up a new minitheory. Minitheory X , which is about Catching Termites, might be able to say 'What kind of *stick* might help to get these pesky termites out of this rotten log?'—but not itself contain very comprehensive information about sticks in general. The sound of the word 'stick', though, would have just the same value as if someone else has used it: it might have become part of the 'call sign' of minitheory Y, which is about Toys, say. Now, for the first time, the Good Things to Play With routine is active at the same time as the Catching Termite routine—and information originally stored in the context of one purpose is now made available for the pursuit of another. A primitive form of 'insight' comes into being.

Thinking

There is, of course, a catch. If you are engaged upon some private scheme, it would be an inconvenience to have to talk to yourself out loud all the time. There may be rivals in the vicinity who could be eavesdropping, and who might then be stimulated to think along the same lines, make the same connections, and beat you to the solution. How useful it would be if you could perform this trick of auto-stimulation, especially when in company, *sotto voce*, so that they would not realize what you were up to. If you could short-circuit the loop that originally had to travel from one minitheory to the other via the open airwaves, and make the connection from 'speaking' to 'hearing' internally, then the possibility of 'industrial espionage' would be forestalled. Luckily this is one of those tricks that evolution has equipped us to be able to learn. 'Thinking', in the specific sense of being able to talk to ourselves on the quiet, is another powerful strategy for boot-strapping our own learning.

In fact, *any* medium through which we can make available the *output* of one part of the mind as a potential *input* to another part, may give us an advantage in the same way. Drawing can be such a device. Diary-writing may be another. Looking at yourself in a mirror or on a videotape, another. And the facility for sensory imagination and fantasy-play can be seen in the same evolutionary light. When a minitheory is activated, one of the effects of this may be to activate the sensory parts of the brain-mind that correspond to the scenes within which its script is habitually played out.

Dreaming and Imagination

Suppose we learnt to be able to reduce the 'threshold' of activity which is needed to fire these sensory parts of the brain-mind until it hovered only just above the level of its habitual priming. Those elements which were also receiving stimulation from particular needs, and/or which had themselves been recently stimulated, might make it over the line, and become 'live', mimicking exactly the effect that would have been produced by stimulation from the outside. The brain-mind would be capable of seeing what it was *interested* in seeing, rather than what was coming in from the outside. This is 'imagi-nation'. And just as, in the speech domain, there is an internal hook-up between speaking and hearing, so the imaginary product—the pattern of activation in the sensory system—of one minitheory could then be available as a potential input to another.

We could even build the foundations of a theory of dreaming on this basis. At night time in a factory there are no trucks arriving with materials and departing with filled orders; no telephones to be answered and minor shop-floor disputes to be sorted out. But this does not mean that nothing is going on. The night shift's job is to tidy up some of the clutter that has accumulated during the day, clean the equipment, and even perhaps to give some thought to the business strategy. Analogously, during sleep the activity of the brain is much less under the control of moment-to-moment inputs from both the outside world and the body. The brain does not close down, but it is 'off-line'. Activity is still flowing around the system, but *how* it flows is rather different. It is guided much more by the inter-nal shifts of priming and bias. Areas that are 'well-primed', but which rarely during the day receive the top-up required to wake them up, stand a better chance of being recruited into the night-time flow.

We could also argue, with some plausibility, that the level of inhi-bition, with which the active pattern normally insulates itself, is somewhat relaxed. During the day, the main job of the brain-mind is to integrate all the different incoming calls, and to make sure that it only allows to be simultaneously active those subsystems that do not interfere with each other. You can digest your food at the same time as walking the dog; but you cannot walk the dog, cook dinner and have your hair cut all at once. During the day, a heightened ten-dency for active patterns to shut off the others makes the competi-tion more fierce, so that when one course of action wins, for the moment, it can be more sure of having the floor to itself.

What this adds up to is a system in which (at night, or when day-dreaming) things that are 'on your mind' are more likely to become fully activated; in which dissonant domains are more likely to be allowed to be active at the same time; and in which the imaginary products of one 'field' of experience are therefore likely to recruit other 'fields', maybe on the basis of an image or symbol which is common to both, but which may not seem to be central to either. Dreaming is a way of using imagery to explore links between different minitheories which may have some emotional or motivational 'charge', and which may have been freshened up—stimulated or primed—during the course of the day. Out of this speculative story drop at least three of the common characteristics of dreams: bizarre associations; emotional charge; and topicality. And it explains the pivotal role that Freud assigned to puns, symbols and ambiguity. These are precisely the small passageways and tunnels that lead from one mental sub-world into another.

As usual, I feel obliged to point out that this theory of 'dreaming' does not require any *conscious* appreciation of the dream content. It simply describes a mechanism whereby the brain-mind uses the still of the night to do some necessary house-keeping and stock-taking. Likewise there is no need to introduce consciousness to account for the value of talking to oneself, drawing or imagination. We are so used to thinking of ourselves as *conscious* beings, with consciousness at the centre of most of our interesting functions, that it takes a slight effort to see that talking to yourself will 'work' regardless of whether anyone 'notices' it or not; and that much of sleep may be devoted to 'unconscious dreaming'.

To explain why *some* of our activities and experiences are associated with consciousness, and what makes them different, requires more understanding of the mind than my story has yet accumulated. The account of dreaming, for example, does not explain why the dreams of which we are conscious are so often cryptic and symbolic. It is almost as if, to put it crudely, two minitheories could be active at the same time, but with only part of each reaching consciousness. As in those children's books where the pages are split so you can see the top half of one animal sitting on the bottom of another, so in dreams we may experience the visual content of one domain coupled with the emotional content of another. You are catching a train...yet the whole performance is imbued with an intense feeling of ambiguity, doubt and anxiety much more reminiscent of the situation at work. As Freud noted, to account for what gets into consciousness, we need such concepts as 'self-image' and 'self-defence' (censorship), and the story has not got that far yet...

Churning Concepts from the Milk of Experience

As we have come to expect, evolution comes up with a solution to one problem—language helping to establish social cohesion, in this case—which then is found, opportunistically, to have unforeseen benefits (and costs). Language, at first designed purely as a social tool, turns out to be the key to solving the increasingly urgent problem of internal communication which the brain set up for itself by opting for an organization based on sub-divisions. Dividing your knowledge up into separate packages was a solution to the earlier problem of accessing an expanding knowledge-base. But as the number of separate 'modules' of intelligence began to explode, so the solution began to create a serious problem of internal house-keeping. Developing language in order to share social knowledge turns out to hold the key to this problem. Out of such accidents and coincidences is evolution constituted.

At first, as we have just seen, a common word was able to put two previously separate minitheories in touch with each other, and from this initial contact, as in a club for 'lonely hearts', a successful and mutually beneficial relationship could blossom. But this is still a hit-and-miss kind of introduction agency, putting individuals in touch with each other if they have both checked the same interest or 'desirable feature' on the application form. A happy couple sometimes results, but society as a whole is not radically affected. However, as it developed, language turned out to have much more wide-ranging potential for integrating the knowledge of the mosaic mind.

As an animal grows up, each of its 'scripts', the scenarios it commonly meets and knows how to handle, becomes more elaborate and subtle. Minitheories become replete with options and possibilities, tricks and manoeuvres, for dealing with the varying realities of the situation. The 'Get Milk From Mum' routine is now able to take account of her moods, whether other siblings are pestering her, her apparent interest in a passing male, what time of day it is, and so on. And as the scripts become (to use Vygotsky's graphic term) 'saturated with experience',[47] so they begin to crystallize into various sub-scripts: elements and interactions that keep reappearing from occasion to occasion. What I have learnt about 'Mum' is portable; it reappears in the Feeding routine, the Playing routine and the

Grooming routine. With the help of the Introduction Agency of language, the trans-situational 'concepts'—for that is what they now are—become crystallized out. When two different domains are activated together, the sub-groups they share receive a 'double dose' of activation and this enables them, by the inherent rules of the neuronal community, to form an especially tight little gang that is less firmly tied to either of the two original sources.

The main form of organization of the brain-mind is now able to take a radical shift. Previously the topography had been defined by the different *situations* that an animal recurrently took part in. Things were associated because they tended to happen together, in both space and time, in everyday life. But with the discovery of stable configurations of experience that could appear in a variety of scenarios, the brain could begin to crystallize out and organize its patterns on a *conceptual* basis. Each 'concept' forms a small vortex of experience that is less firmly 'embedded' in the context of personal history. So it is capable of being associated, via the medium of language, with the related 'kinds' of concepts, and not just with its 'kin'—the family in which it grew up. 'Sticks for playing with' and 'Sticks for catching termites with' could now be grouped together under the general concept of 'Sticks', and these concepts could act as the hubs through which several different scenarios could be linked. The knowledge of each script could now be much more widely available, and the power of the brain-mind to solve problems, to draw on the distillates, the essences, of its experience in flexible ways, to devise novel remedies for unprecedented predicaments, explodes yet again.

So over the minitheory landscape of 'records of personal experience' a new plane, conceptually organized, begins to be constructed. And each of these concepts could be given a *name*. Just as concepts crystallize out of life-scripts, so words began to emerge as having a special status. They were not just a component part of the concept; they were capable of being used to *point to* the concept as a whole. The bellow of a buffalo, or the smell of its dung, can alert you to its presence in your vicinity. The whole Buffalo package can be primed—put on 'stand-by'—so that your senses are tuned to pick up further buffalo-clues, and your muscles are prepared to run their buffalo-scaring routines. But with a word, I can tell your brain to turn on the buffalo-package before you have received any information of your own—and thereby, possibly, save your life.

With words, the 'encyclopedia' of concepts can be organized by categories, indexed systematically, and accessed in the absence of the things themselves. Each word is like a flag planted firmly in the centre of the concept, enabling you to find it in quicker and more flexible ways. And word-flags can be strung together into more elaborate bunting, so that new conjunctions of ideas, never before experienced by you or possibly by anyone, can be conjured up like, for example, a dragonfly out of an oil-tanker. Language comes to form an incredibly powerful 'second signalling system', as Pavlov called it, overlaying and tying together the purpose-built programs of the experiential world.

Thus the evolution of the brain-mind system can be seen in terms of the construction of three layers. At the bottom, comprising the foundation on which all the activities of the brain are built, is the vast intricate network of filaments which are slowly welded by experience into functional groups. When this landscape has become intricate and variegated, the second layer begins to emerge—the extraction of actions, objects or 'sub-scripts' which tend to recur across different domains. Concepts are extracted or 'disembedded' from their particular contexts, and are woven instead into a different kind of tapestry, one organized not according to which things occur together in experience, but with reference to their conceptual, functional or semantic relationships.

And the third level is that of language itself: the superstructure of increasingly abstract terms which begin to derive their meaning, not from the connections they make with the substratum of personal experience, but from the connections they make to other words. In this third realm, syntax may enable me to weave webs of words every bit as pleasing as the webs of spiders, but which may or may not be underpinned by patterns in the plane of personal purpose and experience. Beautiful though they are, they may have little cash value in terms of survival. As we know, the most erudite psychologist is by no means the happiest or most skilful practitioner of the art of living.

The three planes are not, of course, separate. They are multiply, but not completely, interconnected. If I try hard, I may be able to construct a form of words—a poem, perhaps—that will evoke in you a fair copy of my own experience. But often the attempt to talk about 'the human condition' peters out into endless trails of words that keep leading across the verbal landscape, but never manages to drop vertically down into the 'mines' of personal meaning. Likewise, some of my experiential knowledge has made its way up into the worlds of concepts and words; I may from time to time have an 'insight', a spontaneous bubbling up into language of a pattern not previously recognized or articulated. But much, I would venture the vast majority, of what I have learnt about people, gravity, water, justice, cooking and the behaviour of cats stays firmly below ground, exquisitely functional and absolutely inaccessible to word or even thought.

Rumination

It is sometimes dangerous to muddle up arguments about evolution with those about the development of the child. Ontogeny, as psychologists are fond of saying, does not (always, necessarily) recapitulate phylogeny. But in this case I think it might be worth the risk. Andy Clark of the University of Sussex and Annette Karmiloff-Smith in London have recently suggested that it is precisely this ability to distil the general out of the particular, and to do this at an increasingly abstract series of levels, that distinguishes the human brain-mind from its nearest evolutionary cousins.[48] And it is the increasing sophistication of this internal process of distilling and redescribing that characterizes most strongly the developing human child. Karmiloff-Smith has accumulated much evidence to show that children's learning does not stop when they have mastered a kind of task or a particular domain. Rather they 'change gear' at this point and move into a different learning mode, one which plays with what has been acquired, and in doing so uncovers relationships between different domains. They are prepared temporarily to sacrifice success, narrowly defined, in order to bring to light principles and generalizations which had been latent in the original learning.

In one study, four- and five-year-old children were asked to draw a 'real' house, and then a 'silly' or a 'pretend' house. They had mastered the art of drawing stylized houses, but when they cheerfully embarked on the job of producing a 'silly' house, they were unable to produce anything different. Though successful, their 'house-drawing' routine was a single program, unable to be tampered with. Likewise, when they were asked to draw 'a man with two heads', all but one of the children laboriously drew two separate bodies, each with its own head, and though they knew it wasn't what was wanted, were unable to do better. Older children, in contrast, were able to produce non-standard houses, or two-headed bodies, fluently and often creatively.

When children are learning something new, it is as if their brain-minds first lash together whatever bits and pieces they can find that will do the job required, like a person after a shipwreck who collects whatever floats by in order to make some sort of a raft. But later, when dry land has been reached, and the pressure is off, the brain may pull the raft up into 'dry dock', take it to bits and either put it back together again in quite a different way, or use its materials together with others in stock to construct a more sophisticated vessel, capable of undertaking more demanding voyages of discovery. This inherent tendency to seek out links and relationships between different areas of understanding may well explain why children's play, and the *language* of their play, is so symbolic. Metaphors and make-believe are devices for activating two (or more) domains at once, and seeing what happens.

Four points to emphasize about this. First, only a small minority of these improvements are verbally expressed and/or available to consciousness. Secondly, in this tentative process of seeing whether two separate domains can benefit from a partial merger, or whether they should be kept separate, a 'failed' experiment can be just as informative as one that delivers smooth, quick success. Children often seem to go through periods of 'regression', sometimes just for a few minutes, sometimes for days or weeks, which can puzzle or irritate their parents. But the long-term value of this zaniness or 'child-ishness' is, as this discussion makes clear, inestimable, regardless of whether child or parent has any conscious idea of what is going on.

Thirdly, this process of 'learning beyond success' takes time; and how *much* time it takes, and what kinds of activities need to take place for it to happen, cannot be predicted or controlled by anyone, not even the learner herself. It is entirely dependent on what 'state' her brain is in when she starts, and on her own shifting set of priorities. The brain has its reasons, of which the consciousness of the learner knows little, and of the teacher, almost nothing. This boils down to two quite straightforward educational principles: rumination, though vital, cannot be taught; and its development cannot be hurried. As our educational establishments, at all levels from pre-school to university, are preoccupied with the rigmarole of teaching (syllabuses, lectures, textbooks etc), and are always in a rush, there is little hope that the brain-mind will *develop*, in the way it is built to do. Either it flounders and finally admits defeat; or it learns the trick of *laminating* itself, so that layers of half-digested knowledge can be piled on top of one another. The mind becomes an archaeological site, cluttered with fragments of past civilizations. And the unifying potential of language loses out to the impatience of those who, willy-nilly, must 'cover the curriculum'.

Language Lift-Off

Primates, as we have seen, are able to use their non-verbal language to misdirect and deceive, as well as to inform. As the process of dis-embedding concepts from their social contexts, and weaving webs of words with which to express them, expands, so does the capacity for deliberate or inadvertent misrepresentation. As the words for things become interwoven, so it is possible to talk about, or to call up, con-junctions of concepts that have never—and maybe could never—occur together. 'A dog chases a cat' is probably an expression of experience; its ingredients, and the relationship in which they are placed, matches the way things have been found to be. 'A drunken cat chases a professor of Arabic'—that is not the stuff of direct expe-rience, but of literature, of fiction. It is not underpinned by familiar grooves in the brain, but floats a little more freely, capable of being visualized, perhaps, but not of being tied in, directly, to personal or evolutionary history. 'An ambitious but absent-minded cat ran over the President in her Buick'...you have to work harder to pluck con-cepts from here and there, and wriggle them around in order to achieve some semblance of meaning: this is the world of fantasy, of fairy-tale. 'My cat just ate your canary': that, though you do not know it yet, is a downright lie; a wind-up; a partial retaliation for all the grief that your thoughtlessness has caused me.

What about: 'My karma just ran over your dogma'? Well, it is a joke, of course; but does it, could it, *mean* anything? Here language seems to have taken on a life of its own, and the game of trying to figure out whether we are meaning anything, what we might be meaning, and how on earth we are to tell whether one meaning is any 'truer' or more 'interesting' than the others—that can keep us in publications, and on the plane to the next conference, for a blissfully long time. The fine linguistic fabric that floats over the plane of experience can be assembled into semantic castles in the air, supported only by widely spaced pillars that connect them to the ground of experience. If you want to know what a word means, there may well be no linked experience that can help you. You can only see what *other* words it is hooked up to: you look it up in a dictionary.[49]

The Trouble with Words

The linguistic overlay enables the secrets of some of the minitheories to become public knowledge. But, naturally, it is only modules that are hooked up to the linguistic telephone exchange that can ask for and offer help. You have to be a subscriber to get the benefit. And many of our brain sub-systems, intellectual as well as physical, are not. Even those that have been learnt deliberately—like recreational games such as tennis or chess—are not fully articulate. The world chess champion Bobby Fischer, when asked how many avenues he explored in his mind, before selecting a move, replied, 'One—the right one.' And as well as giving knowledge that is incomplete, language also increases our ability to represent information that is unproven or even untrue. The verbal plane comes to be able to speak with its own voice, unwarranted and unmandated by the patchwork terrain of experience that underlies it. Language immeasurably expands our ability to deceive ourselves, and to be deceived.

But language itself is not neutral. It does not need a Machiavellian mind to misuse it. The very nature of language means that it alters the way the brain-mind system behaves in ways that are not always for the best. For example, language exacerbates the intrinsic tendency of the brain-mind towards stereotyping. Remember that it is in the nature of brain-stuff to pick out regularities, and then to register 'near misses' as if they were only variants on the same theme. When a word is attached to a concept, the category becomes more cut and dried; it becomes all the harder to register accurately experience that does not quite 'fit' into existing categories in terms of its uniqueness. We attend to something new only up to the point where there is enough evidence for its name to light up, and then the brain-mind's activity moves on, taking only the word with it. The patient is observed only until the first diagnosis occurs to the doctor, and then the patient herself is no longer of interest, no longer even a person, but just another Latin label for a disease.

So there is a tendency, as the verbal net becomes more and more detached from its perceptual roots, for cognitive activity to take place more and more at that level, and less and less in terms of first-hand observation and experimentation. Once the diagnosis has been made, all the interesting activity takes place in the medical library or in conversations over coffee in the doctors' common room. Treatments and complications are discussed in the absence of the patient, with only the occasional quick visit to the ward to settle a point of dispute. First-hand observation, in other words, is not only reduced, but comes to be driven by concepts and distinctions that are enshrined in language, and not by patient (in both senses) sensitivity to the data.

The upshot of this is that the very existence of language encourages the brain-mind to process the world in a focused, serial way. Recall that the pattern of activation in the brain system can be concentrated to different extents; and that both focused and diffused attention have their uses. Indeed the typical mode of processing would involve pulsing of activation: first diffuse, in order to get a general sense of what is going on; then bunched up or narrowed down in order to collect finer-grain information about some detail; then relaxing again into an open, inclusive, more receptive state, and so on. Because language deals in stereotypes and prototypes, and because it is necessarily a serial medium that extrudes understanding through a narrow one-thing-at-a-time nozzle, it requires the brain to adopt its focused and sequential mode—regardless of the nature of the situation. When the 'default mode' of the brain becomes verbal and serial, it loses flexibility and reduces its ability to see things whole.

It follows that language tends to hasten 'cerebro-sclerosis'—the hardening of the categories. As they become more stereotyped, so concepts and habits of interpretation also become harder to change. When a word has been used as a building block in hundreds of linguistic constructions, it is difficult to try to change its shape without risking the collapse of all these edifices. If you try to persuade me to think of God not as transcendent, which is the basis on which my faith has been founded since Sunday School, but as immanent, present in every moment and every act, it will be hard for me to hear what you say, and hard for me to change what I believe. Too much of my life has been lived and construed through this lens. Too much would need reconsideration. If you want to make *sure* that an old dog will not be able to learn new tricks, first teach it to speak.

And finally, language itself is necessarily passé. The concepts that a language enshrines were abstracted from the brain-minds of people who lived different, often simpler, lives than we do. As Edward de Bono says:

> Language is a museum of ignorance. Every word and concept has entered language at a stage of relative ignorance compared to our present greater experience. But the words and concepts are frozen into permanence by language and we must use these words and concepts to deal with present-day reality. This means we may be forced to look at things in a very inadequate way.[50]

Aldous Huxley summed up this realization that language is, as far as the internal workings of the brain-mind is concerned, a mixed blessing.

> Every individual is at once the beneficiary and the victim of the linguistic tradition into which he has been born—the beneficiary inasmuch as language gives access to the accumulated records of other people's experience, the victim insofar as it confirms him in the belief that reduced awareness is the only awareness and as it bedevils his sense of reality, so that he is all too apt to take his concepts for data, his words for actual things. That which is called...'this world' is the universe of reduced awareness, expressed, and as it were, petrified by language.[51]

2

The
Story of
the Self

EIGHT

The Language of the Self

So wonderful is the organisation of a termite colony that it seemed to some observers that each colony had to have a soul. We now understand that its organisation is simply the result a million semi-independent little agents, each an automaton, doing its own thing. So wonderful is the organisation of a human self that to many observers it has seemed that each human being had a soul, too: a benevolent Dictator ruling from Headquarters.

In every beehive or termite colony there is, to be sure, a queen bee or queen termite, but these individuals are more patient than agent, more like the crown jewels to be protected than the chief of the protective forces—in fact their royal name is more fitting today than in earlier ages, for they are much more like Queen Elizabeth II than Queen Elizabeth I. There is no Margaret Thatcher bee, no George Bush termite, no Oval Office in the ant hill.

Daniel Dennett[52]

The brain-mind contains no special-status ghost or ingredient that tells it what to do. As we saw in Chapter 4, there are simply millions of tiny conduits carrying energy from one part of the network to another. The development of minitheories, and of language, did nothing to alter this fundamental picture. There is no brain-within-a-brain which oversees the work of all the other modules, prioritizes them, or bosses them about. Information is integrated, different parts woken up or put to sleep, claims for the uses of resources assessed, simply by virtue of the way the system-as-a-whole is built. The brain-mind is its own Higher Authority. There is no other.

Yet our experience tells us otherwise. It seems, incontrovertibly, that there *is* something more than this biological black box, some supervisor who is equipped to adjudicate and intervene; and that this 'something' is, essentially, who '*I*' am. The notions of 'self', 'consciousness' and (at least partial) 'autonomy' are key components of our second nature, and are all tied together into a taken-for-granted view of human nature which is in flat contradiction to the story that science has to tell. Part II of the book continues with an evolutionary perspective—though now we are talking more of 'cultural' than 'biological' evolution—in an attempt to show how it came about that humankind developed a 'sense of self' that *seems* to be in executive control—but in fact isn't. It turns out that neither 'self' nor 'consciousness' is what it seems; and that each is a result of a continuing series of evolutionary twists, turns and coincidences. In this chapter we will begin this work by picking apart the idea of a 'self', and showing how the several different constituents of the modern 'self' came about.

The Layers of Self

Prior to the development of 'personal' language, a 'sense of self' would certainly have existed, but it was simple and, crucially, implicit. The 'secret handshakes' of the immune system that we discussed in Chapter 3, for example, still provide the basis on which many of the body's different ingredients can recognize each other, and can make fine discriminations between 'resident' and 'alien' tissue: witness the high likelihood of rejection of donor organs, from the same species and even the same family, in transplant operations.

The muscular counterpart of this is the 'body image': the tacit knowledge of the body's current configuration: its posture, where the limbs are, in what direction the eyes are pointing, and so on. Without this running record of how the flexible, mobile body is disposed, the brain-mind would not know what instructions to give in an emergency. The 'right' movement of the hand, to flap away a wasp, say, depends absolutely on where the hand happened to be the moment before. Without the knowledge of where 'here' is, we could not program ourselves to get 'there'.

Then there is the sense of self which derives from learning to hook up things I can *do* with things I sense. When a baby looks around, for example, there are many things that move regardless of what she happens to be willing or feeling. The steam rises, the cat stretches, the ball rolls across the room. But there are four objects in her world which, she begins to discover, she has a rather different, and much closer, relationship with: her 'hands' and 'feet'. When a hand drifts across the scene, it is correlated, with a very high degree of reliability, with sensations that are arriving in the brain about the position and movement of the relevant arm; and also (unless someone happens to be moving the arm 'passively') with activity in the brain that is telling the muscles of the arm to move. This correlation signals a very different kind of relationship with the baby's hands from the one she has with the cat. She can put her hands around the cat to pick it up, and she can draw on her knowledge of the cat (both first-hand and via gossip) to anticipate how it might react. But however much she knows (or even loves) the cat, she can never have such an intimate, cooperative, reliable relationship with it as she has with the hands that reach out to clutch it.

Similarly, there is the correspondence, which we have already discussed, between the feel of the throat and mouth as I 'talk', the neural commands from the brain that are controlling the muscles, and the sounds that are entering my ears. When I say 'Cat', the internal correlations and cross-checks that are happening are quite different from the way the brain-mind responds to the cat's meow. There are many such correlations between the instructions that the brain sends out, and the kinaesthetic and sensory feedback that come rippling back as a result. Where this special relationship exists, there is a sense of predictability and control that might justify one particular use of the words 'me' and 'mine'.

And more generally there is an embedded sense of my own vantage point with respect to the 'external world', the way in which sounds, smells and especially visual impressions serve to orientate me in space with respect to the supposed *source* of these stimulations. The varying intensities of smells and sounds, and the area on the retina where contours and colours are falling, give information about where best to point my head, body and receptors. 'Me' can be seen as a kind of address, a reference point in space, which the brain-mind has to take account of in computing the strength and direction of a pounce or a swerve. One of the jobs that the brain of a predator (or a footballer) has to perform is the creation of an implicit model of where things are, and what is stable and predicable in the outside world; a background image of locations and expectations against which any change, or any unanticipated movement, will stand out sharply, and will immediately draw attention.

Without this picture of where things are and what they are up to, drawn in terms of the patterns and predictions which the brain has been programmed (by genes and by learning) to make, your attention would constantly be caught by *any* change, however familiar, and you would be unable to devote your resources to the top-priority task of noticing, not just what is new-this-moment, but what is *unprecedented* and *significant*. This constantly updated map of how one is placed, both literally and figuratively, with respect to the world, is a vital survival aid for an animal on the move, and another ingredient of the 'sense of self'. Whether we are feeding, napping, playing with the kids or trying to impress a potential mate, the body-image and the sensory platform have a continuity that needs to be preserved as the range of daily dramas come and go. And of course this backdrop of predictions does not have to be articulated, or even conscious. It is as available a resource to my dog as it is to me.

The Thing-ing of People

And then along came language. For our early ancestors, being able to talk about *people*—their habits, their phobias, their quirks, their moods—was a much more urgent priority, in general, than being able to talk about *things*. Yet the course that language took as it evolved enabled—indeed required—people to talk about other people as if they *were* 'things'. Other members of your community form the most interesting class of objects in your world, but they are, in an important sense, objects. The very idea of a 'thing' suggests an entity—something that is all-of-a-piece, and which rolls through both space and time carrying its identity and its characteristics with it.

To be able to talk about your friends—just as much as about your CDs or your supplies of bamboo shoots—presupposes that they can be seen as collections of more or less stable attributes. Gossip would be useless if one could not recognize individuals again, and if one could not rely on them, up to a point, to behave consistently. If Jane wants to forewarn Sally about Tarzan's touchiness on the subject of his relationship with his pet chimp, she can only do so by talking about him *as* a kind of thing. So any language of people's traits and features—their meanness, protectiveness and passion for chocolate, as well as their small feet and auburn hair—imputes an *identity* to people, and, to a greater or lesser extent, invites people to see each other in terms of their long-lasting traits and dispositions.

Some present-day languages emphasize the solidity of this 'thing-ness'—they put the 'entity' into 'identity'—more strongly than others. Indo-European languages very clearly segment the world into things (nouns) which have characteristics (adjectives) and which meet and interact in various ways (verbs) which do not fundamentally alter their identities. 'The chimpanzee stole the bananas'. 'Zebadee washed his sheets'. We even have to say 'It poured with rain', though who or what 'it' refers to is mysterious. 'It' is forced on us by the form of our language. When someone sits, they create a thing called a 'lap', which magically dematerializes when they stand up again. When they close their hand they form a 'fist', which again can be destroyed and recreated as often as they like.

Other languages, the most famous examples being some of those of the Native American tribes, take a more 'systems' view of things and their attributes, seeing them as stable forms of process, in a world that is essentially dynamic. 'Fist' and 'lap' are represented as actions or events, and so are people and their idiosyncrasies. Mike's taste for spicy food, and his tendency to fall asleep in the movies, are personal traits that are somewhat more stable than his posture, but they differ from the posture, in this linguistic view of things, only in their timescale, not in their kind. But even these languages cannot avoid giving names to individuals, to types of animals and trees, to their identifying features, and to recurrent types of event and interaction, and thereby picking out, as topics of conversation, those aspects of the world that are predictable. This is what lan-guages *do*.

Projections as Templates for Self-Discovery

Personal language enables me to talk not only *about* him and her and you; it gives me the chance to discuss my personality, and yours, directly *with* you. If we are in alliance at the moment, we can co-ordinate our plans better if each of us checks out with the other our impressions of how we are likely to behave under different circumstances. If I think you are a good person to have beside me in a fight, and am therefore inclined to bank on your physical courage, then it will be useful if you *know* that I am making this assumption about you, for two reasons. First, you might wish to dispute my reading of your character, and attempt to put me straight. You may have seen yourself behaving in a much more fearful fashion than I have, and wish to correct the exaggerated impression I seem to have picked up, via the grapevine, about the extent of your 'grace under pressure'. Secondly, you might accept (even if only tentatively, as a hypothesis) my evaluation of your courage. You might 'try it on for size', so to speak, using my 'summary' of this aspect of your character as a lens through which to observe your own behaviour. You can use my view of you as template through which to view yourself, and perhaps to discover a genuine pattern that had not yet come to light.

This second possibility is of vital importance to our understanding of the evolution of the self. When two beings talk to each other about how they see each other, *as objects*, they have to begin to develop the capacity to see themselves in the same way. They begin to develop a new minitheory, a concept of 'self', which represents 'me as seen by others'; me as a thing-with-features, just like all the other things-with-features that I am building up images of through my conversations and encounters.

The effect is useful because you can precipitate out of your experience some labels for your own characteristics which you can then share with potential allies and collaborators. 'Don't get upset if I don't show up for the hunt exactly at two o'clock', you might say; 'I'm not a very good timekeeper, but I promise you I will be coming.' Or: 'I know I have difficulty in showing my tender side. So if I seem to be a bit cold, it doesn't mean I don't love you.' To be able to include yourself as one of the social objects capable of being gossiped about would be of great utility, and another of the serendipitous side-effects with which evolution is peppered.

And this also gives you the opportunity to *deceive* people in a more direct or reliable way, as well. You can tell them you care when you really don't; or that you will honour an agreement you have no intention of keeping—as in the famous fable of the frog who found a scorpion sitting by the side of a stream. 'Please take me across the stream on your back,' said the scorpion. 'I need to get to the other side, but I can't swim.' 'What do you take me for?' said the frog. 'I know your type. You will sting me.' 'Think for a moment,' said the scorpion; 'I couldn't do that, could I, because then we would both drown. Would anybody be so stupid?' The frog was convinced by the scorpion's logic, and so set off across the stream with the scorpion on her back. Half way across the scorpion stung the frog, and as they were both disappearing below the water, the frog gasped, 'Why?' 'I'm sorry,' said the scorpion. 'It's in my nature.'

The trap of deceit is that the benefits tend to be visible and immediate, while the costs are often more remote, more probabilistic, and more nebulous. Changes to one's 'reputation' are usually cumulative and delayed—earlier deceptions may only come to light when a later one is uncovered—so an early run of 'success' may mislead the manipulatively inclined into believing that they have hit on a strategy that is more fool-proof than it actually is. Criminality is a *gamble*, in the chattering classes of the chimpanzees, just as it is in human society.

Social Approval

Primate groups are clearly structured according to a principle of seniority or status. Whereabouts an animal is in the hierarchy determines much of its life: the share of food it is entitled to; who its potential mates will be; who it kowtows to and whose bananas it can get away with stealing. And as this structure was carried forward into the societies of our early human ancestors, so the language of politicking would naturally have been recruited in the service of establishing and maintaining the pecking order. Personal characteristics would have had differing values assigned to them when it came to deciding who was who. Size, strength and skill in combat might still remain the ultimate arbiters of power and prestige; but other attributes would also have begun to emerge as important—skill in problem-solving, sexual prowess or fecundity, physical attractiveness, ability to mediate in disputes, honesty...

So the language of personal attributes would have picked up significant connotations of social approval and disapproval. Selfishness, without the necessary muscle to silence your critics, could push you down the hierarchy; but so could physical cowardice. As people began to apply the language of personal characteristics to each other, and then to themselves, so a socially derived element of *evaluation* would come to accompany it. One not only learns to describe oneself in terms of certain attributes, but also to be able to predict, of oneself and of others, the 'appropriate' place in the scheme of things for which this 'character' fits you (and them).

Thus the 'self-concept' comes to contain various sub-selves: that which is approved of, and will therefore tend to make my social life go more smoothly, and give me status; that which is disapproved of, and which (if the word gets round) will make things tougher for me; and that which is neutral with respect to this process of social ordering. Animals and ancestors who lived in such societies, and who had developed such a psychological language, would be inclined to become 'approval-seekers'. Being of 'good repute' is adaptive, and it is in the interests of a stable social structure for individuals to care about where they stand.

Moral Schizophrenia

But the need to maintain 'respectability', while at the same time promoting one's own private interests, creates another twist in the multi-faceted tension between 'selfishness' and 'altruism'. Individuals can now be faced with the prehistoric prototype of the moral dilemma: to hog the bananas, or to go for the brownie points. It becomes possible to act against their own (and even their species') best biological interests, in order to maintain social approval. At the personal level, the drive for social approval, and the labels that are used to channel and justify it, serve to create a separate centre of evaluation within the brain-mind. An action might be judged 'good' or adaptive when referred to this socially accredited self-concept, but 'bad' or self-destructive in terms of procreation or the protection of existing children.

Such tensions are nothing new in evolutionary terms. The brain-mind evolved to cope with the increasing frequency and complexity of such inner disputes. And while all these claims on the body's resources were legitimate, they could not all be honoured at the same time. The brain-mind was designed by evolution as a way of weighing these claims and arbitrating in a way that was in the best interests of the total community. Just as the Blood Sugar Control System and the Predator Detection System need their voices to be represented at Court, so the Social Approval System presents appeals for action when ostracism or demotion is threatened. Initially the 'competition' is increased by the arrival of the self-concept, but it is not (yet) radically overturned.

But while the claims of the liver on the time and capacity of the whole body-brain-mind system vary from hour to hour, so long as it remains healthy its needs do not escalate significantly over time. The self-concept system in the modern world, however, has developed a very different status. One might almost say that it is diseased from the word go. It certainly becomes a firmly entrenched, and ever more demanding, cuckoo in the mental nest. Instead of being one voice amongst many, it comes to set itself up as an alternative centre of government, like a President that is at loggerheads with its parliament—a Yeltsin, whose area of power and concern is almost exclusively Foreign Policy, dealing with the image of the community abroad, and the negotiation of foreign aid; against the Congress of People's Deputies, whose dominant concern is with Internal Affairs, the needs and tensions within the 'body politic'.

The question of how it is that the self-concept is able to lever itself into a position of such authority, to the point where it threatens to destroy the integrity and balance of the whole community, is one that will be central to the discussion of the next three or four chapters. For the remainder of this chapter I shall restrict myself to some further remarks on the role that is played by language itself. Language cuts the world up, though the world itself is seamless and systemic. It turns a world full of greys and gradients into a rectangular landscape of black and white. Language highlights structure and persistence, though the world itself is constituted only out of process and change. Language demands conventions that refer to nothing in the world of the senses. And language demands an identified 'operator', even where there are only reciprocal interactions within a wider system. All of these characteristics bear on the developing subsystem of the self; on how we come to construe the nature of identity. The tension between the self-concept and the other modules that make up the Central Committee of the brain-mind is not just practical but linguistic, or even philosophical. They compete not just for resources and attention, but are locked into an *ontological* dispute; they disagree profoundly about what it means to exist.[53]

You cannot talk about character and personality in English without calling up the genie of personal identity. You have to say 'I am lazy', or 'I can run fast'; and the 'I' (like the 'it' in 'It is raining') seems, but *only* seems, to point to a persistent, localized entity, a 'subject', who 'possesses' these features and properties. We know intellectually, from science, and the body-brain-mind knows organismically, because it is so constructed, that the individual is ecological: there is no point at which you can accurately say that 'I' stop and 'Not-I', or even 'You', begin. If we remember that it is in the nature of language to misrepresent the world, and that it *has* to do so to be of any use, then it is a good servant. If we forget, then it makes a troublesome master.

Establishing Head Quarters

The European languages take us one more step further away from the ecological, systemic nature of the organism. As well as inviting us to think of ourselves as a self-contained meatball, rolling through space and time, having encounters, acquiring and modifying our characters, and collecting memories, it also leads us to believe that there is an internal controller, a little 'I' behind the eyes, who is in charge. Enshrined in language is the view that a brain-mind on its own is not equal to the task of making wise decisions in a complicated and uncertain world. We are seduced by language into supposing that some mysterious form of intelligence, closely associated with consciousness, is needed as well. Because we are not conscious of the brain-mind's intricate, lightning computations, we cannot believe that it is up to the job, and we add in to the way we think about ourselves the idea of a Higher Authority.

We say 'I chose the fillet steak', when describing a meal in a restaurant, or 'I decided to walk the dog before doing the dishes for a change', and the syntax gives us the sense that we are not just describing what happened, but also somehow taking credit for making things happen in the way they did. What happened was the ordering of the steak, or the walking of the dog; but the use of 'chose' and 'decided' suggest something more than that: that the ordering and walking were only the external products of a prior internal process that 'I' was not only privy to, but actively involved in.

Mistaken Identity

Before the time when the development of 'identity' really took off, the opportunity to use other people's descriptions of us as a way of helping us crystallize out our own attributes was nothing but tentative. If my internal scan fails to find a sub-pattern that matches your projection, I can always go back to you and try to resolve the discrepancy—or just ignore it. However, there must have come a point when one party to this dialogue, A, was sufficiently powerful with respect to the other, B—a high status member of society, or B's mother, perhaps—that A was able to make B an offer he could not refuse, and he incorporated A's judgement of himself into his 'Self System' *even though it did not check out in his own experience.*

Now B is in trouble because, when he takes the Self System—the SS—as a guide to his own nature, and calibrates his actions with respect to this false image, he is now going to be off-target with his actions. He acts as if he had an attribute that he in fact does not, or acts as if he was lacking something that he does in fact possess. Now the misapprehensions that are endemic to language—the sense that 'things' are more autonomous, more clear-cut and more permanent than they really are—are compounded by some very specific errors concerning one's own character.

This would initially make a difference to one's communication, to social relationships. Now one would sometimes lie *inadvertently* to friends and allies, and any joint plans that were based on the mistaken identity would be liable to go (inexplicably) wrong. The strategy for cementing alliances would now be prone to undermine and confuse them. But a far worse kind of mistake is now made possible. If B comes to use the SS not only as a basis for communication, but also as the foundation on which he build his actions, he is going to be at odds with himself, as well as with others. His actions become mis-guided, like the trajectory of a badly programmed missile. When people lay their plans on the basis of an adulterated sense of themselves, they head confidently off in wrong directions, like an explorer with a faulty compass. They become fundamentally disorientated. We shall explore the vast scope for self-deception which this opens up in later chapters. And we shall also have to explain why it is that this disastrous shift in the brain-mind's 'centre of gravity' comes about.

A Summary of Self

What I might call my 'self' thus has representations at each of the three levels of mind that we identified in the previous chapter: first, the foundation layer of filaments grouped according to experience; second, the extraction from their context of things related according to concept, function or meaning; third, the level of language and its potential disconnection from personal experience. In the modular patchwork, therefore, 'I' am implicit and fragmented. My character reveals itself in the style with which I pursue my goals and go about my business. Just as these minitheories must pick up patterns in the world, so they must co-ordinate them with patterns of Me—my appetites, dispositions and quirks. If I am diabetic, or arthritic, or allergic to dairy products, the programs that are designed to feed me must be calibrated accordingly. What I can achieve, and under what conditions, is relative to my talents and my temperament, so 'I' must be represented in the equations that compute my every move: represented, but not delineated; not yet identified as a separate 'variable'.

But as I learn the language of persons, as we have seen, I begin to be able, with guidance, to pick myself out of the line-up. The different aspects of 'self' that we reviewed come into focus and gravitate together, a loose affiliation of bodily systems for recognizing intruders, remembering posture and orienting myself in the sensory world; of aspects of preference and behaviour that have precipitated out of specific scripts; and a collection of attributes that have been imputed to me, and which I have 'bought', as being true descriptions without seeking, or finding, any warrant from them in my own experience. Thus is constituted a motley Self System that spans all three levels: partly verbal and partly tacit; partly general and partly situation-specific; partly accurate and partly wrong.

All of these drift together under the umbrella of my name, which is often abbreviated to 'I' or 'Me', and which confers an aura of coherence, permanence and substantiality which my constituents do not in fact possess. When I say 'I', I can mean a dozen different types of thing. I'm coming. I'm over here. I'm an animal. I'm lazy. I'm British. I'm bored. I'm hungry. I'm worthless. I'm walking the dog (look at me!) I'm going to walk the dog. I walked the dog. I *tried* to walk the dog (but couldn't get it to follow me). I *wanted* to walk the dog (but didn't get round to it). I *can* walk the dog. I *might* walk the dog (if I have time). I *won't* walk the dog. I *thought* of walking the dog (but decided against it). I wouldn't walk that damn dog if it were the last life-form in the universe. I want my Mum. I *hate* my Mum. I hate French. I have a funny feeling in my tummy. I have a funny feeling about Mr Mandrake. I'm having trouble starting (I think my spark-plugs must be dirty)....As Kurt Vonnegut would say, 'and on and on'.

If words are used to point (That's Daddy; that's Fluffie; that's a piano; woops, that's dirty...), what on earth is it that is pointed at by the word 'I' (or 'you', as you call me)? This is a conundrum that has to be solved by every English-speaking child that is far more weird than the square root of -1, infinity and dividing by 0, all rolled into one. Yet all these 'I's seem to point 'inwards' at something. Imagine if you can that you had never seen your face in a mirror, and then found yourself in the middle of a ring of people—friendly people, nice people—all of whom are pointing at an area somewhere above your chest and passing remarks about what a pleasant expression you have, and how pretty, and what a sweet little nose just like her Auntie Madge. They might even help you by pointing to aspects of the meat-ball that each of *them* seems to have balanced on their shoulders. But of an equivalent, in your own first-hand visual experience, there is not an iota of evidence.[54] 'My face', for you, is an idea that exists only in language. (I am ignoring the 'face' you can construct by *feeling* with your hands what is above your chest; this is a very different, and much more shadowy, animal than the one we associate with mirrors.)

Yet, if you persist, you will come to be able to *talk* confidently and acceptably about 'your face', to use the language in approved ways, to echo the judgements of those around you, so that nobody would be able to tell that you didn't have a clue what you were talking *about*. You will, after a while, forget that you have no direct knowledge to underpin your fluent linguistic performance. You will even develop a faint feeling that you could even *see* this face, out of the corner of your eye, if you turned quickly enough...but somehow you never put this vague assumption to a stringent test. The little word 'I' points to a psychological face that is like the physical face in this 'fairy tale', only much more convoluted, and much more slippery.

So all the ingredients of this 'self-concept' are perfectly straightforward, even if some of them are arguable, troublesome or false. It is the fact that they are lumped together and treated, in language, as if they were all 'attributes' 'of' 'the' 'same' 'thing'. I have to use a form of punctuational overkill here, to make it absolutely clear how *questionable* these familiar little words are; how they embody a *theory* of the self which is only tenable because it is invisible; an invisibility which is the almost-inevitable result of long acquaintance.

Anthropomorphism

Because the vocabulary of personality evolved so rapidly, its sophisticated descriptions of character and relationship would have formed the lexicon in terms of which the rest of the world was first discussed. The domains of prey and predators, rivers and mountains, storms and stars would have been approached using the familiar social world as a source of metaphors and relationships. If people's feelings are agreed to constitute sufficient grounds for their actions, for example—if one woman can legitimately curse another *because* she feels wronged—then mountains can have love affairs and crops fail because the gods are displeased. The land is our mother; the trees are our brothers: however we *behave*, the understanding of our place in the cosmos that we articulate cannot but be cast in the image of querulous grandparents, ungrateful neighbours, faithless lovers and disobedient children: that is the only language that our ancestors had.

Western science and technology have 'grown out of' these picturesque metaphors and myths. We have developed over the last millennium languages and theories that enable us to predict and control nature to an unprecedented degree. To reach this level of control, the language of family had to be superseded by a new vocabulary and a new 'grammar' of relationships, one which could no longer be derived from society. A Brave New World of rationality and logic, of empiricism and deduction, was created in culture, and in individual brains, that now had only remote connections with the personal. Thoughts could be had in this world, theories could be proposed, devices could be designed, that were unconstrained by the 'natural morality' of traditional society.

The deeper, older brain-mind was designed to provide continual integration of need and deed; what could be thought was in every moment constrained and guided by an embedded sense of purpose. The 'creativity' that the network allowed was an instantaneous function of the total set of priorities—short-term and long-term, individual and altruistic—that were represented within it. That which was undesirable was literally unthinkable.[55] But with the creation of this disconnected realm of Truth and Objectivity, what could be thought was freed from these implicit ethical constraints, and became limited only by the rules of rationality and evidence. Now you could think what you pleased. You could conjecture a new theory, or imagine a new kind of device, and then there was nothing to stop you trying to split the atom, or to clone the gene, to see if you were 'right'.

As creativity became unfettered, it also became unprincipled. In throwing out the bathwater of 'naive', mythical accounts of nature, we also got rid of the human baby—the implicit checks and balances on human ingenuity that the fundamental social metaphors carried forward with them into our dealings with the natural world. Naive they may have been, but embedded within them was a natural sense of proportion and responsibility; not articulated as a code of conduct, but saturating the metaphors themselves. Just as (most) traditional societies learnt over time to protect their children, respect their elders, tolerate cantankerous grandparents, forgive (up to a point) lapses of manners and derelictions of duty, so these human-scale virtues were carried over into their dealings with crops, animals and natural forces.

When the branches of reason are no longer rooted in the ancient soil of our embodied understanding of ecology and community, then a man can happily work 9 till 5 on a weapons guidance system, and dash home to see the children he loves before they go to bed; a woman can work Monday till Friday for a transnational petrochemical company, and drive down the motorway on Friday evening for a weekend at the country cottage where the air is drenched with honeysuckle; and neither of them notices, as they change into their jeans, that like Superman they are literally turning into different people. Their priorities, reactions, feelings and even identities are changing as the energy of their brains syphons down from one level to another.

As Kurt Vonnegut wrote in *Galapagos*:

Human brains back then had become such copious and irresponsible generators of suggestions as to what might be done with life, that they made acting for the benefit of future generations seem like one of many arbitrary games which might be played by narrow enthusiasts—like poker or polo or the bond market, or the writing of science-fiction novels...

That, in my opinion, was the most diabolical aspect of those old-time big brains: They would tell their owners, in effect, 'Here is a crazy thing we could actually do, probably, but we would never do it of course. It's just fun to think about'. And then, as though in trances, the people would really do it—have slaves fight each other to death in the Colosseum, or burn people alive in the public square for holding opinions which were locally unpopular, or build factories whose only purpose was to kill people in industrial quantities, or to blow up whole cities, and on and on. Somewhere there should have been, but was not, a warning to this effect: In this era of big brains, anything which can be done, will be done—so hunker down.[56]

In this chapter we have assembled a number of the ingredients of the 'self'. Each of these emerged gradually as language seemed to offer new avenues for meeting the ever more complex demands of living in society. And, because they were all linked together with a common *name*, they became bound together as a new, separate subcompartment within the brain-mind—the 'Self System', or the 'SS'. Instead of 'self' being distributed across all the different minitheories, all the scenarios in which a person took part, it became precipitated out as an ill-defined set of general personal characteristics, a language-based conglomeration of features associated with a nebulous sense of inner authority, of being able to instigate, direct or veto various lines of thought and action. But this is just the beginning of our troubles. With the invention of *leisure*, things took another turn for the worse.

NINE

Affluence, Leisure and Learning

A camel is stronger than a man; an elephant is larger; a lion has greater valour; cattle can eat more than a man; birds are more virile. Man was made for the purpose of learning.

El-Ghazali

The wisdom of a learned man cometh by opportunity of leisure; and he that hath little business shall become wise.

Ecclesiasticus 38:34

The Golden Age of Homo Sapiens

At a certain point in the history of a successful species, life becomes easy. A new capacity evolves which permits the colonization of a vacant niche, or a definitive triumph over a rival species. An increase in ability makes available a resource that was previously inaccessible or unusable. A new technique enables the exploitation of an existing resource in a more powerful or productive fashion. Or simply a change in climatic or other conditions means that, for a while, resources are plentiful, and threats are rare.[57]

The formidable intelligence of our human forebears made life in many places relatively easy between 10,000 and 20,000 years ago. Tool use—for hunting, fishing, harvesting, cooking, clothes-making and so on—had become sophisticated. Robust shelters and store-houses were routinely constructed. And social groups had evolved stable forms of organization, which enabled, for example, the coop-erative collecting, transporting, preparing and sharing of food. Many hunter-gatherer societies, for instance, did not lead the back-break-ing subsistence life that one might expect. Given a bit of luck in finding a congenial climate with plentiful food supplies and few competitors or predators, life could have been luxurious. Marshall Sahlins, summing up his research on aboriginal Australians, argues that:

> A good case can be made that hunters and gatherers work less time than we do; and, rather than a continuous travail, the food quest is intermittent, leisure abundant, and there is a greater amount of sleep in the daytime per capita per year than in any other condition of society.[58]

If needs are few, and satisfied with relative ease, as is clearly the case for such groups, then it makes sense (as Sahlins does) to refer to them as 'the original affluent societies'. We are reminded of Rousseau's 'noble savage':

> the closer to his natural desires man has stayed, the smaller is the difference between his faculties and his desires, and consequently the less removed he is from being happy. He is never less unhappy than when he appears entirely destitute, for unhappiness consists not in the privation of things but in the need that is felt for them.[59]

We now take this communal approach to food so much for granted that it is easy to underestimate what a major step forward—even from the lifestyle of the chimpanzee—this was. Primatologist Glynn Isaac suggests that 'if we could interview a chimpanzee about the behavioural differences separating us, this might well be the item that it found most impressive—"These humans get food and instead of eating it promptly like any sensible ape, they haul it off and share it with others!"'.[60]

The Glimmerings of Choice

Where there is abundance, there is variety. The Natufians, for example, were a sedentary people living in northern Syria from about 12,000 to 10,000 B.C., who had a much more varied diet than their predecessors. Daily life involved choices and preferences as well as necessities. For meat they could choose from gazelle, fallow deer, ibex or fish, and they supplemented these with all kinds of wild cereals and pulses.[61] Their descendants were among the first to domesticate and cultivate the cereals, gradually ensuring an even greater reliability and variety of supply. They were able to ask 'What shall we have for dinner tonight?'. Likewise they and other civilizations were increasing the range of styles of dress and ornamentation: they were able to ask themselves 'Which shoes shall I wear this morning?', or 'Is this a leather jerkin or a woollen coat type of day?'

And as well as these everyday decisions, individuals could have begun to select more enduring idiosyncratic lifestyles. Within these societies of, let us suppose, 100–150 people, it would have been possible for social roles to become differentiated. Not everyone had to cook, or to butcher meat, or to tend the goats, or make moccasins, or to plan the next raid, or make and decorate pottery. Different individuals are suited by their chromosomes and by their personal history for different roles. They have different passions, talents, preferences and tolerances. So the niches that people come to fill are determined partly by happenstance, but also partly by their own predispositions. There is a greatly increased opportunity for individuals to choose, and to continually renegotiate if they wish, their way of life.

So in times of stability, abundance and variety, the answer to the age-old evolutionary question 'What shall I do next?' is no longer, on many occasions, dictated by the exigencies of survival. The highly developed, sophisticated brain-minds are less often kicked into action by the sudden appearance of a predator, or a crisis in the food supply. These brains were produced by evolution to solve multifactorial survival problems 'on-line'; their design specification required them to integrate a limited but constantly fluctuating agenda of survival needs with the repertoires of capabilities, and current opportunities, available; and to do it quickly, 'on the hoof'. Now these powerful computers would sometimes find themselves in a very different situation: one where there were no pressing survival needs to be addressed, an increasing range of non-survival related options to be considered, and plenty of leisure to think about things. The human brain-mind in this situation would be, so to speak, 'all dressed up and nowhere to go', with masses of spare capacity and time on its hands.

There are a number of possible solutions to this predicament—this *embarras de richesse.* One would have been to follow the lead of the juvenile sea squirt who, you remember, wandered the sea-bed until it found a desirable residence, and solved the problem of its now redundant brain by eating it. The problem with this 'solution' is of course that it is irrevocable; by achieving a measure of happy veg-etable-ism, you have also removed your ability to respond to diffi-cult challenges when they *do* arise. The other two options are learn-ing, and identification. In the rest of this chapter I shall indicate the nature of the learning option, and the consequences for a society that adopts it, perhaps overenthusiastically. In the next chapter I shall return to the second option, that of identification, and show how the Self System can be hooked up to a person's Survival Systems so that it magics into existence a new gamut of threats, and therefore an endless succession of new 'pseudo-problems' to be solved.

Play-Time

When no obvious threat is demanding your attention (and you are well rested and in good health), one useful way of filling your time is to go looking for a new challenge. By investigating either the implications of what you have learnt already, or physically going exploring, you may uncover latent possibilities and patterns, the knowledge of which will stand you in good stead if and when they actually jump out at you in 'real life'. The first route involves the cultivation of thought, imagination and reflection—the kind of abil-ity which we have already shown is present even in quite young children when they are 'chewing the cud' of their experience. Through the medium initially of symbolic play, and later of logical thought, links can be made and generalizations extracted from the mental mosaic of specific encounters.[62]

It is natural, and useful, for these ruminations to pay special attention to any possible threats that may be uncovered. But, as with every survival strategy, it has its time and its place, and if it becomes compulsive, it becomes counter-productive. No situation is absolutely safe. If you scrutinize it for long enough, and let your imagination run free, there will always be something that can go wrong. Thus it is that bored and restless brains construct scenarios in which loved ones who are late home have been involved in horrific automobile accidents; in which a slight crack in the bedroom ceiling might mean that the house is falling down; and in which a colleague who failed to laugh at our best joke is sure to be plotting something to our serious disadvantage.

A corollary of this tendency is to use thought and imagination to try to improve on *past* encounters, rerunning the tapes and inserting different endings that would have been more to our advantage. As Osho Rajneesh said in one of his lectures: 'Before, you are wise. After, you are wise. In between, you are otherwise. And in the middle is *life.*' [63] If the computer is programmed to extend its search for adverse possibilities to the limits of probability, it will end up jammed with its own remote alarm calls.

Exploration

The internal sifting over of knowledge to uncover potential links and weevils is mirrored by an increase in the 'off-line' search for, or creation of, challenging situations in the real world. The quest for knowledge can take many forms. Some of them involve putting yourself directly in situations that will provoke further learning, without (hopefully) containing mortal challenges that you will not be able to meet. You can set off in a boat to seek what lies beyond the horizon, and if you are lucky, will return not only having colonized a new land, and captured its resources, but also with enhanced skill in navigation. Alternatively, you can explore vicariously, by putting yourself in other people's shoes. For the more timid, the more patient, and the better off, there are sting-drawn echoes of these adventures available as roller-coaster rides, horror movies, bungee jumps and packaged air-conditioned safaris.

The opportunities that a culture provides to explore vicariously its fears and threats are called 'entertainment', and the entertainments that it offers are therefore symptomatic of what it reveres and what it disdains. Circuses enable you to see real people overcoming their fear—*your* fear—of heights, wild animals and looking ridiculous. Soaps flip over the stone of family or corporate life, and show you people behaving as badly—jealously, meanly, violently, stupidly, resentfully, lustfully—as you, your family or your colleagues would sometimes like to be, but dare not. You can see what it might gain you, and what it might cost you, to behave with less restraint. Game shows and quiz shows celebrate the intensity with which our culture confuses knowledgeability, intelligence, a good memory, and personal worth, and hold out the delicious possibility that someone might end up looking, in front of millions of people, as stupid as we often feel. And 'sports' offer images of dedication and fitness, but more importantly of what it is like to be obsessed; to dedicate yourself to the point where there can be no excuses, and yet to 'fail', to only get the silver medal. Televised spectating *seems* to offer us models of human behaviour and feeling, yet perhaps they have become only a tease, an avalanche of images that are too many, too fast, too superficial for us to do anything with. They arouse, but cannot satisfy the powerful urge for vicarious learning.

Literature and myth offer powerful stimuli for this vicarious exploration. Novels reach through words to the concepts and scenarios that structure our understanding of social life, and compose on those personal strings new harmonies. The notes are endlessly familiar—fear, misunderstanding, deceit, love, rage—but our fascination with the range of chords that can be struck seems similarly inexhaustible. From Beryl the Peril to Jude the Obscure, there is someone out there, in a comic or a book, who is facing what we hardly dare to face; hanging in there when we are set to flee; finally doing well in situations that are even worse than our own. They encourage, they inspire, above all they inform; they show us through actions and thoughts what the inside of another human being feels like.

And there is also the option to develop knowledge at several removes from the chalkface of human interaction—to become a scholar, a philosopher, an academic. If you end up in cancer research or weapons research, biotechnology or intermediate technology, you can follow the thread back from your lab-book to a concern with human survival and welfare. But if your field is the origins of life, or the history of the subjunctive, or the behaviour of the brown trout, or the theory of numbers, then the trail may be so faint as to be invisible. The thrill of the intellectual chase is no longer means but end. The process of enquiry has come to constitute its own reward.

The problem with the strategy of endless knowledgeability is again that it may become addictive. Once the collection of knowledge, unrelated to immediate need, becomes a priority, there is no end to it. When we learn in the context of an immediate personal need, what we learn becomes automatically bound in with the mental module that is operating at the time. Gradually it may be distilled out of its original context so that it is available more widely; but the process of 'disembedding' leaves it still linked in with the brain's intricate networks of access and retrieval. But when we bombard the brain with a constant stream of fragments of information, items on the news, gossip, opinions, Amazing Facts and Trivial Pursuits, it becomes not modular but granular, a jumble of unstructured, undigested impressions, impossible to make use of and hard to retrieve. Our culture has increased the rate of feeding while leaving us with brain whose 'digestive system', designed by evolution for less hectic times, refuses to be hurried.

The Invention of Science

Out of increased leisure, and the increasing facility for thought and imagination, came the ability to ask, and sometimes to answer, a particularly powerful question: How Come? The 'natural learning ability' of the brain-mind is excellent at uncovering correlations. It is a beautifully designed pattern detector, which enables you, on the basis of experience, to predict what happens next—and therefore how to intervene in the flow of events to alter what happens next to your own advantage. But an effective *explanation* for why a domain (a motorcycle engine, falling objects, mother-and-baby) behaves as it does amplifies the power of prediction enormously.

There is nothing so practical as a good theory. You can trace and identify an unprecedented fault in the engine; you can design a communications satellite; you can help the mother understand her depression, and its effect on her child. Some patterns may be too long-term or diffuse for even the brain to pick up. The correlations between childhood leukaemia and radiation from a nuclear plant, or between endemic dysentery and dumping your waste in the stream, may simply never dawn on you. But a successful *theory* that links health to the two different kinds of pollution may enable the 'mind' to see what the 'brain' cannot.

But today we are witnessing again a helpful servant metamorphose into a monstrous master. What starts out as a valuable use for a leisured brain-mind turns out to possess no natural brake to its activities. If some is good, more must be better, goes the cultural logic, and the evolutionary brain-mind is unable to govern what has become a runaway machine, spewing out theories, opinions, attitudes and ideas without ground and apparently without end. Let me leave it to Kurt Vonnegut, in another quotation from his book *Galapagos*, to sum things up with his usual sharp pathos:

> Darwin did not change the (Galapagos) islands but only people's opinion of them. That was how important mere opinions used to be back in the era of great big brains [i.e. *now*]. Mere opinions, in fact, were as likely to govern people's actions as hard evidence, and were subject to sudden reversals as hard evidence could never be. So the Galapagos Islands could be hell in one moment and heaven in the next, and Julius Caesar could be a statesman in one moment and a butcher in the next, and Ecuadorian paper money could be traded for food, shelter and clothing in one moment and line the bottom of a birdcage in the next, and the universe could be created by God Almighty in one moment and by a big explosion in the next— and on and on...
>
> Even at this late date, I am still full of rage at a natural order which would have permitted the evolution of something so distracting and irrelevant and disruptive as those great big brains of a million years ago. If they had told the truth, then I could see some point in everybody's having one. But these things lied all the time![64]

Projects and Plans

The last one I wish to point out here is the opportunity for formulating long-term goals, interests or plans. At first these would have centred, as usual, on the social sphere. Instead of thinking in terms only of single encounters with other individuals or groups, there would be advantage to be gained from planning ahead. These longer-term plans were at first almost certainly communal (as we shall see in a moment), but there is no reason, as with other cognitive abilities, for them to stop there. It would not take much to realize their potential at the individual level. And they need not all be based around the manipulation of others for personal gain.

The shift from a concern with the immediate 'tactics' of survival to the development of longer-term strategies and campaigns would have been of immense benefit in the competition between different tribal groups for territory and resources. Planning campaigns or raids involves complex calculations and projections, if they are to stand a good chance of success. The choice of opponent is vital. Wars have habitually been won by a combination of superior technology and an astute choice of victim.[65] And a good campaign is one that does not just result in a victory, but in the acquisition thereby of valuable resources. So information is needed about the 'enemy's' assets, which can be offset against the costs and risks involved: how many warriors will we need; how long will it take us; what supplies will we need; whose support can we count on; and so on. The amount and kind of our arms will depend not only on the state of our own technology, but also on the anticipated armoury, and methods of defence, of our foe.

Empathy and War

But most importantly of all, from the cognitive perspective, the best-laid plans are those that take into account the way your rivals might be thinking, because this enables you to mount a pre-combat campaign of misinformation. If We know that They are short of a certain resource, We can avoid their attentions if We pretend to be poor in that respect as well. If They are nervous of attack, let Us pretend to have our eye on quite a different tribe all together. If We suspect that They have cracked our code, then let us keep using it to broadcast misleading information...but We must do it subtly, so that They do not twig that We *know* that They have broken the code. This kind of disinformation reached a pinnacle of sophistication in the complicated attempts at deception by both sides in the Second World War.[66]

This ability to mount intricate campaigns of deception requires yet another development in social intelligence. Not only do you need to have a model of the character—the desires and fears, perspectives and habits—of the Other; you also need to be able to construct the kind of model of the world—and specifically of *you*—that such an Other—a society or an individual—would construct. You have, in a word, to develop 'empathy'. A child playing hide-and-seek needs to 'know' (at some not necessarily conscious level) that it is not sufficient for her not to be able to see you. She has to develop an internal model of the room, the sofa she is trying to conceal herself behind, *and* of what you can see from where you are standing. Then she can place herself in a way that takes into account your point of view, not (just) her own.[67]

On a larger scale, the person planning a major coup of disinformation will have to build into it what she knows of the enemy's suspicions, how they *think*, so that the deception can contain plausible answers to their likely questions. And what is more, this entails that you can draw a sketch of *yourself*, within the other person's picture, which not only represents what *you* know of yourself, but also is modified in the light of the others' knowledge of you. Your sketch of yourself will be successful in helping you determine which way other people are likely to jump, or to interpret your signals, to the extent that it represents accurately the way they see you.

It has been suggested that it is this ability of the brain-mind to construct models of other people's viewpoint that required evolution to play its trump card, and bring forth *consciousness*.[68] There is no good reason to suppose this. The brain, as we have seen, abstracts 'concepts' (of classes, groups and individuals) from the accumulated records of personal encounters, *and* the hear-say evidence it has received, and represents these as loose, 'fuzzy' packages of attributes. When the concept is sufficiently activated by its inputs, the whole structure tends to light up; but the *specific* pattern that is activated depends on the pattern of priming that was there before. When you hear the word 'dog', the actual pattern of units (octopuses) that fires (wakes up) will depend heavily on whether you have just seen a Pekinese or a Great Dane, or on whether the context has led you to suppose that the animal is tame or fierce. Each concept has a 'core' of features that will always light up (unless explicitly denied); what Marvin Minsky calls its 'default values',[69] and a more diffuse penumbra of associated features from which the context, via the priming mechanism, will select what 'fits' and what is needed.

So the precise pattern of activity that any event gives rise to depends on what other concepts are already active, or have recently been so. When I am trying to see how you, my opponent, will react, the brain-mind first lights up the concept I have developed of you. This concept then sends out its characteristic pattern of priming to other parts of the network, including my *self*-concept, so when this is turned on, the actual pattern of 'Me' that lights up will necessarily be 'Me-in-the-Context-of-You'. The particular characteristics of me that are activated will be precisely those that—according to my model—*you* are looking for. Now the brain-mind is able to compute a course of action that either highlights, or masks, those attributes. Thus the ability to 'see yourself from another person's perspective' is another example of what the brain-mind is built for and good at. There is no need to wheel out the Big Gun of consciousness—not just yet.

We have seen in this chapter various examples of the way in which the capacity for imagination and exploration can get out of hand. But how is this unbalancing of the brain-mind's priorities possible? It is useful to be able to anticipate a rival's responses; but when you are so preoccupied with the next business deal that you absent-mindedly walk out into the path of a bus, things have clearly got out of kilter. It is to this key question that we turn in the next chapter.

TEN

Identity and Survival

When our ruling passion is no longer survival it becomes comfort. To someone whose passion *is* survival our preoccupation with comforts is ignoble and trivial, utterly selfish; there's no way it can be justified. It can't even be understood.

Nicholas Freeling[70]

On Deciding Who to Be

For organisms other than human beings, the issue of survival is (on the Darwinian view, at least) clear-cut. The evolutionary imperative is for your *offspring* to survive, carrying your genes forward into the next generation. And for this to happen, the most important thing is for *you* to survive until your children are born and raised. Survival means *physical* survival.

But the way twentieth-century Western human beings behave makes it clear that, for them, this is very far from being the end of the story. On the whole people still care about their physical well-being. But they also seem to care about an enormous number of other things as well; and, on occasion, they appear willing to risk their lives for the most surprising reasons. A starving woman may refuse a cup of warm milk, because her identification with the cause of A United Ireland is stronger, at that moment, than her interest in life itself. A man may expose himself to injury or death in a duel, because his 'good name' has been impeached, and life without honour is not worth living; or move to a new country and adopt a new 'identity' when evidence of his fraudulent research is published. Clearly the partial vacuum created by the scarcity of life-threatening events has been filled with a host of other concerns. Instead of opting to cash our evolutionary good luck in terms of leisure and learning, we seem to be more busy, more worried, more *threatened* than our ancestors: more even than our domestic pets. How this came about is a reflection of the other option that humankind discovered for keeping itself amused: what I referred to in the last chapter as *identification*.

Wiring Your Self up to the Mains

The second major solution to the excess-brainpower problem is to hook the Self System (the development of which we began to trace in Chapter 8) directly up to the Fundamental Survival System; give it a hot-line to the Commander-in-Chief of the Armed Forces. Now anything that comes through to Allied Headquarters on the red telephone from the SS is *ipso facto* a matter of national security. Any appeal for help to the brain-mind that comes with the authorization of Self, that has the right code-word—*that* is what gets priority. If the SS is sufficiently elaborate, it will be constantly on the phone, and the Big Brain will have cracked the problem of boredom. So the preservation of the Self System becomes the engine for survival, taking precedence, if needs be, even over the interests of the physical body—even over the survival of the species. *Whatever is included within the working definition of my self, that is what the survival resources of the whole mind-brain-body system are mobilized by and dedicated to.*

This inner process of hooking some additional aspects of the brain-mind system up directly to the survival machinery is called *identification*. My 'identity' comprises whatever is inscribed within the charmed circle of the self; and whatever is written therein, that features on my list of things to be preserved. Its protection, validation and development become 'my business'. This wiring-in of different aspects of self-knowledge to the mechanisms of survival is what Freud referred to as 'cathexis'. Any part of the system that is 'cathected', when threatened, can—indeed must—call on the full defensive forces of the community as a whole. An assault on my reputation can now have exactly the same over-riding impact on the whole system as an attack of malaria or the burning-down of my grain-store.

There is no mystery about how this is achieved within the brain-mind. If I have decided that being laughed at, for example, constitutes a threat, I simply commit a continual stream of priming, long-term, to the sensory patterns that recognize laughter, so that they are 'set' to detect it and to analyse it carefully for tell-tale signs of ridicule or disdain. And then, if the Contempt Detectors fire off, they activate whatever parts of the Face-Saving System has proven successful in deflecting or neutralizing the 'threat'. I create a diversion by spilling my drink, determine never to go to parties again, bop you on the nose, start plotting your downfall...whatever.

A large part of what makes people so interesting is the different ways in which they respond to these emergencies. As Alexis de Tocqueville put it:

> I have always thought it rather interesting to follow the involuntary movements of fear in clever people. Fools coarsely display their cowardice in all its nakedness, but the others are able to cover it with a veil so delicate, so daintily woven with small plausible lies, that there is some pleasure to be found in contemplating this ingenious work of the human intelligence.[71]

When the SS is given 'top priority' in this way, it is enabled to jump the queue. No longer do all the self-related needs and threats have to compete for attention in the general prioritizing market-place of the brain-mind; like one of the permanent members of the United Nations Security Council, it has powers to push through its own concerns, and to veto the concerns of others, regardless of what those concerns happen to be. Thus the proliferation of different needs that we have discussed over the last few chapters does not just make the implicit decision-making of the brain-mind more complicated; it actually turns it on its head, and changes it in kind. The trivial can take precedence over the biologically fundamental. People can kill, even kill themselves, in order to avoid embarrassment, or to gain a material advantage that they do not really need.

The image that you have developed on the basis of your own experience of yourself is a flexible summary of the way you tend to see things and the ways you tend to react. It is open, always capable of being updated, even surprised, as you meet new situations and experiment with new ways of being. But once you 'identify' with this provisional precis of your self, it becomes a roster of injunctions that have to be preserved and obeyed. Instead of being motivated by the desire to *improve* your knowledge and skill, to keep up with the play, you are now condemned to hang around constantly *proving* to yourself and anyone who will stop to listen, that you are who you have decided to be.

And when we include in our list of things that must be preserved at all costs some or all of the labels that other people have attributed to us, but which do not fit, then we are bound to devote a lot of energy to trying to be, or to pretending to be, somebody we are not. Someone (not necessarily a man), for example, might struggle with a self-definition that prohibits (what it calls, pejoratively) 'weakness'— the natural impulse to cry, and seek physical contact with another member of the same species, when sad, overwhelmed or confused. If, *in extremis*, such an impulse becomes too powerful to inhibit, he feels 'mortified'—a word that rather gives the game away. When we are mortified—off the end of the scale of embarrassment—we are literally experiencing a little death. A fragment of identity has been disregarded (even if only temporarily), as we see ourselves flouting one of its sacred conventions. For a few minutes we are an outlaw. The Amazing (literally, 'confusing') Technicolour Dreamcoat of fictional identity is not just too small; it was cut for someone of quite a different shape, with a different taste in cloth.

Dying to Stay Alive

The beauty of identification, as a strategy for keeping busy, is that it poses problems that are, in fact, insoluble; and so as long as this remains unrecognized, we can keep ourselves running round and round in circles like a dog chasing its tail. There is no way of becoming that which it is not in our nature to be—immortal, for example. Yet people will identify with an image of themselves as youthful and firm, healthy and fit, and therefore struggle mightily against the irresistible ravages of illness, age and death.

The body-brain-mind system, of course, is dedicated to the survival of the physical being. But after the age of reproduction, when the most vital evolutionary obligations have been fulfilled, and when the main roles of the elderly—to aid the bonding of clans and dynasties, to help make sure that the vulnerable new generation make it through to maturity, and to moderate some of the wilder creativity of the youth—have been fulfilled, the hold with which the physical body clings to life naturally becomes less tenacious. As the fabric of the body ages, so its constitutional attachment to living lessens.

But not so the mind. Identity, as a set of constructs, ideas and opinions, clings on as tightly as ever. There is no necessary loosening, so it seems, of the straight-jacket; no clues built in to the ageing process that say 'Time to ease up'.[72] The body and its brain are built to look after themselves, and when the time comes, to give in gracefully. But if a *concept*, idealized or arrested in time, of the body and its functions has been inscribed within the circle of identity, then ageing is going to be a tiresome process, filled with anger and distress and vain (in both senses) attempts to stop the rot. The biological *tendency* to persist is transmuted into a *compulsion*, and survival is infused with an air of desperation.

The Proliferation of Needs: Part III

Leisure and abundance naturally give rise, as we have seen, to many choices that are only remotely, if at all, related to physical survival. People can develop, to any degree of refinement they like, their aesthetic preferences, their sense of 'style'. If these, too, get hooked in to the matrix of identity, then preferences can be upgraded to necessities, and 'taste' to a matter of life and death. If 'I am what I like', then not getting what I *want* can be as much of an emergency as not getting what I need. In fact, when I start writing in to my self-concept the fine details of my whims and foibles, I can no longer tell the difference between a need and a want.

Once the survival-machine has been programmed to seek and destroy any opposition to my 'will', then failing to persuade Mummy to fork out for an ice cream is registered as no less important to my well-being than being swept out to sea on my rubber-ring. Parents who (almost from the word go) offer their children endless choices, and who try to discern in their every move a preference or a trait, are educating them to become lifestyle addicts. Children, vitally keen to join in any game that makes them feel connected to those around them, start to identify with their impulses, and thus to engage in the life-and-death struggles to 'be' what they 'want' that are said to characterize the 'Terrible Twos'.

The Horizon of Fashion

One more step into busi-ness and bewilderment is taken when we transmute into 'needs' wants that are inherently inflationary; when we 'need', for example, to stay ahead of people whose 'need' is to catch us up. Such a step was taken in eighteenth-century Europe, and has now infected almost the entire world.[73] As economic historian Nicholas Xenos puts it: 'The European eighteenth century saw the invention of the steam engine, the jigsaw puzzle, and the toothpick. It also witnessed the invention of scarcity.' Prior to that, people's needs had been separable and, at least in principle, satiable. The basic needs—food, water, warmth and so on—appear cyclically and are satisfied by different means. A blanket is no good if you are hungry; a glass of water will not help you reproduce. And these basic needs are not addictive. We do not build up tolerances which require us to consume or copulate more, over time, in order to assuage the need.

But what happens when you mash people's social, psychological and material needs together, so that it becomes possible to gain prestige on the basis of your possessions or your achievements—but only if these are in some way *outstanding*, if they conform to the ever-changing dictates of what is 'classy'. Now your goals, originally distinct and intermittent, become homogenized and insatiable. Your needs are capable of infinite expansion. 'For us, the denizens of this world of desire, it is no longer a question of episodic insufficiency; out of our affluence we have created a social world of scarcity.'[74] As Jean-Jacques Rousseau commented:

> The object which at first appears to be at hand flees more quickly than it can be pursued. When one believes that one has reached it, it transforms and reveals itself in the distance ahead of us. No longer seeing the country we have already crossed, we count it for nothing; what remains to cross ceaselessly grows and extends. Thus one exhausts oneself without getting to the end, and the more one gains on enjoyment, the further happiness gets from us.[75]

Eighteenth-century London, in the grip of the Industrial Revolution, emerged as a hotbed of style. A high proportion of the English population either lived in London at some stage of their lives—one estimate puts it at 16 per cent—or passed through from time to time, and were thus exposed to the fashions of the court. Copies of the current fashions were available to the wealthy, and especially to the 'country gentry', for whom a London town-house was becoming *de rigueur*, and who could then take them back to their country seats to be the envy of their friends. Thanks to the new means of mass production, their servants could buy cheap imitations, and so the new game of 'keeping up with the Joneses' could spread downwards through society as well as outwards geographically.

The entrepreneurs of the day were not slow to realize what we now call 'the elasticity of demand': that the job (for that is what the 'game' quickly became) of keeping ahead could stimulate endless desire for the new 'in thing' in such everyday objects as clothing, crockery, furniture, transport...you name it. Pottery baron Josiah Wedgwood (like the computer barons at Apple-Macintosh three centuries later) knew the value of keeping the prices of each new design high, to stimulate the snobbish appetites of those who would 'love to be able to afford one'. Only once a design was well established would Wedgwood put it into mass production and drop the price—while simultaneously introducing yet another new 'top of the range' model.[76]

Because each of these goods had a price, all you needed to possess them was money—not good breeding, learning or any other of the traditional virtues—so they became available, at least as objects of desire, as dreams, to anyone. Who knows, even *you* could win the lottery. Aspiring to *own* was a game that everybody could play, at least in their minds. And because everything had its price, this desire for a prestige that could be seen reflected in the patina of one's possessions, could be, it seemed, satisfied in any one of a dozen different ways. One can swank about anything provided your neighbours want it and have not yet got it.

It was Rousseau, again, visiting London as the guest of the philosopher David Hume, who saw most clearly the inevitable culmination of this social trend, not just in endlessly escalating consumption and disappointment, but in competitiveness, aggression and deception. He observed that:

man, who had previously been free and independent, is now so to speak subjugated by a multitude of new needs....Consuming ambition, the ardent desire to raise one's relative fortune less out of genuine need than in order to place himself above others, instills in all men a black inclination to harm one another.[77]

Evolution has made us social animals. It has made us want to *belong*, and has equipped us with big brains designed to enable us to do so. But when 'having' and 'showing' become the main ways in which we gain public esteem and private satisfaction, the web of social cohesion begins to disintegrate. Interactions become competitive, but worse than that they become superficial. For thousands of years, people have been honing to a razor's edge the skill of reading each other: of discerning another person's character from an acute observation of their behaviour, as well as from the fallible tittle-tattle of gossip. But in the society that Rousseau was observing, these delicate whispers were being overwhelmed by the cries of 'wealth' and 'taste'. People were coming to advertise themselves in the tabloid headlines of the latest wig, or the most stylish carriage, and were learning to conceal the small print of their 'true characters' behind the increasingly elaborate facades of etiquette and 'propriety'.

The Thrill of the Chase

In the end the process of acquisition itself becomes an integral part of the Scarcity Lifestyle: it not only results in the possession of the desired object, but the 'thrill of the chase' develops an addictive quality. Sending off for the catalogues, saving up, trailing round the shops for Saturdays on end looking for the perfect lampshade to go with the newly decorated living room—all of these provide ample opportunity to express preferences, to nourish the sense of style with which one is identified.

The promotion of these marginal matters from the brain-mind's 'chorus' to its centre stage seems to offer manageable opportunities for the Self to experience its pivotal feeling of *autonomy*. In a world where we are daily reminded that at least 99 per cent of the things that affect us are beyond our control, it can be reassuring to focus intently on the 1 per cent that is currently represented by the choice of curtains for the spare bedroom. When looking up at the mountains reminds us uncomfortably of how little we can truly influence, exaggerated concern with some molehills (even though we may complain about the time and the cost and the sore feet) may have a tranquillizing effect. 'I shop—I compare, I choose, I buy, I cut off the horrid fringe thing, I own—therefore I am.'

Being Right

One elegant refinement of the game of judging people by their possessions can be achieved by the simple expedients of viewing *knowledge* as a possession, and opinion as a commodity, as subject to the whims of fashion as the length of skirts. When survival comes to depend on a generalized ability to have answers to all conceivable questions, and the 'right' opinions about all conceivable subjects, then the tail of the mind is tucked into its own mouth. 'Being right' is now elevated from being a means of survival to an end: political, social and epistemological correctness for its own sake. The *purpose* of the mind now, beautifully, paradoxically, becomes its own survival.

Any piece of knowledge or belief can be made a subscriber to the survival hot-line, and then *its* preservation becomes the business of the system as a whole. If 'I am what I think', then even my half-baked views on politics or football or the best seats to have on a jumbo-jet *have* to be right. If such an opinion turns out to be wrong, then *I* am wrong, and that is another little death. So the full majesty of the brain-mind's power can be turned on by even the merest suggestion that I could be just a teeny-weeny bit wrong. There are people who react even to being questioned with a furious mixture of anxiety and rage that would do credit to Attila the Hun in full cry.

Whereas the original function of the mind—all its knowledge, all its processes—was to expand the capacity of the brain to help the body-system as a whole to co-ordinate and defend itself, *now* the inversion of priorities is complete, and it becomes the job of the whole system to protect the mind. When a belief becomes one of the things that I am committed to protect, it becomes sacrosanct, a shibboleth, a sacred cow. Learning is finished. New information is a threat of invalidation, not a promise of deeper understanding. The cogs of cognition are jammed. Survival is now jeopardized by the very engine whose job it is to promote it. Humankind is finally hoist with its own petard.

ELEVEN

Accentuate the Permanent: the Narrative Self

Our fundamental tactic of self-protection, self-control and self-definition is not spinning webs or building dams, but telling stories, and more particularly concocting and controlling the story we tell others—and ourselves—about who we are. And just as spiders don't have to think, consciously and deliberately, about how to spin their webs, and just as beavers, unlike professional human engineers, do not consciously and deliberately plan the structures they build, we (unlike *professional* human storytellers) do not consciously and deliberately figure out what narratives to tell and how to tell them. Our tales are spun, but for the most part we don't spin them; they spin us. Our human consciousness, and our narrative selfhood, is their product, not their source.

Daniel Dennett[78]

The Origins of Fiction

As we saw in Chapter 8, one of the basic functions of language is to enable people to develop and communicate 'minitheories' about each other. And we also suggested that this ability to formulate hypotheses about the reasons why people acted as they did came to be used reflexively by individuals to explain their own actions. Just as I can spin a hypothetical story to account for *your* funny little ways, so am I able to theorize about myself. Particularly when one of my actions seems not to fit with the expectations of the Self System, the 'How come?' story generator—the 'Narrator'—could be called on to try to build a plausible account out of the same conceptual vocabulary that I apply to others.

Now suppose that these stories begin to get strung together into an increasingly continuous narrative. The activity of generating putative explanations for what I am doing might come to take on an almost addictive quality. It becomes like a radio in the background, featuring an internal 'commentator', continually adding a description (in words) of the action which is shot through with interpretations, suggestions, judgements and asides. The personal narrative, constantly spewing out like ticker-tape, reinforces the view of the Self as a lone general, sitting in head-quarters, receiving intelligence, planning the campaign and issuing orders. Many languages now are so saturated with this view of human nature that any child who wants to join the speakers' club has to accept it. It is not that English *presents* a psychology. It embodies it so completely that a child never has a chance to question it. If she wants to speak properly, she has to *infer* for herself the theory which her language presupposes.

The basic features of the mythical 'I' are separateness, autonomy and persistence. 'Things' have boundaries, they have inherent qualities and characteristics, and they move through space, and exist through time. The stories of the Narrator helps to solidify—to give apparent credence to—all three of these core features of the self. The language of inner traits *is* the language of things and their distinguishing marks: pretty, needy, hopeless at maths, whatever. The language of folk psychology—wishing, desiring, regretting, choosing, deciding—as well as the complicated weaselly modal verbs like do, can, try, will and so on that we have already discussed in Chapter 8, conspire to point ever more forcefully at some experiencer behind the experience, doer behind the deed, chooser behind the choice.

And the linked episodes of the Narrator's tale stretch back into the past, like a long-running soap, and in all of them 'I' am the star; there is a common presence, a character called 'Guy' whose story this is. It seems so obvious that it is the same real 'me'—somewhat greyer and stouter, I must admit, than twenty years ago, but still going strong—that it is perverse to point out the difference between the character and the actor. The same *character*, with the same name, keeps showing up, sure, just as Daisy the pantomime cow delights the children with her antics night after night. But could there not be a whole team of actors taking it in turns to 'be' the front and the back legs? The name and the costume give the illusion of continuity; but the body-brain-mind-world system, which is the only *real* actor in the show, may be constantly changing, and is certainly no more visible than the people inside the cow.

What could possibly cast doubt on the conviction that the actor and the character are the same? Why should 'I' entertain the possibility that it was in fact a whole string of actors who played the lead in all those old memory clips? Of course it was 'Me' who fell into the brook when 'I' was eight; 'Me' who lolled self-consciously on the walls of darkened rooms clutching a paper cup of cheap red wine at student parties; 'Me' who got married and had the 'reception' in a fish-and-chip shop.

The most fundamental reason—the theme of this book—is that science, from one end, and mystical experience, from the other, give us descriptions of the 'actor' that are quite unlike the 'character' that I experience and remember myself to be. For the true actor is (like the people inside the pantomime cow) in practice unknown to us, and in principle unknowable—whereas I think I know the 'character' rather well. And the true actor is a system that included much of what I think of as 'Me', but is much wider and deeper. The 'character' is individual, while the actor is ecological. Who we are is fundamentally misrepresented by the Narrator.

The Story-teller's Craft

But there are more specific ways in which the stories that the Narrator tells are skewed versions of events. The stories have to be built around those personal traits that I consider to be mandatory. If I believe myself to be an abject failure, then the Narrator cannot suddenly come up with a story in which I am a brilliant success. All other things being equal, the Narrator's job is to present 'Me' in a favourable, or at least a sympathetic, light. But though I am usually the star, the role I play may be victim, or even villain, if the Self System so dictates.

But sometimes the demands of the Narrator to tell a convincing tale can actually override the SS and cause it to change so that it falls into line with the story. In an experiment by Goethals and Reckman,[79] American high school students were asked to rate their opinions on a number of social issues, including—one of the controversies of the time—the busing of school students to different schools to achieve a better racial mix, and therefore to promote, it was hoped, racial harmony. A week or two later, students were brought together in groups of four for a discussion of the busing issue.

Unbeknownst to the students, each group comprised three members who all shared the same strong, either pro or anti-busing, view, and one other member who was armed with a number of persuasive arguments in the contrary direction, whose job it was to try to win the others over. After the discussions, the three 'naive' students were asked to rate their views again, and were found to have shifted markedly towards the opposite camp. Then they were asked to recall what their opinion had been the previous week. Control students who had not had the discussion were able to recall their opinion very accurately; but those whose view had shifted grossly misremembered what they had previously believed, and showed no recognition that this had happened. They were convinced that their views had *not* been changed by the discussion. In order to preserve a key assumption of the SS—that it is consistent and reliable—they had rewritten the records, in line with their new position, and tactically failed to notice that they had done so. Their view was that the discussion had been very interesting, but had basically supported the position they had always held!

The Narrator is bound by the constraints of any author. He has to tell a 'good' story. It has to seem to make sense, to be coherent, so even when causes are complicated, muddled and unknown, there is always a neat tale to be fabricated. It has long been known, since the pioneering experiments of Sir Frederick Bartlett in Cambridge in the 20s and 30s[80] that memory tends to distort strange or inconsistent stories—ones, that is, that are not of its own making—recalling them as neater and more coherent than they originally were. It may well be that this characteristic of memory for fiction is a generalization of the way it *has* to treat personal, self-justifying stories. We are all familiar with the tendency of the Narrator not only to neaten, but to dramatize, stories that are to be made available for public consumption: the exaggeration of key details; the rearrangement to create a 'better' story with greater suspense; the relegation to minor roles of other people who, in *their* versions of events, were the stars of a production in which *you* were only a spear-carrier; and so on.

The Pitfalls of Narration

The neuropsychologist Michael Gazzaniga has recently offered several examples of the 'compulsion to narrate' at work in the field of mental disorder.[81] Consider the debilitating condition known as schizophrenia. In this condition, people experience their world as bizarre; full of mysterious ambiguities, disharmonious or threatening relationships with other people, and delusions and hallucinations, primarily auditory and visual, which are not (usually) experienced *as* illusions but as a genuine, weird, reality. In the grip of a schizophrenic episode, people will behave in eccentric or self-destructive ways—perhaps isolating themselves, or hurting themselves, and will often seem to be cut off from their own 'normal' emotions.

There have been attempts to explain schizophrenia in many different kinds of ways, from seeing it as primarily a biochemical disorder of the brain, through to seeing it as a sane but desperate response to conditions in family or society that are literally driving the 'patient' mad.[82] Gazzaniga, however, argues persuasively for a multi-level approach, in which unusual states of the brain produce unusual feelings or actions, which are then 'interpreted' by the Narrator, according to its normal constraints. However these constraints force the Narrator to come up with explanations that make the self, and the world, look very odd, and these accounts are then fed back into the image of the self which the person holds, creating for him or her a bizarre reality. Let us see how this could work.

One of the most plausible biochemical theories of schizophrenia proposes that it may all start with a specific disorder in the production and metabolism of a certain chemical—dopamine—in the brain. For some unknown reason, the part of the brain that manufactures or controls the release of dopamine goes on the blink, too much of the substance is available in the system, and this biochemical accident then causes the brain to behave in an unusual way—the sufferer has her first psychotic episode.

Something goes wrong perhaps with the way the person experiences her social world. Since babyhood we have built up strong expectations about how (by and large) people respond to us, and we to them. They smile when they see us, ask us how we are, laugh or groan at our jokes, reassure us when we look sad, and so on. We see a friend across a room or a street and we feel a pleasurable sense of anticipation about the interaction to come. But what if the brain stopped sending out these messages of familiarity, fondness and security? Flooding certain parts of the brain with dopamine may somehow have swamped the mechanism that enables us to tell friend from foe, and to predict how each will relate to us. (It is known that the part of the brain that deals with the emotional and motivational 'aura' of events—the limbic system—receives a particularly rich input from dopamine-generating cells.)

This creates difficulties not only directly, in terms of navigating through the social world, but also for the Narrator. What is going on? The Narrator has no access to the brain, so it cannot find an explanation in terms of what has *actually* happened. So it can only assume that something has changed in the social world itself. 'I am feeling confused and vulnerable because people who I had thought were my friends are now revealed in their true colours; they do not like me after all, and are not to be trusted. They fooled me all this time, but not any more. I shall be on my guard.' The Narrator dreams up for me a strange and dangerous view of 'reality' which 'accounts' for the radical change in my responses, but at the cost of dramatically shifting my relationship with the world.

The original glitch in dopamine production might have been just a temporary interruption to the smooth running of the brain, like a speck of dust in the carburettor causing a brief loss of power in a car. But once the Narrator has got to work, the person is left with a new perspective on the world *which is capable of becoming a self-fulfilling prophecy*. The function of the brain-mind returns to normal, but still there is that nagging suspicion that people are not as friendly or as trustworthy as they appear to be. The processes for exploring safe situations until they give up their hidden threats can now get to work on these normal, routine interactions with people, and sure enough, if you look carefully, you will find evidence to support your suspicions.

I am standing in the queue for the cafeteria cash-desk, waiting to pay for my lunch, and out of the blue a cheerful-looking young woman behind the counter says 'Anything I can do for you, my love?' What does she mean? Why the endearment? Is she making fun of me, or offering a sexual opportunity? Has she been put up to this by her friends? What is going on? The world which had been stable, while I was in my reverie, suddenly lurches and tips. I am precipitated onto thin ice, where any response I make is fraught with the danger of being inappropriate or ridiculous. I drop my tray on the floor and blunder out of the hospital canteen, knocking people out of the way in my panic.[83]

Where is that Voice Coming From?

One of the commonest experiences associated with schizophrenia is auditory hallucinations. Gazzaniga quotes this excerpt from the case notes of a young woman called Georgia:

> Georgia was reporting that the hallucinations had become more frequent and were occurring throughout her waking hours. Hearing voices several times a day led to inevitable and obvious personality changes. These became profound. She slowly withdrew into the world of her auditory hallucinations and constructed a complicated paranoid delusional system around them. She believed that these voices were intruding into her head and controlling her will. In fact she began believing that all her thoughts were public knowledge and that anyone could read exactly what she was thinking.[84]

In the schizophrenic state, the outpourings of the Narrator are experienced as 'inpourings'. We might say that, for some reason, the Narrator system becomes de-coupled from the rest of the Self System, so that its *sotto voce* commentary is no longer interpreted as 'talking to myself'. The only other possibility, given that somebody, or something, *is* talking, is that I am hearing the vocalizations of other people who seem, on the basis of all other evidence (visual, the reactions of third parties) not to be present. Again, the quest for a 'reasonable' explanation by the Narrator—in this instance, paradoxically, of the sound of its own voice—leads it inexorably to postulate a very different world from the one that underlies normal 'sanity'.

What if one were to attribute the voices of the Narrator to the Outside, but happened to live in a community who shared this interpretation, and who generally heard the voices offering interpretations and guidance about human affairs, rather than attempting to account for experiences that were lonely and frightening? Would not the Narrator, in this situation, assume that there were genuine but

WISDOM BOOKS MAIL ORDER

I would like to receive the latest Wisdom Books Catalogue Supplement as well as information regarding the Wisdom Books Mail Order Service.

Please print clearly.

NAME _____

ADDRESS _____

_____

TOWN/CITY _____

POSTCODE _____ COUNTRY _____

WISDOM BOOKS

402 Hoe Street

London E17 9AA

England

invisible external forces or presences that were overseeing, perhaps even supervising, the running of the community? Sometimes these voices would produce, through individuals, judgements of criticism and condemnation; sometimes of wisdom and compassion. Would not these indeed be the Gods? Julian Jaynes of Princeton University has suggested exactly this: that as little as three thousand years ago, when the Narrator was installed in the mind, but had not yet been incorporated within the Self System, its commentary was routinely heard as being received by the mind, not generated by it. And why not? It makes perfect sense.[85]

What has happened to Georgia is that she has temporarily reverted to this earlier way of interpreting the Narrator. The de-coupling of Narrator and Self represents one more vital twist in her self-destructive tale. The commentary becomes more and more entangled and mad, and as the Narrator struggles to make sense of abnormal events in the brain, so it constructs an ever more terrifying world. There comes a point where the Narrator can no longer bear to attribute the manufacture of this mad world to the self—to accept it as being self-generated—for to do so would involve admitting the madness of the self. Thus to *protect* her self from the imputation of madness, Georgia has to adopt a desperate measure: that of attributing her thoughts to external agencies...and thus, of course, *appearing* 'mad'.

It is interesting to note that schizophrenia appears to be a modern disorder, first detected in the early nineteenth century. Before then there is no historical record of anything that resembles the syndrome that is today, especially in Western cultures, only too familiar. Perhaps it is only very recently in our cultural evolution, and only in the European cultures even now, that the incorporation of Narrator into Self has become a routine facet of child development. And perhaps it is because it is a relative newcomer into the nest of the self that it can, in troubled times, be kicked out again.

The Community of Selves

As we have seen, the self-concept is a loosely interwoven collection of characteristics. Some of them remain partially attached to the particular scenarios in which they were learnt or developed, so that they are somewhat situation-specific. Some of these personal attributes are more fully 'disembedded'; they tend to follow us around wherever we go. They are our 'core personalities', we might say. We could envisage the self-concept as a flower, with our optional or situation-specific traits as the petals, and with the core, compulsory traits at the centre. 'Who I Am' is a fluid and changing constellation of qualities. Every new situation gives a shake to the kaleidoscope of my personality.[86]

Just as a physicist can get a long way with the aid of the fiction that a body has a centre of gravity, a single point where its weight may be supposed to be concentrated, so it can be helpful, provided you remember what you are doing, to postulate a 'centre of *narrative* gravity' for yourself or another human being.[87] Unfortunately the Narrator, with its perpetual conjecturing of a stable, central character to the unfolding story, doesn't see it that way. It likes to create a fiction of coherence and consistency. It seeks to add another injunction to the set of core characteristics by which I am bound: 'Thou shalt stay the same'. And this means that I am constrained to see my 'core' not as a rough precis of my general nature but as an accurate and complete account of All of Me.

Sometimes, for some people, this injunction is only weak, and mercifully ineffective. They are able to 'be themselves' in a variety of different ways without having to apologize or cover up. At the most they might feel obliged to say 'I don't know what came over me', or 'I must have been beside myself', when they have surprised themselves or others by the 'self' that popped up. But for others the need to preserve the fictional consistency of the self is stronger. What do you do when required to present your self in a way that flies in the face of the facts? You are obliged to inhabit the community of sub-selves sequentially, only one at a time, and when we are 'being' any one of them, we have to ignore the existence of the others, or create a distorted picture of them that is acceptable to the vantage point currently espoused. As philosopher Jacob Needleman puts it:

Beneath the fragile sense of personal identity, the individual is actually an innumerable swarm of disconnected impulses, thoughts, reactions, opinions and sensations, which are triggered into activity by causes of which he is totally unaware. Yet at each moment the individual identifies himself with whichever of this swarm of impulses and reactions happens to be active, automatically affirming each as 'himself', and then taking a stand either for or against this 'self', depending on the particular pressures that the social environment has brought to bear upon him since his childhood.[88]

In extreme circumstances it may be necessary to work a more difficult trick: to separate out a number of different sub-selves, and keep them in watertight compartments, to all intents and purposes oblivious of each other's existence. In such cases clinicians speak of 'multiple personality disorder', though the strategy only emerges as a 'disorder' if it is creating trouble. In the classic cases, one or more of the constituent personalities may behave violently or irresponsibly, thus bringing the whole community into disrepute—quite unfairly, the other residents would rightly argue. (There have been some interesting legal cases in America in which the 'innocent' sub-personalities have protested the injustice of being sent to jail for crimes 'they' did not commit. Unfortunately no-one has yet found a way of incarcerating a 'self' without its associated body.)

The Self in Sum

In Chapter 1 I raised one of the puzzles that mysticism has set for science. Mystics from every religious tradition, and none, have agreed that their experience reflects a loss of self. They see more clearly, kindly and wisely because a great weight of personal selfishness seems to have dropped away. But if the self is so dysfunctional, as they claim, how could it have ever come about in the first place? If the self is not part of our inescapable biological endowment, but was 'invented' along the way, must there have not been a time when the sense of self looked like just the thing that was needed?

We can now give an answer to this paradox. The self is neither a biological necessity, nor an acquired impediment. It is not one 'thing' at all. It cannot be understood or judged as a whole, because it is not a whole, but a curious collection of originally separate parts that have grown together. The self is like a mass of entangled vegetation which looks like a complex 'system' but which turns out to consist of different parts that have become confused.

Evolution invents new capabilities to aid survival, but these always bring with them as yet unrealized potential for both good and ill. As the different constituents of the self, which we have been tracing back to their roots over the last four chapters, grew, so they revealed unintended properties. And as they grew *together*, so these properties became interwoven and interdependent, and eventually became the Self System that has so colonized and misdirected the Western brain-mind.

The 'solution' to the problem which this monstrous house-guest poses, for both individual well-being and global survival, cannot lie in clearing away this Self System root and branch, because its original constituents are still functional parts of the total life-support system. What is needed is a process of disentangling, gently teasing apart the different strands of self, and undoing some of the damage that their confusion has caused. Luckily we have been provided with the means to do this, which I shall return to at the end of the book. But the next step, before we can fully appreciate this unexploited resource, is to tackle head-on the issue that has been lurking behind many of the previous discussions: the enigma of consciousness.

3

The
Emergence of
Consciousness

TWELVE

Alarums and Excursions

It is doubtful whether the generalisations and categories of folk psychology...carve Nature at her joints....The brain undoubtedly has a number of mechanisms for monitoring brain processes, and the folk psychological categories of 'awareness' and 'consciousness' indifferently lump together an assortment of mechanisms

Patricia Churchland[89]

It is now time to embark on the story of consciousness: why it evolved; what (if anything) it is for; and why it contains the motley assortment of contents that it habitually does. Almost all of the pieces of the puzzle have been introduced. But one key piece remains. Nothing that we have discussed so far—or almost nothing—*requires* us to talk of consciousness. The proliferation of needs, the elaboration of language, the extraction of concepts, the assembly of the Self System, and even the increasing volume of verbal ticker-tape produced by the Narrator: none of these required our ancestors, nor do they require us, to be conscious. A moment's introspection, for example, will reveal that we frequently produce language without any conscious awareness of either the process of production or the product. One can talk without hearing oneself talk. And one can just as well think without being conscious of it. Try tracing your way from any momentary thought to its predecessor, and its predecessor's predecessor, and you will most commonly grind rapidly to a halt. The trail is so cold that it might never have been.

Yet we undeniably are conscious, we know we are, and many of the products of mental activity do make fleeting appearances in what seems to be the illuminated room of consciousness. So where did consciousness emerge from in the first place, and why? And what determines which aspects of experience are rewarded this, apparently privileged, status?

On the Importance of Being Arrestable

We need to retrace our evolutionary footsteps to the time when animals—probably mammals and probably those that were capable of a reasonable turn of speed—were appearing. They had evolved, let us suppose, intricate and differentiated bodies, each subsystem of which contributed specialized functions to the body community, and each of which, in turn had its own needs. All of them needed oxygen and nourishment; some of them needed a special diet, specialized maintenance and so on. The animals as a whole needed to feed, to drink, to find shelter, to defend themselves as best they could, to rest, to groom, to repair injuries, to find mates, give birth and raise their young. They had brains to co-ordinate information about the state of affairs both inside and outside the body, and to select or construct appropriate courses of action. And they were able to modify their responses, up to a point, in the light of experience.

But they needed one more system, one which would enable them to detect and respond to emergencies. They needed to be capable of being interrupted in the middle of satisfying one set of needs, to stop, take stock, and, if required, to head off on quite a new tack. And they had to be able to do this quickly. If you were quietly resting, digesting a recent meal of wildebeest, cleaning your fur and keeping an eye on the cubs, you would not be a very successful survival-machine if you could not detect the odour of a skulking hyena, or a glimpse of a man with a spear, and instantly reorganize the entire system of internal priorities to respond.

You need a procedure analogous to that of a teacher in a busy classroom, where groups of students are working on different projects, who needs from time to time to give the class as a whole some new instructions, or to stop for a general discussion. First she bangs on the desk with the blackboard eraser. All activity stops; all attention turns to her; silence reigns for a moment as they wait for the next thing to happen. (I am assuming an ideal class, for the purposes of this analogy.) *Then* she and the class are able to act in concert. Either they all have to march out into the playground for the fire drill; or she gives them a new idea to think about, or simply reminds them that there is only ten minutes left, and they go back to their diverse tasks and projects.

This is exactly, I suggest, what began to happen in the brain-mind of a startled animal. For a brief period, all the lines are open and vigilant: ears pricked, eyes scanning, nose twitching. If this early-warning alert confirms the threat, and gives a preliminary diagnosis of it, then send a rush of adrenaline through the body, moving all systems on to 'action stations', and focus the pool of sensory activation in the detection systems which are most likely to pick up further information. (If the first scan determines that it has been a false alarm, then the all-clear is sounded, the off-duty crew go back to bed, and normal service is resumed.)[90]

This mechanism was probably a development of the more basic strategy of freezing when threatened, a prevalent response throughout the animal kingdom. Physical immobility would, on the forest floor, have rendered you much less conspicuous (though in the bottom of a white enamel bath it does nothing for your chances). But this inhibition of all overt activity would have had the added benefit of making more neural activity available to the sensory systems (in rather the same way that people who lose one of their senses are said to gain acuity in the others). Thus freezing turned out to have the unintended side-effect of enabling a more detailed and complete perceptual picture of the situation to be painted. And this intensified data-gathering can only have been of benefit in dealing with many unusual situations. (Of course, if you are about to be carried off by a bald eagle, or washed down the plug-hole by a nervous householder, both your freezing and your concentration will have been in vain.)

The Startled Brain

In neural terms (or rather in terms of the simple analogies I have been using) this general alert requires all non-essential systems to be shut down, temporarily. Their activation is withdrawn. Part of the liberated energy, if necessary, goes to inhibit the systems which were previously active, and part of it is sent back to 'central resources' to enable the sensitivity of the detection systems to be raised to the utmost. Under these exceptional circumstances, activation can build up in active areas of the network faster than it can be redirected, so that for a brief period they become 'super-excited', we might say. When the source of the threat is identified, its associated patterns in the network receive a huge power-surge of activation. This forms a new focus of activity which now supplants any other, and which locks on attention in a highly focused manner. Other areas are initially inhibited, giving one intense 'hot spot' which stands out starkly against the suppressed surround. And then, when the identification of the threat is clear, the concentrated 'knot' of activation swiftly relaxes and diffuses out into the associated 'action' systems, to initiate the best responses to the new situation.

This sudden arresting of on-going functions, and bunching up of activity in an area of the network *into which it would not have flowed naturally*, given the activities that were ongoing at the time, would have been a very valuable trick for dealing with unwelcome surprises. You want the alarm to be able to break the continuity of action, and start 'from scratch', so that the emergency has the power to reset the switches in the network, and determine the priorities that the different subsystems should have—regardless of the pre-existing state of activity of those subsystems. Without the rapid centralization and mobilization of brain resources which this evolutionary move made possible, you would have had less activity available, and you would have had to wait longer for activation to make its way, by recognized channels, into the requisite area. And by then it might have been too late.

There is an additional way in which this alarm reaction would have been helpful. You will recall that Marcel Kinsbourne has suggested that each minitheory of the brain, when it is active, tends to protect itself from 'interruption' by surrounding itself with a ring of inhibition which serves to prevent its own share of activation leaking away. By this means, each active area is able to 'disable' other areas that might threaten to compete with it. But disrupting these semi-autonomous subsystems is precisely what an effective response to emergency has to do. Unless these subsystems are closed down, and their ability to suppress competing areas thereby withdrawn, they may effectively cut off parts of the total network that could have been useful, or even vital, in coping with the new situation.[91]

One of the great values of being in this state of heightened but contained arousal is that your diagnosis of the situation is acute. But also, by flooding the appropriate areas of the brain at the same time as you dam its instinctive outflow channels, you might discover *new*, more 'creative' possibilities of response. (I explained this mechanism in more detail in Chapters 3 and 4.) Instead of going with the first impulse that 'comes into your head', the build-up of activation may uncover alternative pathways, just as a dammed stream backs up into a lake, and may overflow into a channel that leads in a different direction from the original. The mechanism of intense activation, surrounded by a ring of intense inhibition, enables the network to discover and cut new channels in exactly the same way. Creativity is made possible without any 'creator' other than the network itself.

The Dawn of Conscious Awareness

It was these temporary 'hot-spots' in the brain that were associated, I suggest, with the emergence of conscious awareness. Conscious awareness had no function in its own right. It did not emerge 'for a purpose'. It came along with the developing ability of the brain to create these transient states of 'super-activation' as a useless by-product, of no more functional interest than the colour of the liver, or the fact that the sea, under certain conditions, bunches up, rolls over and turns white. It was, in the philosophical jargon, an epiphe-nomenon.

Though its plumage is clearly a signal, the flesh of a pheasant does not taste the way it does (to me) for a purpose. Though it helps to maintain the lineage of the cow, its milk does not need a reason to be white. Evolution is not about the survival of the 'tastiest', or the 'whitest and creamiest'. Both pheasant and milk are made of stuff that turns out to have these incidental properties for no good reason at all. But though they had no *original* purpose, once they had appeared these properties may very definitely have repercus-sions, and may even be capitalized upon, opportunistically, by both the owner and their exploiters. It is a mixed blessing to the pheasant species that its flesh tastes good to some jaded human palates. Cows would not occupy the place in the scheme of things that they do if their milk, though equally nutritious, had been grey, lumpy or bitter. (We do not drink pigs' milk, for example, though some cultures drink the milk of mares.) Likewise we do not have to explain what vital property of consciousness brought it about; but we may wonder about the consequences of having it.

So conscious awareness was associated, from the start, with a state of disruption and imbalance in the life of the organism. As Lancelot Law Whyte has suggested: 'Consciousness is like a fever which, if not excessive, hastens curative processes and so eliminates its source.'[92] Like Whyte, I am suggesting that the original moments of consciousness were intermittent, normally brief, and, if all went well, self-eliminating. Consciousness originally had the quality of a violent sneeze, or an orgasm perhaps (events that are themselves associated with intense levels of consciousness).

I need now to define my use of words a little more carefully. By *awareness* I shall mean the responsiveness of the brain-mind system to a stimulus, as inferred from its, or the animal's, behaviour, without any associated conscious experience. I shall bank this for the moment: the idea of unconscious awareness, which this is, is going to become invaluable in a little while. By *conscious awareness* I mean the quality of 'being known' to an experiencer of an experience; ordinary common or garden seeing, hearing, smelling, tasting, feeling, sensing of inner and outer experiences as they happen. This is what was originally made possible by the appearance of the cerebral hot-spots. And by *consciousness* I shall mean the full-blown, complicated mess of sensation, interpretation, inner talk, fantasy, memory and the rest, each ingredient constantly shifting in and out, foreground to background...the conscious mind at work as we know it from the inside today, here, now. These categories are themselves imprecise in rather important ways, but they will serve to make the rough distinctions that we need for the moment.

The Frequency of Interruptions

Once this emergency mechanism has begun to evolve, there is a problem, for each species and each individual, about how finely or coarsely to 'set' it—like a burglar alarm on a car. Do you want it to go off at the slightest nudge, or do you want to reserve it for full-blown, unequivocal emergencies, and take your chances with lesser surprises? There are good reasons for keeping the frequency of your emergencies down. If you are constantly being interrupted by every little noise, you will never be able to get on with your everyday business. And the process of putting the body on fight-and-flight stand-by is costly. It takes energy to make and stock-pile the reserves of adrenaline that are released every time the alarm goes off. And it is wearing on the fabric of the body to be constantly subjected to *false* alarms; fired up for action, and then 'stood down' without any action having taken place to release the tension.[93] A car treated in the same way would quickly wear out, and so does the body.

However, despite these arguments in favour of a 'coarser' approach to emergencies, there are other, even more pressing, reasons why one should be prepared to 'freak' more often. There are obvious evolutionary advantages to taking even the faintest whiff of a threat, or an unknown, seriously. While a false alarm may take its toll, long-term, on the body, one emergency undetected may mean the end right now. There is no point in having an alarm that will only detect surefire emergencies, when it takes only ignoring one 'possible emergency'—the one which turns out to be 'real'—to finish you off.

This pressure to set the alarm bells to go off at the slightest thing is one aspect of what American psychologist Susan Mineka calls 'adaptive conservatism'.[94] Another is an in-built tendency for the categories of events that bring on the startle reaction to broaden. When one of a kind has been treated as a possible emergency—especially when it has turned out to require some self-protective reaction—anything vaguely similar will come to call out the guards as well. Interestingly, experimental research shows that, if the original trigger turns out, on further investigation, to be safe after all, the fearful, vigilant reaction to similar events tends to remain. Treating something as a possible emergency is a reaction that generalizes widely and easily, but shrinks only slowly and narrowly. Once one has been mugged by a tall thin white man with a zapata moustache, one tends to see them everywhere, and not to be too fussy about the precise shape of the facial hair, either. The receptors get 'set' to detect such stimuli, and it is very hard to un-set them once this has happened. So for all these evolutionarily good reasons, the frequency of startlement rises in the population.

If you want to be really on the safe side, you do not even wait until you are picking up the traces of what may turn out to be an emergency. If you remain totally absorbed in your lunch until the sun is obscured by a looming shape, you may already be as good as lunch for someone else. So the next escalation in the frequency of alarms is when you begin to startle yourself. If you are a small herbivore, used to grazing in open areas of long grass, you are at your most vulnerable when you are hunkered down searching out the tenderest shoots. If you spend too long without rearing up on your hindlegs for a good look around, stopping munching so you can hear the slightest sound, and sniffing the breeze, you are liable to get crept up on. The brain becomes programmed to initiate a stage-one alarm reaction every few seconds—regardless of whether the receptors say it is necessary or not. Anxious and cautious beings tend to live longer in such a world.

The ability to startle yourself would have paved the way for a whole new area of learning: deliberately seeking out, or creating, *controlled* emergencies of your own. As we saw earlier, investing some of your 'leisure time' in devising (hopefully manageable) adventures may pay off handsomely if you ever run across 'the real thing'. Practising how to kill an as-good-as-dead rabbit enables you to sharpen up some of the skills you are going to need if you are ever to catch one that is vitally alive and violently kicking. Teasing a senior member of the troop reveals useful information about how adults react when they get angry. And every such adventure—if it is a *real* adventure—is bound to contain shocks and surprises that are sufficiently strong to set off the alarm. In fact part of the purpose of such 'playing with fire' is not only to learn about the particular domain, but also to get used to, and to tune, the Alarm System itself, under circumstances that are hopefully less genuinely hazardous than those which are truly unexpected.

Adventures are ways of creating prolonged contact with the unknown, and they are therefore going to create concomitantly longer periods of conscious awareness. In learning mode, routine activities are suspended in order to make available the large pool of 'free brain energy' that will enable you to sense things very keenly, be prepared to break off the encounter instantly if it should turn nasty, and, while you are hanging in there, to be making all the useful brain-mind connections that you can. When a threat suddenly appears in the normal course of events, you will leap into flight-or-fight-mode as quickly as you can. The moment of arrest, of suspended animation, will be minimal. But when you are exploring, you are deliberately staying in that state for a longer time, hovering on the brink of flight, but restraining the impulse to flee till the last possible moment, flirting with danger, in the interests of finding a way of dealing with it that will reduce its status as a threat in the future.

As we saw in chapters 9 and 10, one of the motifs of human history is the way in which safe situations are increasingly transmuted, by a big brain looking for some 'action', into dangerous situations. This is achieved by the development of imagination and exploration, so that more and more subtle threats are discovered; and also by the act of 'identifying' with the Self System, so that any potential invalidation of the SS is interpreted by the system-as-a-whole as a threat to its survival. Thus paradoxically, as a result of our relative affluence, and the way we have responded to it, the frequency and duration of the alarms that humankind experiences have not decreased but increased.

In the life of Rousseau's 'noble savage', needs are few, and emergencies correspondingly sporadic and well defined. But if you have been offered a sought-after promotion at the other end of the country, where house prices are higher, the weather is colder and the schools for your teenage children have an uncertain reputation, then the emergency that this convoluted conflict creates may well last for weeks. And if your well-being is dependent on keeping ahead of the Joneses in the stylishness of your home-furnishings, then the occasions for 'alarm' and 'adventure' can become virtually continuous, running into one another like watercolours on wet paper.

Thus the conditions in the brain-mind system that generate conscious awareness have become ever more frequent and long-lived. Whereas originally conscious awareness emerged as an accompaniment of brief, sporadic alarms, now it develops into a state of semi-permanent low-grade emergency. Brief bursts of intense excitation in the brain become strung together into protracted periods of suspended animation and focused attention: a response which was fine for dealing with a potential predator, but is hopelessly unequal to the task of resolving a mid-life crisis.

The repertoire of potential threats is now so large, and contains so many inherent conflicts and ambiguities, that it may only rarely be possible (when drunk; absorbed in a romantic movie; making love; possibly not even then) to stand down the guard. (If your self depends for its safety on being popular, avoiding physical harm *and* on acting with courage and integrity, then life is going to be full of opportunities to grapple with the awkward, irresolvable fact that you cannot always have all three.) The consciousness that we human beings prize so dearly turns out to be a symptom of a *chronic* fever of the mind.

Note incidentally that, as the number of possible emergencies increases astronomically, so the *intensity* of consciousness that accompanies them tends to diminish. This follows from the basic design-specification of the brain. It has a relatively fixed pool of mental energy that is available to it at any time. But remember that many of our self-related needs can only be represented in the brain by setting up a constant trickle of priming. So as the number of these threats increases, the proportion of the brain's activity which is freely available to flow around the network effectively drops. Thus though there is still enough energy available to create the local levels necessary to produce the phenomenon of conscious awareness, the overall level of this intensity, and hence of consciousness, goes down. Specific moments of real danger will recreate the old intensity of experience, but mundane consciousness will look dull by comparison.

The Body of Consciousness

As emergencies proliferate and blend into one another, so it is not only the mind but the body that is affected. When the alarm goes off, the body is first frozen, and then is prepared for action in characteristic ways. As American psychologist and writer Sam Keen says:

> When we perceive danger the body immediately prepares itself for fight or flight. Glands and muscles switch to emergency status. Adrenaline courses through our system, the heart rate increases, and we assume a 'red alert' stance. In the natural course of things a threat arises and recedes, the lion approaches and retreats or is killed. But a culture that is at war, or constantly preparing for a possible war, conspires to create the perception, especially among its male citizens, that the threat from the enemy is always present, and therefore we can never let down our guard. 'Eternal vigilance is the price of liberty'. So men, the designated warriors, gradually form 'character armour', a pattern of muscular tension and rigidity that freezes them into the posture that is appropriate only for fighting—shoulders back, chest out, stomach pulled in, anal sphincter tight, balls drawn up into the body as far as possible, eyes narrowed, breathing foreshortened and anxious, heart rate

accelerated, testosterone in full flow. The warrior's body is perpetually uptight and ready to fight.[95]

And as we know only too well, our hospitals and clinics are full of
people whose bodily systems have finally broken down or rebelled at
the unrelenting state of vigilance that the Self System has indirectly
required of them. Psychosomatic medicine, and its impressively titled
offspring 'psychoneuroimmunology', have documented irrefutably
the dozens of ways in which protracted stress can result not just in
distress but in damage to the tissues: dermatological, respiratory, circulatory, digestive, urinogenital and neuromuscular disorders of all
kinds.

THIRTEEN

Feelings and Seeings

Some truths are so near and obvious to the mind that a man need only open his eyes to see them. Such I take this important one to be, viz. that all the choir of heaven and furniture of the earth—in a word, all those bodies which compose the mighty frame of the world—have not any subsistence without a mind.

Bishop Berkeley

In a world of no eyes, the sun would not be light. In a world of no tactile nerve ends, fire would not be hot. In a world of no muscles, rocks would not be heavy; and in a world without soft skin, the rocks would not be hard.

Alan Watts

The Feelings of Conscious Awareness

We have not yet mentioned one of the most important features of the alarm reaction: its close relation to feeling and emotion. Our basic 'negative' emotions are responses of the whole bodily system to different kinds of threat, disruption or injury. Emotions are the consciously felt aspects of the ways in which the system as a whole responds when it is blocked or frustrated. When plans are upset, that is the time when 'we' are upset. And different basic kinds of upset produce different emotional tones.[96] Each of these emotional states represents the way the body-brain-mind system as a whole responds to the instantaneous diagnosis of what kind of emergency it is facing. The precise response that is made depends on further analysis, which may refine or even overturn the original snap diagnosis.

Fear we might see as corresponding to the appearance—usually sudden—of a known threat: a predator, restriction of movement, imminent disclosure of a past indiscretion. Fear is associated with the preliminary judgment that the appropriate response might well be to make a run for it. The sensations of fear are associated with mobilization of the body for flight. *Anger*, on the other hand, is the way the body 'feels' when it is preparing to stand its ground and if necessary fight it out. It is aroused by the appearance of a threat from which, for one reason or another one is unable or unwilling to run: an attack on a child; a challenge for territory or mate; being cornered; being prevented by 'pride'—the belief that running away is 'cowardly'—from doing the sensible thing and going to ground. Anger is usually directed towards an animal of the same or another species, who is seen as presenting a threat to a cherished object or resource. The related feeling of *frustration* occurs when an ongoing activity is blocked for reasons which are not seen as being the work of an animate enemy or rival. Frustration signals the systems's readiness to adopt either a primitive (kick it, shake it, scream at it) or a more sophisticated (take it to bits, consult the manual, ring up the shop where you bought it) kind of strategy to remedy the fault or remove the blockage.

Grief and sadness reflect the loss of a cherished possession, ability or companion. The loss is perceived as irreversible, and therefore the 'problem' is one of adjusting many aspects of life to take account of the unfillable hole. *Disgust* is a basic emotion reflecting the sense that the body has been, or is about to be, invaded by hostile objects, substances or experiences. The body is preparing to resist this invasion, by tightly closing the relevant orifices, or to expel what had already been absorbed. While it is not usually classified as an emotion, physical *pain* can usefully be included in this listing as a catch-all term for various kinds of body reaction to other kinds of invasion, subversion or injury. Different types of pain can signal the need for swift action (to prevent being punctured further by the drawing pin on the chair), for a period of uninterrupted rest to allow natural healing to occur without risk of further trauma, or for a loud cry for help (to assist in beating off the attack, preventing further blood loss and so on).

Finally *anxiety*, the prototypical feeling of alarm, accompanies the appearance on the brain-mind's radar screen of an unidentified object, with respect to which the course of best action is not yet clear. It is related to fear, but is related too to *excitement*, for the stranger may turn out to be (in the words of the poster) a friend you have not met yet. If you always run from the first intimations of the unknown, you will tend to be safe, but also to have less fun, and learn less, than if you dared to hang around for a bit longer. On the other hand, if you always go rushing in where others fear to tread, you will have a happy life, but a short one. Of all the basic feelings, anxiety is the one that is characteristic of human beings' advanced level of evolution. If you were not in part constituted out of an impressively malleable nervous system, and therefore did not know the value of learning, you would not experience not-knowing as an opportunity as well as a threat. You would not find yourself suspended, sometimes for considerable periods, in the exquisite, agonizing state of indecision as to whether to approach or avoid.

Even when the 'emergency' is one of those home-grown, stretched-out, low-grade kind, associated with a period of adventurous play, the emotional tone is still there. As Dennett says:

> As usual in evolution (animals) cobbled together these new systems out of the equipment their heritage had already provided. This history has left its traces, particularly on the emotional or affective overtones of consciousness, for even though higher creatures now became 'disinterested' gatherers of information, their reporters were simply the redeployed warners and cheerleaders of their ancestors, never sending any message 'straight', but always putting some vestigial positive or negative editorial 'spin' on whatever information they provided.[97]

Confusion

As needs and threats get more numerous, more convoluted and more psychological, so the emotional hues that conscious awareness can take on also become more varied. *Confusion*, for example, acquires an unpleasant tinge which it did not originally have, by virtue of the compulsion to have a continual mental commentary. If the Self System contains an injunction to keep the narrative going at all times—if the self has learnt to recognize itself in the narrative—then confusion becomes aversive, and the mind's job is therefore to construct an explanation—*any* explanation—that will satisfy the craving for a mental story. In the absence of such a story, a kind of intellectual panic takes over, which can only be pacified by an account, however flimsy or dubious, that can be used to paper over the crack.

Being prone to this panic makes people easy prey for those who hawk apparent certainty, and this vulnerability can be exploited either for good or ill. On the one hand it makes it easy for us to be persuaded by politicians who are plausible, confident story-tellers. We will tend to prefer someone who has a simple, reassuring tale to tell, to someone who tells us that things are hard to understand and largely out of his control. We choose the lie and the liar over the truth. This need for a story—if not our own, then one we can borrow from someone who seems to have a nice one for rent—makes politics into a circus of personalities, and ensures that we will elect the most plausible rogue.

On the other hand, there is the chance to put this hunger to therapeutic use. Milton Erikson, the famous psychotherapist and a master trickster in this respect, devised what he called 'Erikson's confusion technique'.[98] There is a type of 'client' (I marginally prefer this to 'patient', and both to 'customer' in the context of psychotherapy) who *seems* to listen to what the therapist has to say, but who in fact takes nothing in. In a way, they are sabotaging their own recovery. Erikson made use of the Narrator's need for a story to get over this obstacle. First he would act in a way, or say something, that utterly confused the client. If the client earnestly asked, 'Doctor, I'm desperate. Do you think I will ever get better?', Erikson might look at his watch and say in a kindly voice, 'It's 10.45pm'—a time which it clearly isn't. In the context of the therapeutic relationship, there was no way in which this response could be understood. It does not compute. The client suddenly, out of the blue, finds herself tumbling into a pit of confusion, which raises her anxiety to such a pitch that she will cling tightly on to any piece of apparent sense that comes her way. And this opens her up to taking on board, in a deeper way than usual, whatever it is that Erikson says next.

It hardly needs saying that such a therapeutic device only works, and only works for the good of the client, in the hands of someone who has great sensitivity, considerable wisdom, and the client's best interests at heart. Milton Erikson was also a great exponent of the therapeutic use of hypnosis, another technique that is able to side-step the Narrator and its voracious appetite for superficial understanding, and to put the brain-mind system in a state in which it is able to 'hear' at a level which can make contact with the knotted part of the Self System which is actually causing the client's suffering.

Embarrassment and humiliation are the kinds of fear associated with the public revelation that I am not what I am supposed to be. Such revelations, real or imagined, acquire the status for us that the appearance of a sabre-toothed tiger had for our ancestors. Actions that are not up to the standards prescribed by the injunctions are 'predators'; when I make a fool of myself it is as if I had a tiger by the tail. If I am committed to being a success in school, I am always at risk of being mauled by a silly mistake or a forgotten answer. And the mauling is all the worse, of course, when the audience share the values that make me squirm.

Guilt is the kind of fear created by not living up to standards of honour or generosity. If the injunction says 'Thou shalt do what other people want', it preempts the subtle brain-mind computation that decides whether it is best for selfishness or altruism to win *on this occasion*. I am no longer free to decide each case on its merits. Maybe this time I really did need to take the last piece of cake; and maybe it was OK with Auntie Beth. But the injunction does not enter into this delicate process of decision-making; it stands outside it and criticizes the result. It does not contribute to the cerebral debate; it waits to use its veto. An emergency is created by the simultaneous need both to take, and *not* to take, the piece of cake, and the emotional aroma of such impasses we call guilt. The obverse of guilt, of course, is resentment, a variant of anger which is directed towards another person who is held responsible for the conflict. If the selfishness wins the fight, I feel guilty. If the injunction wins, I feel resentment.

The Compassionate Gene

The early humans were genetically committed, up to a constantly debatable point, to being sociable. Altruism was not a luxury for our ancestors, a matter of higher virtue to be practised, or indulged in on the odd occasion when it was not going to cost them anything. It was a died-in-the-wool genetic trait. There was no question about *whether* to be a helpful person or not; only when, in what ways, and how much. Members of chimpanzee troops show altruism as well as machiavellianism; and it has been demonstrated that human babies, before they have been 'got at' by conventional morality, show sympathetic distress to another distressed child.[99] Compassion is hereditary. We are endowed with Good Samaritan genes as well as Selfish ones.

So emergencies, for our forebears, would have been precipitated by hearing cries of alarm or distress from other members of their family or clan. Their sense of identification—what it is 'my business' to protect—would have extended outwards to embrace family, friends, other members of the species, and all living and non-living elements of the wider ecological system of which they were part. Sometimes the immediate commitment to personal survival would have temporarily taken precedence over these more diffuse aspects of the 'personal support system'; but, all other things being equal, it is in 'my' interest to look after my community and my environment, because, fundamentally, they are not really 'other'. Thus the feeling of sympathy for another (or of distress at the wasting of a useful resource) would have become one of the 'emotions of consciousness'.[100]

But the more complex and demanding the Self System becomes, the more this 'enlightened self interest' is shrunk and skewed, until it comes to seem that compassion is an unsustainable luxury, rather than a regular part of the maintenance that our living room requires. In contemporary America it has been found that the likelihood of any one member of the public going to the aid of someone who is taken ill on the street or the subway platform is inversely related to the number of people around. The risk of being conspicuous, or 'looking stupid' (if the person turns out to be merely drunk, or a student playing the fool) is greater the larger the audience, so the 'need' for self-protection rapidly overtakes the more primitive 'need' to go and help. For our ancestors the analogous situation would not have created such a conflict of interests. To go and help you might have had to put down the bundle of firewood you had just laboriously collected, and thereby run the risk of a bystander running off with it. But the decision would have been about practical priorities, of which helping other people would have always been one: not a matter of 'image'. Our ancestors would not have tried to fade into the background, or hide behind their newspapers, in a barely-felt paroxysm of anxiety and confusion.

The Positive Emotions

And what of the so-called 'positive emotions'—happiness, joy, love and so on? These are either associated with the resolution of an emergency, or with the suspension of certain kinds of belief and identification within the Self System. The latter I shall come back to towards the end of the book. The former are various kinds of fleeting feeling of *relief* or *relaxation* that occur with the passing or the successful handling of an emergency. The surge of ecstasy that is felt by sportspeople as they cross the line in front of their arch-rival, or score the winning goal, floods into conscious awareness because it is the feeling of fundamental relief that accompanies achievement. But by the same token, such positive feelings are famously ephemeral, much more fleeting than the 'negative emotions', because while fear, anxiety and so on are created by the *existence* of a hot-spot, which may last as long as the emergency is sustained, the happiness of winning can only be conscious briefly, because it is associated with the dissipation of the hot-spot, and the standing-down of the bodily action systems. That is why setting up this feeling as a goal to be sought in its own right—searching for the next 'rush' of pleasure or success—is a life-strategy that guarantees frustration and disappointment.

The Sensory World

We saw earlier in Chapter 3 that one of the brain-mind's functions is to weave a dynamic and constantly updated tapestry of expectations and predictions, against the backdrop of which anything unprecedented or unanticipated would stand out in sharp relief. Originally, before the take-over of the human brain-mind by the compulsive habits of learning and identification, conscious awareness would only have accompanied these shocks and surprises. But when life is lived in a state of chronic emergency, nothing, not even the stable, manageable world woven out of our past experience, can be relied upon. We behave like mild versions of the schizophrenic in the cafeteria, freaked out by an innocent remark. And the more anxious we are, the higher this sense of imminent threat, and the more the entire sensory world is suffused with consciousness. Indeed the state that we call 'self-consciousness' is one in which the apprehension of social threat is so intense—and therefore the interpersonal parts of the brain-mind in such a state of heightened excitation—that there is not enough left over to sustain the normal activities of the body, and one breaks plates, loses one's train of thought, and develops ulcers.

Worry

Modern Western consciousness has developed a 'feel' that is very different from its original state. Nowhere is this more apparent than in its restlessness. Its contents—those areas of the brain-mind that are associated with current hot-spots—keep shifting as one source of anxiety after another is attended to, but cannot be resolved. This constant movement, you recall, is characteristic of the basic brain-mind itself, as each neural gang which is awake at any moment quickly tires and gives way to another. Only in an acute emergency does activation get held for longer in the relevant areas of the network, while information is gathered and plans formulated. But if *no* plan of action can emerge—because of inherent conflicts and contradictions—tiredness still builds up and ensures that the flow moves on within a few seconds.

When nothing is arriving from outside the central brain-mind to call its activity in a certain direction, then the flow can travel round and round familiar problems, like a circular subway system, stopping at each one for a brief (but useless) commentary from the Narrator before shuttling on to the next stop. This compulsive work of 'worrying' or 'fretting' is, in the case of those problems that keep reappearing, unproductive—if they could have been solved by 'thought', they would have been by now. And it can only be stopped by capturing the activation and taking it elsewhere, so that it cannot, for a while, fall back into the endless Escher waterfall. This is why television and the 'mindless' collection of trivia become addictive. They provide enough stimulus to require processing, and they therefore capture the train of consciousness; and they are sufficiently unrelated to anything of real importance in our own lives to keep the train chugging along tracks that do not threaten to deliver us back inadvertently at the familiar stations we are trying to avoid.

The Quality of Consciousness

We are now in a position to summarize some of the characteristic features of conscious experience, and to see how these reflect both the *original* nature of consciousness, and the way in which this has become adapted, overlaid and distorted by subsequent developments—especially those that concern the Self System. At first, conscious awareness came in short sharp intermittent bursts; now it is more continuous. At first it was intensely emotional; now it has become dulled and smothered by a variety of other qualities. At first it was located in the body and the senses; now it has become more frequently verbal and conceptual. At one time its 'voices' were heard as if they came from the 'outside'; now we have decided to treat the Narrator's commentary as if it were the inner voice of the Self.

But there are yet other ways in which our experience and appreciation of consciousness have changed over the centuries, which we shall pick up in the following chapters. Let me conclude this chapter by focusing on the one that we shall pursue in the next. Originally consciousness was continuous with unconsciousness. Brief periods of conscious awareness emerged from, and died away into, a resting state of diffused awareness that was not associated with anything like the consciousness that we inhabit today. The modern mind focuses only on the clear bright centre of consciousness, and tends not to notice the shadowy margins and the unclear origins of whatever is centre-stage.

Still today it is as if there were a chorus of potential contents at the back or the sides of the stage, or even off in the wings, any one of which could suddenly step or slowly sidle into the limelight, and then fade back into the background again. Some sensations can hover around for a while before being admitted: the faint cry of a full bladder while you are deep in a good book; a nagging feeling of something not done, before you realize that it is your mother's birthday. In neural terms, even as one area of the network is the focus for a build-up of activation, to the point where it emerges as a hot-spot, a range of other areas are also being primed and stimulated, one of which may quietly fade again, like a wave that threatened to break but then gently subsided, while another may accumulate sufficient strength to oust the first, and take its place in consciousness. Yet—as we shall see in the next chapter—we have grown to ignore the margins and horizons, and have done so at some cost.

FOURTEEN

The Circumcision
of Consciousness

It may...be wrong to think of two *realms* which interact, called the conscious and the unconscious, or even of two contrasting kinds of mental *process*, conscious and unconscious, each causally self-contained until it hands over to the other. There may exist, as I believe, a single realm of mental processes, continuous and mainly unconscious, of which only certain transitory aspects or phases are accessible to immediate conscious attention.

Lancelot Law Whyte[101]

It is clear from the evolutionary story that consciousness is not, and cannot be, a window on the mind. It is a product of the mind, designed to aid (but subsequently evolved to frustrate) physical survival. Originally associated with a marvellous mechanism for spotting and responding to basic emergencies, it has become, through an interlocking series of evolutionary accidents and coincidences, primarily a mechanism for constructing dubious stories whose purpose is to defend a superfluous and inaccurate sense of self. The most powerful device in evolutionary history once found itself kicking its heels because life had become easy. Now it finds itself embroiled in a deadly serious game that it cannot win, because the problems it tries to solve are products of its very own misapprehensions.

The Integrated Psyche

Up until about 350 years ago, humankind did at least preserve an accurate sense of the relationship of conscious to unconscious aspects of mind. The eighteenth century had not yet completed the transmutation of scarcity from an occasional emergency into a perpetual threat—and with it, the degradation of consciousness into an experience of chronic low-grade emotional distress. Consciousness could still be seen as one product of the mind, of no more or less significance, ultimately, than any other product. The sense of identity was still capable of being diffused throughout body, society and nature. For many people 'my' well-being remained so intimately bound up with that of the community and the harvest that 'I' could simply not conceive of my self as separate from them or without them. I no more saw myself as my thoughts than I did the beating of the heart, the gurgling of the stomach or the subtle flexing of the nostrils in response to a faint whiff of smoke. Each is a manifestation—capable of reflecting either health or illness, growth or decay—of the inscrutable multi-layered system with which 'I' am associated. At the end of the sixteenth century John Donne was able to write his famous 'No man is an Island, entire of itself; every man is a piece of the Continent, a part of the main.'[102] This sentiment, I suggest, captured not a special state of mind, but merely a mundane reality.

And if consciousness was not yet seen as the special residence of the self, unconsciousness, the essential unknowability at the heart of existence, was not yet denied or disenfranchised. Indeed so seamless was the continuum between conscious and unconscious that before the sixteenth century there had been no cause to talk, or think, of 'the' unconscious or of 'unconsciousness' at all. As Lancelot Law Whyte says in his book *The Unconscious Before Freud*:

> Prior to Descartes and his sharp definition of the dualism there was no cause to contemplate the possible existence of unconscious mentality as part of a separate realm of mind. Many religious and speculative thinkers had taken for granted factors lying outside but influencing immediate awareness....Until an attempt had been made (with apparent success) to choose *awareness* as the defining characteristic of an independent mode of being called mind, there was no occasion to invent the idea of unconscious mind as a provisional correction of that choice. It is only after Descartes that we find, first the idea and then the term, 'unconscious mind' entering European thought.[103]

As the Oxford philosopher Kathleen Wilkes says: 'We have in classical Greece a great and glorious psychological understanding. It is not necessary to argue for this: the works of Euripides and Aristophanes alone prove the point. Yet there is no term that *even roughly* translates either "mind" or "consciousness'".[104] The term *psyche*, from which we of course have taken our 'psychology', refers much more broadly to the quality of being alive. Grass and amoebas have *psyche* just as much as human beings do. And neither *psyche* nor any other Greek term enables us to single out consciousness as a particular facet of this 'being alive'.

In fact in the first 1500 years of the Christian era, there was a general appreciation of the continuity, and the unity, of conscious experience and the unconscious ground that gave birth to it. And the sense of 'self' was not yet restricted to the clear centre-stage of consciousness, but embraced its shadowy and inscrutable margins. Who 'I' am embraces the ineffable. Knowing and unknowing are equally part of my experience. The emergence of thoughts and feelings from the Unknown was 'a mystery to be lived; not a problem to be solved or denied'.

Many writers throughout this long period of history noted and recorded this continuity. Plotinus, the third-century philosopher, held that 'the absence of conscious perception is no proof of the absence of mental activity'; and he made the observation, which we could have credited to any contemporary psychotherapist, that 'feelings can be present without awareness of them'.[105] St Augustine, the great Christian philosopher, provided us in the fourth century with one of the quotations with which I prefaced Chapter 1: 'I cannot totally grasp all that I am...the mind is far too narrow to contain itself'. And nearly a thousand years later, St Thomas Aquinas wrote: 'I do not observe my soul apart from its acts. There are thus processes in the soul of which we are not immediately aware'. Montaigne, from the sixteenth century, reminds us how many of our feelings and even actions do not seem to have anything to do with the conscious, deliberate Cartesian 'chief executive': 'we have many motions in us that do not proceed from our direction...so falling people extend their arms before them by a natural impulse, which prompts our limbs to offices and motions without any commission from our reason'.

Shakespeare, of course, in the same century, was perfectly at ease with the sense of not-knowing at the core of human experience. His plays are littered with references to various aspects of our psychological inscrutability, such as, in the first three quotations, the inability to give rational explanation of our feelings.

> My affection hath an unknown bottom,
> like the bay of Portugal.
>> *As You Like It, Act 4, Scene 1*

> My mind is troubled, like a fountain stirr'd;
> And I myself see not the bottom of it.
>> *Troilus and Cressida, Act 3, Scene 3*

> In sooth, I know not why I am so sad:
> It wearies me; you say it wearies you;
> But how I caught it, found it, or came by it,
> What stuff 'tis made of, whereof it is born,
> I am to learn;
> And such a want-wit sadness makes of me,
> That I have much ado to know myself.
>> *The Merchant of Venice, Act 1, Scene 1*

In *King Henry IV, Part II* (Act 4, Scene 5), he anticipates by 300 years Freud's 'discovery' of unconscious motivations, and the ways they make themselves known in our mental life:

> Prince: I never thought to hear you speak again
> King: Thy wish was father, Harry, to that thought.

And in an equally well-known extract, this time from *A Midsummer Night's Dream* (Act 5, Scene 1), he sketches out a theory of creativity that is still the psychological front-runner.

> The poet's eye, in a fine frenzy rolling,
> Doth glance from heaven to earth, from earth to heaven;
> And, as imagination bodies forth
> The forms of things unknown, the poet's pen
> Turns them to shapes, and gives to airy nothing
> A local habitation and a name.

(In fact it is hard to resist putting this account of the creative process alongside corroborating statements of more recent vintage. Albert Einstein, for example, musing on his own creative process, says: 'The words or the language as they are written or spoken do not seem to play any role in my mechanism of thought. The physical entities which seem to serve as elements in thought are certain signs and more or less clear images....Words intervene...only in a secondary stage.'[106])

To the human mind up until the sixteenth century, so far as we can tell, the fact that it could not see its own bottom, that those things which formed the contents of conscious awareness obviously and naturally danced onto the stage from wings that were beyond one's ken, was neither remarkable nor threatening. Certainly the sophistication of the mind had proceeded to the point where one was, so to speak, displaced somewhat from the mysterious core of life. Consciousness was becoming prominent, and much of its content, as well as much of the computing power of the brain-mind, was dedicated to the maintenance and enhancement of self-esteem and social status. But there was no reason for the mind to lie about itself.

Enter Villain, Stage Left

Not, that is, until Descartes, in a mere two pages of his *Meditations*, published in 1641, drove a pernicious wedge between conscious and unconscious, and issued to the European intelligentsia an invitation which it found itself unable to refuse: to identify itself exclusively with consciousness. Contrary to popular supposition, Descartes' most resounding achievement was not to sue for the divorce of mind from matter, or even of mind from body, but to tender a view of the mind as iceberg tip without iceberg bottom—as conscious, self-sufficient, all-embracing, explicit and rational—and to assert that the only and proper home of human identity is in this conscious realm.

What then am I? A thing which thinks. What is a thing which thinks? It is a thing which doubts, understands, conceives, affirms, denies, wills, refuses, which also imagines and feels.[107]

And when pressed to define thought more precisely, he tells us that:

Thought is a word that covers everything that exists in us in such a way that we are immediately conscious of it. Thus all the operations of will, intellect, imagination and of the senses are thoughts.

And so that there shall be no doubt at all about the matter, Descartes writes in a letter to Mersenne:

> As to the proposition...that nothing can be in me, that is, in my mind, of which I am not conscious, I have proved it in the *Meditations*.

Mind is now carved out from the psycho-physical unity of *psyche*, and is identified exclusively with consciousness. The unconscious body-brain-mind is denied its existence and leached of its intelligence, which is appropriated instead by an ever-conscious bubble behind the eyes. Into his creditable attempt to find for himself, in the first-hand facts of his experience, the foundation of his identity, Descartes slips a whopping—and unlicensed—assumption: that behind his thoughts there *must be* one who thinks, the *res cogitans*, a thinking kind of 'thing', and that this is who he must ultimately be. If he had been as rigorously scientific an explorer of inner space as he claimed, he could not have made that jump. He could only have said 'There is thinking (seeing, imagining, remembering etc)', or 'Thinking is happening', for more than that represents an inference for which there is no independent evidence.

Having denied that the source of his conscious thinking lies in unconscious processes, processes that are inherently invisible, he has to fill the explanatory vacuum with a cypher: the lead character in the internal soap opera, 'Me', is now given additional magical powers. 'Me' is not just a personal cartoon character that gives the narrative its sense of continuity. Now he/she/it is given the job of running around behind the scenes (replacing the sacked biocomputer) 'seeing', 'thinking', 'deciding' and 'willing'. Identification with this fictitious character is finally complete; the 'Me' is transmuted, in good alchemical fashion, into 'I'. Instead of an unspeakable mystery at the centre of my being, I have been persuaded to identify instead with a species of elusive manikin.

And I have also been bewitched into a corollary misinterpretation of my own consciousness. No longer it is to be seen as a peculiar, and in some ways peripheral, product of the extended biological mystery that I truly am. Now it is to be treated as a privileged window through which 'I' can look *out* at the world 'as it really is', and *in* at myself 'as I really am'. What I can see through the porthole of consciousness is real and true. What I cannot see does not exist.

This philosophical sleight-of-hand soon found plenty of fans. By 1690 John Locke was able to say that 'it is altogether as intelligible to say that a body is extended without parts, as that anything thinks without being conscious of it'. And he consolidated Descartes' identification of a person's very essence with this conscious mind:

(A person) is a thinking, intelligent being, that has reason and reflection, and can consider itself as itself, the same thinking thing, in different times and places, which it does only by that consciousness which is inseparable from thinking, and, as it seems to me, essential to it; it being impossible for any one to perceive without perceiving that he does perceive....Consciousness always accompanies thinking, and it is that which makes every one to be what he calls self...[108]

And David Hume could simply assert that 'the perceptions of the mind are perfectly known', and 'consciousness never deceives'.

Pathologizing the Unconscious

Before Descartes' preposterous rejection of mystery had wormed its way into 'common sense', there had been no need to have a special term for *un*conscious processes; it was, as we have seen, taken as self-evident that self-knowledge was patchy and cloudy. But after the Cartesian coup, anyone who wanted to dispute that 'consciousness was all' had to have their own vocabulary to fight with. And so 'the unconscious' had to be invented as a partial corrective, a way of reasserting the existence of that which we do not know. As the mystics and poets had always known, unconscious mental processes are an unavoidable inference from experience. By waving his linguistic wand, Descartes had been able, like a magician with a top-hat, a rabbit and some sleight of hand, to make them vanish, but this did not mean that they had actually dematerialized.

So words had to be found to remind us that they were still there 'really'. In 1751 the word 'unconscious' appeared in English, and over the next hundred years—with the help of such writers as Goethe and Schiller—equivalents gradually became common in French and German as well. The adjective 'unconscious' became reified as 'the unconscious', and so the notion of a separate, inscrutable storehouse of the mind began to take hold. In trying to reestablish the existence of unconscious *aspects* of the mind-body system, these well-intentioned writers fell into the unavoidable verbal trap of implicitly postulating a separate new department of the mind—one which was in some sense antagonistic to, or subversive of, conscious reason.

Thus the ground was prepared for a rapid takeover of 'the unconscious' by those interested in mental pathology. From a hundred years before Freud, and almost up to the present day, the unconscious has been seen predominantly as the lair of dark and wild forces which are a threat to the established order and clarity of reason. 'Day was challenged by Night, the enlightenment of reason by the tempests and conflicts of intuition and instinct, the soul of man by a dark and frightening, but desperately attractive, inner spirit of temptation and surrender, ready to take over....'[109] Instead of being an intrinsic, valuable, even vital, ingredient of *psyche*, the unconscious became seen as both a contentious hypothesis, and a source of disruption and disorder, associated with mad and violent storms that could threaten the civilization of mind and society.

Into this climate of scepticism and anxiety stepped the pioneers of psychiatry and psychotherapy, offering themselves as guides, lion-tamers and shamans: ready, willing and able 'to boldly go' where others feared to tread. Freud, his fore-runners and his followers, filled the storehouse of the unconscious with disowned, repressed aspects of personality, and showed how these rejected children of the mind come back to haunt us in bizarre and terrifying ways. The unconscious was simultaneously declared to exist, pathologized, and ripped away from the mainstream of life. Sure, there were party-games one could play with dreams, and fun to be had with Freudian slips. But 'normal' people could mostly afford to feel sorry for those whose unconsciousnesses were playing up, while safely ignoring their own. As well as being pathologized, the unconscious was marginalized: it became an idea that could be played *with*, like a child peeping through her hands at a horror film.

This shrunken, demonic version of 'the unconscious' served to obscure even further the generic Unconscious: the unfathomable source that lies behind *all* experience. Freud gave us back a *version* of the unconscious, but one which focused entirely on the costs of 'tactical ignorance', and ignored, equally entirely, the deep, calm pervasive unconscious that is the very foundation, the *sine qua non*, of conscious life. By defining the unconscious in the way he did, he presented it as the antagonist of mental health; a repository of wild forces which could only be civilized and integrated into the personality by being brought into the light of consciousness. When we had finally emptied the cupboard of skeletons, optimal well-being would be ours, and the power of 'the unconscious' would be reduced to zero. Freud never saw the possibility that therapy could be a prelude to a passionate love-affair with Mystery.

The pathologizing of the unconscious makes it frightening, and inclines us even more strongly to ignore its existence. We are like children who will not sleep in their own snug beds because they are fearful of the bogeymen and monsters that (might) lurk (unseen) underneath. The Freudian imagery speaks of wildness and danger. 'The experience of the inner darkness, as Freud described it, is the vivid confrontation with one's own repressed nature. *The beast emerges from his lair* where he has long lain sleeping, and a man has night terrors, awakens in a sweat....One meets face to face the *perverse and amoral creatures* who have been inhabiting other parts of the building [emphasis added].'[110] No wonder we do not feel inclined to 'go down to the woods today', if we are sure of *that* kind of 'big surprise'; and we become oblivious even of the existence of the woods—'Unconscious? I can't see any unconscious'—using our defences of projection and rationalization to reinterpret the inner growls or cries as Outside, Of No Consequence, Nothing To Do with Me.

C.G. Jung, to his credit, was able to see the effect on the popular imagination of this scary image of the unconscious. In *The Undiscovered Self* he rather gleefully reveals that Freud himself was peeping through his own fingers:

Resistances to psychological enlightenment are based in large measure on fear—on panic fear of the discoveries that might be made in the realm of the unconscious. These fears are found not only among persons who are frightened by the picture Freud painted of the unconscious; they also troubled the originator of psychoanalysis himself....It is this fear of the unconscious psyche which not only impedes self-knowledge but is the gravest obstacle to a wider understanding and knowledge of psychology.[11]

Jung seems at times to have the mundane and ubiquitous view of the unconscious that modern science endorses:

> For more than fifty years we have known, or could have known, that there is an unconscious as a counterbalance to consciousness....There is an unconscious psychic reality which demonstrably influences consciousness and its contents....All this is known, but we still go on thinking ourselves to be innocuous, reasonable and humane....It is frivolous, superficial and unreasonable of us, as well as psychically unhygienic, to overlook the reaction and standpoint of the unconscious. [pp83–4]

Why is it 'psychically unhygienic' to overlook the unconscious? Because it is still, for Jung, as for Freud, the centre of dissociated madness which, if not brought within the civilizing purview of consciousness, can strike out in harmful, maybe even 'evil', ways. The unconscious manifests itself 'mainly in the form of *contrary* [emphasis added] feelings, fantasies, emotions, impulses and dreams'. And to reject these is to fall prey to a disastrous illusion.

> Since it is universally believed that man *is* merely what his conscious knows of itself, he regards himself as harmless and so adds stupidity to iniquity. He does not deny that terrible things have happened and still go on happening, but it is always 'the others' who do them. And when such deeds belong to the recent or remote past, they quickly and conveniently sink into the sea of forgetfulness, and that state of chronic woolly-mindedness returns which we describe as 'normality'. In shocking contrast to this...the evil, the guilt, the profound unease of conscience, the obscure misgiving are there before our eyes, if only we would see. Man has done these things; I am a man, who has his share of human nature; therefore I am guilty with the rest....Only the fool can permanently neglect the conditions of his own nature. In fact, this negligence is the best means of making him an instrument of evil. [pp95–7]

So for Jung it is not that 'the unconscious' is inherently a pit of snakes, as the popular image would have it. Rather it is the state of dissociation, of identifying oneself too narrowly with a sanitized consciousness, that leads to trouble, as the conscious mind struggles to maintain a view of its self which is ultimately, and eternally, untenable. It is not one's nature—comprised integrally of conscious and unconscious—which is at fault; it is the doomed attempt to live by a false impression, a black-and-white caricature, of that nature which has been pasted over, and now obscures, the more pastel shades of reality.

In this Jung is undeniably right; it is the proper business of psychotherapy to attempt to deal with some of the wilder thrashings of a strangulated unconscious, by persuading sufferers to take their hands away from their own throats, and allow themselves to breathe the air that they are terrified will poison them. Yet even here the unconscious is still identified, albeit in a rather different way, with troubled emotion and 'contrariness' of thought and will.

Jung's great advance on Freud was the insight that daring to live close to the unconscious was an essentially religious stand. 'When the individual is willing to fulfil the demands of rigorous self-examination...he will have taken the first step towards the foundations of his consciousness—that is, towards the unconscious, the only accessible source of religious experience....The unconscious is the medium from which the religious experience seems to flow. As to what the further cause of such an experience may be, the answer to this lies beyond the range of human knowledge.' At root, for Jung as for the mystics, staring into the darkness is not only an act of courageous self-healing; it is an invitation to the divine.

But though Jung's view of the relationship between conscious and unconscious was broader and more balanced than Freud's, it nevertheless preserved the feeling that the unconscious was something 'special', apart from the mundane realities of washing up and feeding the cat. It could perhaps be sacred, as well as profane, and for reopening this possibility Jung deserves the heartfelt thanks of disenfranchised mystics—the 'inglorious Wordsworths' of everyday religious experience—everywhere. But the unconscious still felt arcane: more the wildness of Saturday night, or the piety of Sunday morning, than an average day at the office. The 'collective unconscious' was introduced as a repository of transcultural wisdom, to balance the individual childhood knots of the 'individual unconscious', but it was still another separate, speculative box in the head, at least as it diffused out into popular culture. And still the aura of psychological muck—albeit now tinged with mythology and magic—hung over it.

The therapists' unconscious remains 'hot and wet'. The Unconscious that was cast aside by Descartes is 'cool and dry'. It is this one we need to recapture, and we should accept no substitutes. To think of the unconscious as a locked cellar (as Freud did), within which we have stashed away our guilt secrets and bad memories, is to limit and distort the mystery. To see it as a kind of seed-bed of our potentialities (as Jung did), fallow land that contains and nurtures the germs of our future character—'the earth or ground of one's new being, the part which is *in potentia*'[112]—is to fail to appreciate how vital a part the unconscious brain-mind plays in the creation of every moment of experience, right here and now.

Fear of Losing what We Never Really Had

The deeper reason why we have become oblivious to our own unconsciousness is that its existence is threatening to the phoney images thrown up by the Self System, which are all to do with Consciousness, Clarity and Control. If 'I' am essentially identified with the content of consciousness; if I see consciousness as the mind's Executive Headquarters, and as a non-distorting peephole through which 'I' can spy on my own workings; and if 'I' has mistaken the ability of consciousness to (sometimes) *predict* what the system as a whole is going to do for an ability to *determine* and *control* what is going to happen...then the suggestion of a big fat engine behind the scenes that is *really* doing all the interesting work, is not going to go down too well. The conceit and the conspiracy can only be maintained by denying the existence of any such machine, and ensuring that what the Mind's Eye sees is what it is *meant* to see.

To an 'I' that has come to see, and to need to see, itself as in charge, the idea that it isn't (and maybe has never been) can only be felt as a shock and a threat. The idea that this sense of control is an illusion, a form of self-deception, does not compute. For years I have been construing my experience in terms of this model of Consciousness sitting in the driving seat; it isn't an *idea*, it's *true*. Because the beliefs are dissolved in my experience, every moment seems to bring further proof—if more were needed—that control is an incontrovertible fact. And if I am persuaded to take your idea seriously, the only way I can make sense of it, from behind the bars, is as a genuine *loss* of that which, up till now, I have genuinely had. The proposal is therefore either preposterous, or terrifying. If 'I' am not driving the car, what on earth *am* 'I' doing; and who *is*? If I am forced to imagine myself in the back seat, I simply cannot see anything (or anybody) up front. We are in danger of careering off the road—of running amok or going insane.

(One is reminded of the famous cartoon of two rats in a 'Skinner box'—an experimental apparatus in which rats are rewarded for learning new tricks—one saying to the other 'You know, I've really got this guy in the white coat where I want him. Every time I press this lever, he drops in a pellet of food!' From Rat's point of view, she is in control. From Professor Skinner's point of view, he is. Who is right; and who is deluded?)

The Mind's Petard

Once the twin Cartesian assumptions become taken-for-granted—that whatever makes its way into the central spotlight of consciousness is what is *real* (or 'valid'), and that whatever is conscious is *me*—then the mind truly is hoist with its own petard, for its job becomes the defence of whatever is conscious, and the editing of consciousness to fit with the definition of self. What appears in consciousness is automatically referred to the underlying definition of my self—my unquestionable assumptions about my character, my worth, my personhood—and if anything seems not to fit, then it has to be ignored or explained away. It is no longer just my actions that have to fall into line with my self-definition; my conscious experience too has to be submitted for approval to the panel of internal censors. Or rather the censors have to be given power of veto during the process of consciousness *making*, for once an antagonistic thought, impulse or feeling has already appeared in consciousness, the damage has been done; the threat to identity or self-esteem is real. As a result of the Cartesian identification with consciousness, the nature of consciousness becomes even more *unlike* whatever is going on behind the scenes.

Originally conscious awareness occurred in a state of alarm, and it was associated indelibly with an uncomfortable emotional tinge that signalled the urgent need to resolve the apparent emergency, in just the way that physical pain enters consciousness as a biological call to arms (or to rest). But deprived of the vivid emotional stimulus, we are in danger of allowing conflicts and dangers to persist, to our own detriment, just as those patients who lack the ability to 'feel'–that is, to be conscious of–pain fail to notice, and therefore to respond to injuries, or to take appropriate remedies for their ailments. In one famous case, a 'Miss C' from Montreal failed to experience pain, and so did not react to noxious stimuli. She never moved while sleeping, never shifted her weight from foot to foot while standing, and adopted various unhealthy postures. As a result, her joints became malformed and diseased, and she contracted various infections that led ultimately to her death.[113]

Thus in a curious way the Cartesian split caused us to lose touch with one form of unconsciousness–the essentially mysterious ground out of which experience wells like a spring–and at the same time requires us to manufacture a second form of unconsciousness– a kind of selective inattention to those aspects of experience which, if allowed to become conscious, would be construed by the mind as threatening to the Self System. If a macho self is committed to 'keeping cool' under all circumstances, then the experiences of fear, anxiety or confusion–all parts of the human birthright–must be denied. One manages, through intelligent action, to keep the appearance of these unwanted feelings to a minimum; but it is not in our power to remove the conditions that prompt them entirely. There are always going to be surprises, misfortunes and disappointments. So the only alternative that is left to us, if we cannot bear simply to *suffer* them, is to ignore them and hope they will go away.

FIFTEEN

The Cultivation of Ignorance

The range of what we think and do
is limited by what we fail to notice.
And because we fail to notice
 that we fail to notice
there is little we can do
to change
until we notice
how failing to notice
shapes our thoughts and deeds.

R.D. Laing

The subtle menace of repression is the silence with which it occurs. The passing of pain out of awareness sends out no warning signals: the sound of repression is a thought evaporating.

Daniel Goleman

I have argued in Chapter 13 that consciousness is irredeemably emotional, and that the faint sense of persistent dis-ease which the Buddhists call *dukkha* is an inevitable feature of modern consciousness. But surely this gloomy view cannot be accurate (you could reasonably ask); after all, most of us, much of the time, feel reasonably cheerful. Is not this insistence on the ubiquity of anxiety an exaggeration? Yes it is, and for two possible reasons. Some of the time the Self System is in abeyance or unstimulated, so that we do, if we are lucky, have periods of respite. The wiser we are, the less frequent and the less intense are our feelings of unsatisfactoriness. As Montaigne said, 'The most manifest sign of wisdom is enduring cheerfulness'.

The other reason for the reduction in consciousness of unwanted feelings, however, reflects not wisdom but self-deception; and it is to the processes whereby we are able to edit and expurgate our own minds that this chapter turns its attention. To be unhappy or unsettled all the time is psychologically painful and practically unhelpful. If we are to function, while burdened with sadness or guilt, and cannot eradicate the cause, perhaps we can at least learn how to *ignore* the discomfort, somehow blot it out from awareness, and carry on. The cost of this, of course, is that consciousness then becomes an even more unreliable guide to what is going on than ever.

If the circumcision of consciousness that we discussed in the last chapter—the detachment of its bright core from the shadowy ring that surrounds it—makes consciousness un-holy, then the process of expurgation makes it very holey indeed. It becomes peppered with no-go areas, the insides of which are thereby rendered invisible. And the fact that there are such areas is somehow itself concealed, so that one is presented, in consciousness, with a work that appears seamless, and from which all evidence of the censor's knife has been removed. We are left with a consciousness that does not acknowledge its own edges and its birthplace; and does not see its own holes.

But if the very existence of these blind-spots is denied to consciousness, how can we know they are there? Perhaps the most famous method for revealing them is the classical Freudian technique of 'free association', in which the mind is allowed to ramble around, or is gently 'prompted', until it suddenly seems to hit a brick wall. By removing the guiding hand of conscious intention, the stage is set to allow the concealed threats and attractors to exert their influence. The significant moment arises not when the person produces a bizarre or intriguing riposte, but when no association comes at all. It is at the point when the mind goes blank, when the train of thought suddenly disappeared into a black tunnel, that Freud knew there might be some fruitful digging to be done. As in the case of that other great detective, Sherlock Holmes, Freud's ears would prick up when he heard that the dog did *not* bark in the night.

More recent work in clinical psychology relies on the fact that, while consciousness is purged of the unwanted feeling, unconsciously a threat can still be registered very clearly. Recent work by Andrew Matthews at the Applied Psychology Unit in Cambridge has highlighted this almost paradoxical coupling of the 'unconscious fascination' of threats with apparent conscious denial.[114] As we saw earlier, anxiety tends to be self-perpetuating, in that, once an area of threat is established in the mind, the relevant perceptual thresholds are permanently primed or lowered, so that events which are related to that threat are preferentially detected and processed. But this detection, for some people at least, does not result in any *conscious* experience of the threat.

Matthews has found that some highly anxious people give evidence of having registered the threat, but do not 'know', consciously, that they have done so. Other people who show an equally high level of physical anxiety do not seem to have learnt the 'knack' of conscious denial, and may be recurrently—or even continually—swamped with all-too-conscious feelings of fear or dread. When one of the former type of people meets a situation in which the intensity of anxiety reaches tidal wave proportions, and is strong enough to breach the wall of silence that has been erected around it, then they may experience the inner chaos and destruction of a 'nervous breakdown'. So if you are scared of spiders, one of two things may happen. Either you notice every single little spider, cobweb and spiderlike ball of fluff wherever you go. Or you just get tense as you enter a strange bathroom, and don't know why.

At an everyday level, we can often see when someone else's body is giving the lie to their apparent insouciance: the jiggling foot, or the patch of sweat under the arms, gives them away. We swear 'blind' that things matter to us which truly do not; that things which really concern us are of no consequence at all. Detecting discrepancies between what consciousness 'publishes', and what the unconscious 'leaks', is the stock-in-trade of the psychotherapist. And this is one area in which we can be helped to see ourselves more accurately by science. A psychological test can pick up evidence of the *body's* registration of a threat, even when consciousness has managed to concoct a convincing cover-story. A recording of the electrical activity in the brain, or the conductivity—i.e. the sweatiness—of the skin, or the size of the pupils, will frequently show that a threat has been recorded, even though no mention of it shows up in the despatches of consciousness.[115]

The editing of consciousness is the domain of the well-known psychological defences. While *denial* is the fundamental defence, its use alone leaves us vulnerable to noticing that there *is* a hole or a blockage somewhere. The cover-up is more complete if we add in other ploys such as distraction, projection, rationalization, sublimation, the use of muscular tension, and the rest. To see how the whole process of the sanitizing of consciousness works, let us follow an example.

Suppose that one of the areas of tension in my Self System concerns loneliness. I have incorporated in this system the idea that mature, healthy people are gregarious and relaxed, always capable of meeting new people in a cheerful, friendly, positive frame of mind. Now suppose that my reality is, sometimes, rather different: I experience anxiety, tension, and a tendency to avoid people's gaze and to want to run away. These (perfectly natural) responses are evaluated negatively with respect to the idealized image of self. They seem to provide evidence for 'weakness' or 'immaturity'. Thus they become tinged with a shameful quality. Shame itself, however, is a feeling that is also anathema to the image of self with which I am identified, and so it sets up another loop of uncomfortable emotional reverberation. I feel anxious about feeling ashamed. So the whole package of resonances tends to be excluded from conscious recognition.

Now suppose that I, who have come to appreciate the benefits of keeping to myself, am asked by someone (at just the kind of cocktail party that I find difficult) whether, in my solitary lifestyle, I don't sometimes get lonely. Already feeling (unconsciously) on edge, 'lonely' looms out of the conversational haze, threatening (still unconsciously) to remind me of this whole entangled, uncomfortable mess of feelings and judgements. The defence mechanism of the brain, on recognizing the danger signal, immediately sends a large squirt of inhibitory activity to this complex, which effectively prevents it from being able to accumulate enough excitation to become conscious. The damper is put on this potential route, so that the conscious train of thought cannot progress further into this threatening territory.

But it is not necessary to stop the train of thought entirely, only to make sure that it does not chug down the track labelled 'Here be dragons'. So *other* associations to the word 'lonely' become relatively more accessible—even though they are not primed to the same degree—and with scarcely a break in the conversation, the points are switched and the train of thought—*conscious* thought—careers off down a safer track. I start telling you about all the benefits of a solitary lifestyle, how nice it is not having to take other people's feelings into account, how you can do things at your own pace, switch the light on and read in the middle of the night without upsetting anyone else, and so on. With the smoothness of a practised conjurer,

I distract your attention from the sudden threat and substitute an anodyne story that probably bores and hopefully reassures us both. I plug the cavity with an instant filling.[116]

The job of expurgating consciousness of threatening feeling is made all the easier if the muscles of the body are employed to dampen the sensations of fear 'at source'. Instead of having to wait until the brain is in a state of alarm, and only then trying to smother consciousness, it is possible to tense the parts of the body that are being mobilized for fight or flight. Thus the 'hollow' or 'sinking' feeling in the stomach, which is typically associated with anxiety, or the changes in breathing pattern associated with anger, can be attenuated by clamping the muscles of the chest or abdomen. This form of muscular self-abuse, as well as dampening the feeling, has the added advantage of inhibiting the external *signs* of the feeling, so that they are not communicated to anyone else who might scoff or take advantage of the transparent 'weakness'. The prototypically English male response to fear or sadness involves bracing the muscles of the face, so that one does not give oneself away, resulting in the famous 'stiff upper lip'.

Such ploys may be adaptive in certain situations, when other people are really liable to censure or exploit our state of apparent alarm. A schoolteacher on a bad day might genuinely be better advised to 'tough it out', than to run in tears from the classroom. Police or paramedics at the scene of a horrific motorway accident may need, if they are to get their job done, to suppress their feelings of distress. But if the tension, both physical and mental, is not subsequently released, and is allowed unconsciously to persist, or even to accumulate—when a crisis management technique is turned unwittingly into a habit—then a breeding-ground is established for the whole host of so-called 'psychosomatic' disorders. Unrelieved clamping of the gut eventuates in the ulcerative colitis; inhibition of the impulse to run may result in chronic pain in the lower back, hips or legs; tension in the neck, designed to prevent the head from turning anxiously from side to side as the eyes search for an escape route, breeds the persistent headache; and so on.

The Narrator is often recruited by the Self System to spin a tale, for conscious (or public) consumption, that reinforces the image of how I am *supposed* to be, by denying or distorting the unconscious reality of how in fact I am. In 'reversal' or 'reaction formation', the storyline represents me not just as different from, but actually as the opposite of, how I am. If I am congenitally messy and untidy, and have learnt to *hate* myself for my sloppiness, what may eventually surface in the conscious story is a view of myself as fastidiously clean and neat—a view that may actually be supported by a behavioural overlay of obsessional tidiness. If I am full of anger and resentment at an elderly, demanding parent, I may develop an impenetrable 'act' of calm and concern; an act that may only reveal itself in an uncomfortably overprotective quality to the care, or an air of heavy martyrdom. And if challenged about my underlying motives and feelings, methinks I might protest too much that you are quite mistaken.

Reversal often chooses as its partner the defence of 'projection'. If frequently I am angry, but the Narrator denies that I am, then I may be prone to see all this anger not in myself but in the world around me. Anger is there, but its source is displaced to some outside condition or agency. Why do I have to live in such a hostile world, I may complain, when I would never hurt a fly? It is so *unfair*. And all the while the Narrator is keeping up its comforting commentary of 'rationalization', explaining to me, you and anyone who is unwise enough to stop and listen, why it is that I am sane, calm, rational and mature, despite certain (*entirely* misleading) indications to the contrary.

If necessary the Narrator will script a little pantomime for me to act out to convince you. Jonathan Miller, the director and physician, tells of seeing a man in Oxford Street in London who waved for a taxi that failed to stop. Immediately he realized that his gesture had 'failed', instead of letting his raised arm fall to his side, he bent his elbow and scratched his head in a vigorous fashion. This innocent little 'displacement activity' was, suggested Miller, a carefully crafted performance designed to put the record straight for a streetful of strangers, none of whom (with the exception of one eagle-eyed student of human nature) had probably noticed the event at all. 'In case any of you are suffering from the mistaken impression that I have just produced a failed taxi-stopping gesture,' his mime was saying, 'let me reassure you. What I in fact was producing was a—slightly flamboyant, I admit, but none the worse for that—very successful head-scratching gesture.' Thus he could go about the business of looking for another taxi, released (somewhat) from the unfelt fear that a dozen or so people who he did not know, and would never meet, might be *thinking badly* about him.

If a forbidden impulse keeps recurring, constantly threatening to disrupt the soothing commentary with its cries and growls, then a longer-term ploy is to divert the energy into an interest—even a career—that gives license to a disguised version of the impulse, or allows you access to the taboo object of your desire, while not acknowledging its full force or its real intent. These are the Freudian defences of 'sublimation' and 'displacement'. A woman channels her greed into a career with the World Bank. A man with a 'morbid' fascination with blood and injury loves his job as a nurse in Casualty. The soprano nightly sublimates her urge to scream. The man who denies his sexual interest in children is the first to volunteer to join the search-party for the missing little girl.

The Mechanism of Ignorance

It is quite simple to give an account, in terms of our brain-mind model, of how these defences were crafted out of the evolutionary resources of the body-brain-mind system. To do so, we need to go just a little deeper into the mechanisms for juggling with the relative levels of excitation and inhibition.

The control that can be achieved by the operation of two antagonistic forces, like the brake and the accelerator in a car, is much finer and faster than is provided by only one system on its own. The stopping power of a car without brakes in notoriously slow and uncertain. So it is not surprising that the animal body should have discovered the advantage of this kind of opposition, and have developed a variety of mechanisms that capitalize upon it.[117] One of these paired systems controls the intensity of pain and aversive feelings. The excitatory Alarm System tends to turn them up, and another inhibitory 'Anaesthetizing System' turns them down.

The Anaesthetic System has its origins quite early in the evolutionary story: a primitive version is found even in molluscs. A particular class of neurotransmitters can be released which start off a chain reaction that effectively blocks or dampens painful stimuli. The substances are called 'endorphins', and are chemically very similar to the 'opiates', drugs such as heroin and morphine. As we would expect, the release of endorphins in the brain has been shown to be produced not only by physical pain, but also by the other evolutionary alarm calls: fear, uncertainty, being cornered and the like.[118] And it is the inhibitory pain-*reduction* system that can be called upon to help with the persistent emotional headache that consciousness itself has become.

The central characteristic of this antagonistic set-up is that excitation and inhibition do not necessarily cancel each other out, like a credit and a debit added together. They can co-exist, and at quite high levels. The brake and the accelerator of a car do not cancel each other out directly; what they do is oppose each other's *effects*. One tends to speed the car up, the other to slow it down. You can press both pedals together, and the result depends on the relative strengths of the 'irresistible force' and the 'immovable object'. Thus, in the brain-mind, it might be possible for excitation to reach high levels, but for an equal-and-opposite level of inhibition to prevent there being a strong-enough *net effect* for the excitation to become conscious. This hypothesis says, in effect, that the body-brain-mind system is affected by the gross or absolute level of excitation, while access to consciousness is a function of the net or relative level of excitation, after the inhibition has been 'subtracted'.

Shock

The experience of fear or pain, followed by a complete shut-down of consciousness, is clearly demonstrated by the phenomenon of shock. In a situation that is overwhelmingly frightening or life-threatening, a person may feel almost literally as if a switch has been thrown which cuts off their feelings, leaving a rather eerie calm in its wake. A vivid description of the state of shock was provided, more than twenty years after the traumatic event itself, by the Scottish missionary Dr David Livingstone (of 'Dr Livingstone, I presume' fame).

I heard a shout. Starting, and looking half round, I saw the lion just in the act of springing upon me....He caught my shoulder as he sprang, and we both came to the ground below together. Growling horribly close to my ear, he shook me as a terrier does a rat. The shock produced a stupor similar to that which seems to be felt by a mouse after the first shake of the cat. It caused a sort of dreaminess in which there was no sense of pain nor feeling of terror, though [I was] quite conscious of all that was happening. It was like what patients partly under the influence of chloroform describe, who see the operation but feel not the knife.[119]

For Dr Livingstone, the perceptual areas of the emergency are spared; he is able to see and feel what is happening to him. But consciousness is expurgated of its terror. It is as if the direction of the 'action' had suddenly been handed over from Michael Winner to Walt Disney.

Breakthrough and Breakdown

Thus, in a variety of intricate ways, are the Shadow and the Persona constructed. By sending to a danger zone an amount of inhibition that is greater than the excitation which it is attracting, it can be kept from erupting into consciousness, in a state of suspended animation. By keeping lower the thresholds of safe associates, the flow of mental current can be diverted into other channels. By raising the thresholds of those pathways that could lead not to consciousness but to real action, the impulse can be contained. By keeping other thresholds lower, and by recruiting various groups of muscles (including those for speech) to help with the charade, a public front can be created that masks the wild, the selfish, the hurtful and the mad. The production of disinformation, for both public and private consumption, becomes not just an intermittent tactic but a strategic cornerstone of lifestyle and personality. (Interestingly I just mistyped 'lifestyle' as 'liestyle'. I am glad to see that—even as I sit here at the word-processor—I am exemplifying my own analysis!)

But the ability to edit consciousness turns out to be a double-edged weapon. By being able to ignore threats, especially the home-grown variety, we create a consciousness that is patchy and counterfeit, an unfaithful image of what the unconscious biocomputer is up to. But worse than that, the strategy of tactical ignorance leaves the underlying threats in place, unexamined and untested. It may have been that ignoring something was a necessary coping response earlier in our lives; but ignorance is self-perpetuating, because you can never discover that what was once dangerous is now safe. You have to keep on *assuming* that it is still a threat, because you never get close enough to find out. As Mark Twain said, a cat that has once sat on a hot stove will never sit on one again; but neither will it sit on a cold one.

But whereas loss of stove-access will be an insignificant limitation to the cat (unless its sadistic owner decides to put its food bowl on top of it), we constantly find our attention both being drawn to, and veering away from, the same set of psychological hot-spots. The brain develops a condition of chronic restlessness, in which it cannot find a place of equanimity and equilibrium.

SIXTEEN

Stupidity:
the Retardation of Perception

Stupid, Wanting in or slow of mental perception; having one's faculties deadened or dulled; deprived of apprehension, feeling or sensation; destitute of consciousness; insensible to pain or sorrow; stunned with surprise, grief etc.

Shorter Oxford Dictionary

It takes time to see. The content of consciousness does not appear as an instantaneous miracle; it arises as a result of an enormously rapid process that involves the activation and integration of thousands of circuits within the brain. But because these micro-movements of mind happen unconsciously, and happen so fast, it is very hard to become aware not just of the time that they take, but of the very fact that they comprise a process that happens in time.

To some extent this myopia towards our own perception is inevitable, even productive. In evolutionary terms, perception needs to pick up changes that matter, and which we can do something about. We have evolved eyes that are sensitive to falling rocks and charging elephants; ears that are attuned to crying babies and snapping twigs. We are not designed to hear what bats hear, or to detect the movements of glaciers.[120] The speed of normal perception, like the beat of a hummingbird's wings, is too fast to be aware of. And indeed it would be an odd instrument that was designed to register its own changes, like a clock that told not the time, but the speed of rotation of its own cogs.

The tacit assumption that perception is instantaneous is strengthened all the more by the acquired tendency of the Western mind to fasten only onto what is happening in the limelight of consciousness, and to neglect the hazier activity that precedes and surrounds it. We fail to notice that consciousness is a developmental phenomenon, its contents forever arising, unfolding, and passing away, like breakers on the sea. It takes, in the first instance, an act of imagination to 'see' our own seeing as the culmination of a virtuoso behind-the-scenes performance, involving a host of choices and decisions. Let me illustrate.

Seeing in Slow Motion

Imagine the minimal, artificial situation in which you are told to close your eyes, let your mind go blank, and then to open them and look at the new, solitary object that has been silently placed in front of you. Now even though you may have been successful in letting the previous contents of consciousness fade away (and this is no easy thing to do to order), the brain-mind's network of connections is still going to have its shifting pattern of excitations and inhibitions smeared across it. At the moment at which you open your eyes, a patterned wave of activation starts from the retina and rolls quickly up the neural pathways, where it adds to and modifies these pre-existing currents, like a river running in to the ocean. The original pattern of inflow is soon lost, yet it modifies the way the ocean as a whole is behaving in a characteristic way.

Soon, as your receptors analyse the scene in front of you, its different attributes begin to home in on a small number of hypotheses about what might be 'out there'. As the field of candidates narrows, so their underlying circuits ('octopus gangs') accumulate the lion's share of the activation, and this begins to prime *other* attributes—the ones that are not (yet) being activated strongly from the outside. Thus any of these other features that are actually present will require less incoming energy to get them to fire off, and if their presence is confirmed, they will then add their weight to the overall level of excitation of the concept that predicted them.

Suppose that what has actually been placed in front of you is a spherical glass bowl containing water and some long slivers of carrot that are kept gently on the move by an electric stirrer. The hypothesis that quickly emerges as the front-runner, after the first wave of activity hits the brain, is that this is a bowl of tropical fish. If this *is* what it is, then, according to the brain-mind's store of fish-knowledge, the candidates for fish-hood should have V-shaped tails that are wagging in a familiar way. These bits of knowledge are not, of course, articulated in such neat propositions; they are embedded in the way the network is connected up, so that the hypothesis 'fish', as it accumulates more activation, automatically starts to prime these expectations about what *other* features of fish, water and bowl are likely, on past performance, to be present.

If you are being cautious and attentive, you will find (assuming I have not been too careful in crafting my carrot slices) that this prediction is *not* confirmed, and this will cause you to call off the current bets, and pay renewed and less selective attention to what is actually coming in. But if you are being lazy, or you are too tired or upset to see clearly, or if my lab assistant happened to tell you while you were waiting to take part in this little test that I, the tester, am a tropical fish enthusiast, then the extra processing may well not get done, and you 'see' the hypothesis that is to your mind the most likely.

If you have taken it for granted that what is 'really' in front of you is a real bowl of water with real fish in it, then you are in for a nasty surprise when I walk in, casually dip my hand in the bowl, pop one of the little orange slivers into my mouth, and start chewing. You will experience real disgust, or genuine outrage, at my shameless disregard for the feelings of both you and the 'fish'. You may even—consciously or unconsciously—conclude that psychologists (as you have suspected all along) are callous brutes, and, twenty years later, when this episode has long sunk below the surface of conscious memory, you will startle and confuse your seventeen-year-old daughter with the vehemence of your reaction when she announces that she is thinking of reading psychology at university.

On the failure to keep collecting evidence long enough to tell the difference between carrot and fish may be built a whole superstructure of reaction, assumption and belief which can generate emotion, confirm prejudice, rupture relationship and poison the future. If the context had been different, different parts of the brain would have been primed, and different trains of unconscious thought may very well have been set in motion. If I had been introduced to you as a magician, rather than as a psychologist, the feeling that the brain would have thrown up would probably have been amusement, or intrigue, rather than disgust, and twenty years on your daughter would not have retired to her bedroom hurt and defiant.

We're All Naive Realists Really

If we were not so enamoured of our own consciousness, we would not place such great reliance on it. Our reactions and responses would be understood, at some deep level of appreciation, as products of the shifting currents and tides of the unconscious brain-mind, not as the unequivocal truth. But, being Descartes' children, and being therefore conditioned to identify ourselves and our image of 'reality' exclusively with whatever is printed out on the screen of consciousness, we are bound to over-estimate the accuracy and the authority of these conscious pictures and stories. Whatever is printed out in the bold lettering of consciousness is taken to be who I really am, and how the world really is. And once we have made this judgment of authenticity, and conferred on our conscious experience the status of the 'real', there is no going back.

After all, when we call something 'real' we are effectively denying the fallibility of our own perception. We are saying that who I am, what I care about or am afraid of, what I was thinking about the moment before, my scars and my dreams...all of this is entirely irrelevant to the world as I now see it—the *real* world. Having decided that one of my perceptions is 'real' or 'true', I now have to stick by it. If it is real, I cannot change my mind about it, because my mind had nothing to do with it in the first place. Everything that happened on the perceptual production line *before* the moment of consciousness is taken as reflecting the objective reality of the world, not the contributions of the brain-mind itself. If I take myself to be 'really' clever, any suggestion of a mistake has to be contested. If Wittgenstein 'really' is profound, then all obscurities have to be further evidence of his profundity. If the carrot 'really' is a Fish Called Wanda, then eating her is a real sin.

Our everyday, spontaneous behaviour is saturated with unconscious inferences; it is only when they every-so-often turn out to be wrong that we become aware of them.[121] For example, people who live in cities, especially those whose misfortune it is to travel daily to work in the centre of London from such Northern Line underground stations as Highgate and Archway, will have experienced the 'stationary escalator effect'. If you are used to negotiating moving escalators, the sensation getting on and getting off one that happens to be *not* moving is a curious one. As you get on, you have the sensation of being suddenly slowed down or held back by an invisible force; while at the other end, as you step off the stationary escalator onto *terra firma*, you feel propelled gently forwards. Though the effect may wear off if the inconvenience is experienced regularly, it is not at all easy to overcome with an effort of will, or of concentration.

What is happening is that, as we approach the escalator, the visual clues cause us to prepare ourselves, quite involuntarily, for the sense of acceleration we have learnt to expect as we step on to the moving stairs. This preparation involves quite complicated recalibrations of leg muscles, the balancing mechanism in the inner ear, and so on. We are all set to compensate for the acceleration forwards, so much so that when it does not occur as predicted, what we *experience* is a deceleration. The stationary strip of staircase is actually moving *backwards* relative to our (unconscious) expectations. Similarly at the end, we delicately prepare for a slowing-down that does not happen, and experience the result as a surge forwards. It is the brain-mind that is setting us up to respond, incorrectly on this occasion; yet we feel as if there were something funny going on in the world.[122]

So there is always a delay, however brief, between energy hitting the retina and 'a goldfish bowl' appearing in consciousness. But the actual thickness of this small slice of time (beyond the irreducible physiological minimum), and what precisely happens in it, is open to variation. Some of these variations are due to the needs of the moment. If the costs of making a misidentification are high, a final decision can be delayed (automatically, by the way the brain-mind's thresholds are set) until enough evidence has been collected to make sure that a mistake is very unlikely. Or the threshold of things that would meet a particular need can be lowered so that when one of them comes along it will have a head-start in the processing stakes. If I am starving, the faint smell of a bacon sandwich leaps into consciousness ahead of the words of the lecturer.

Perceptual Lethargy

But there is also the possibility that people develop different *habits*, in the way their brains respond, which may alter, as a matter of course, the moment and/or the content of consciousness. In fact, I want to suggest that the modern Western mind suffers from a kind of mental lethargy which routinely delays the moment at which we 'taste' our experience in consciousness, and which therefore allows all kinds of hidden ingredients to be stirred in. Let me explain how this could work.

We talked in the last chapter about the way in which the brain-mind's behaviour is controlled by the 'tension' between the Alarm System and the Anaesthetic System, or, more simply, between excitation and inhibition. Suppose we add one more twist to the relationship between these two systems, and suggest that excitation and inhibition originally tended to build up in the brain-mind at different speeds. There is evidence that, in an emergency, the intensifying of awareness occurs immediately, while the effects of the Anaesthetic System may not be apparent for a few seconds or even longer.[123] Thus the brain-mind would have been prevented from getting 'stuck' in a state of alarm for too long,[124] but you would still have been left with uninhibited—and therefore conscious—periods of pain or anxiety. The anaesthetic would work eventually, but not instantly.

So if you were really intent on reducing the experience of (psychological) pain as much as possible, it would be necessary to speed up the effect of the inhibition—or to slow down the build-up of excitation. If a film of inhibition is overlaid on the neural network *as a whole*, it will take longer for excitation to reach the threshold for consciousness. And if the whole process is retarded, the chances are increased that a potentially disturbing direction of flow can be anticipated, and a burst of specific inhibition sent to the danger zone to suppress it. (If you can slow the bandits down, there is a greater chance that you will be able to head them off at the pass.) Slowing down the rate at which the world is perceived, or reducing the speed of the train of thought thus gives the intrinsically slower Anaesthetic System a chance to inhibit the experience of distress before it has entered consciousness at all. Consciousness offers an even more distorted and unreliable image of what is going on behind the scenes, but at least it doesn't hurt. We can make ourselves *stupid* in order to avoid feeling *bad*.

We usually use the word 'stupid' these days to refer pejoratively to people who are slow on the uptake, lacking in the mysterious commodity 'intelligence', or loath to think in the way everyone is supposed to—politically incorrect. The earlier meaning of 'stupidity' though, as the excerpts from the dictionary suggest, referred more to perception than to thought. Stupidity was a slow, ponderous, coarse, quality of mind, in which the contents of consciousness were some-how low-grade, sketchy or retarded. But it is not just bad luck to be born with a sloppy mind; stupidity is *motivated*. It has a purpose. And the purpose, like that of 'ignorance', which we discussed in the last chapter, is to protect consciousness from the presence of experiences that are threatening to the inflexible sense of a calm, rational, sane self.

The Sophistication of Experience

The trouble with the strategy of stupidity, though, is that it allows time for more monkey business on the production line. If it takes longer for something to gain enough energy to become conscious, there are more ways in which it can have been tampered with before it gets there. The final product may get overworked, convoluted, *sophisticated* in the original dictionary sense of:

> mixed with some foreign or inferior substance; adulterated, corrupted; the product of specious or fallacious argument; ren-dered artificial, less genuine or less honest; falsified by unau-thorised alteration; no longer having or liking simplicity in pleasures, art, social behaviour etc; critical, cynical, blasé; deprived of simplicity or naturalness.[125]

There is a famous story of a man who wanted to hang a new picture in his house, and having no hammer of his own with which to fix the hook, decided to go next door and ask to borrow his neighbour's. On his way, though, he recalled that he still had the man's screw-driver which he had kept forgetting to return, and felt a little guilty. Then by association, he recalled the time when he had lent his lawn-mower to this same neighbour, who had kept it for a fortnight and then returned it in a filthy state. That must have been about the time when the neighbour had started getting home earlier from work and pinching the only parking space left in the street, so he, the picture-hanger, sometimes had to park several hundred yards away. And then there was that party where Hammer-owner had talked in far-too-friendly a fashion to Picture-hanger's wife....By the time Picture-hanger had walked up next door's path, he was in such a state that, when his innocent neighbour opened the front door and enquired pleasantly what he could do, the picture-hanger exploded: 'I'll tell you what you can do. You can keep your fucking hammer!'

The more we are unaware of these voices-off, these associations that load perception with all kinds of troublesome feelings and remote senses of threat and desire, the more sophisticated our perception becomes, and the more complex and demanding life keeps turning out to be. The more we contrive to delay the moment of 'coming to', of admitting into consciousness our concoction of experience, the more scope there is for the Self System, the Narrator, and Uncle Tom Cobley and all, to throw in their two-pennyworth. In another of those evolutionary ironies with which we have become familiar as this story has unfolded, the attempt to make consciousness safe has opened up possibilities for making it all the more bitter and bizarre.

Instead of sitting attentively by the source of our conscious experience, watching it as it wells up from the buried spring of the body-brain-mind, we sidle downstream and sit, half-heartedly bemoaning the pollution and cross-currents that the stream already seems to have picked up, and trying ineffectively to clean it up with the right hand, not noticing that it is the unattended left hand, upstream of our conscious gaze, that is, as if in a trance, busy ladling in the very rubbish that we long to be rid of. As long as we do not see that this is our predicament we are trapped: trapped by the fact that the right hand does know what the left hand is up to; trapped by the assumption that the steam's pollution is none of my doing; trapped, like a manic hamster, on the wheel of *samsara*, which is only rotating *because* I am running.

The Invisible Self

The Self System, as we have seen, comprises beliefs about who we are and how we should behave. If these beliefs appeared in consciousness, we would have a chance of appraising them and, if necessary, changing them. But as a rule they do not make these personal appearances in the mind's eye; instead they prefer to do their work upstream, prior to consciousness, and thus they bias and tilt the contents of consciousness without themselves becoming visible, in just the same way as a computer program determines what appears on the screen without itself being manifest.

A while ago I was travelling on the London Underground in the same carriage as three boys, aged about 8, 11 and 12. The two older boys were amusing themselves by jumping up and swinging from one of the handrails attached to the ceiling. They started to encourage the younger one to join them, but he was reluctant to join in. Finally they persuaded him to have a go. He stood under the bar—which was well within his reach, I thought—and made a couple of pathetic little hops. He looked at the other two with a kind of sheepish defiance, which seemed to say 'I tried; I really did. You saw me. I did try, didn't I? I did my best. But it was just too far for me. I'm only little. OK?' His aim was to put on a good display of having tried, and getting general agreement that he had tried (so as not to run the risk of being thought a wimp), and even to think, himself, that he had tried, while actually failing. 'I can't do this' was on this occasion upstream of 'I want to do this', and therefore the outcome was never in doubt. For him to succeed, in an area in which he had committed myself to being a failure, was to risk an invalidation of self—a little death.

Flybottles

Wittgenstein once famously said that the purpose of philosophy was 'to show the fly the way out of the fly-bottle'. In Victorian times a fly-bottle was an ingenious trap. It was a bottle whose neck and mouth were turned back inside the body of the bottle. This created a kind of funnel with its wide end open to the outside, and its narrow nozzle terminating inside the bottle itself. Some fly-delicacy like a bit of meat was put inside the bottle, and the rest was simplicity itself. The fly, attracted by the smell, was drawn into the (quite safe-looking) funnel, and eventually, by following its nose, it exited into the bottle itself. Having dined, and wishing to move on, however, the fly finds itself in a bit of a fix. The only way out is via the same narrow opening through which it has arrived. But seen from the inside of the bottle, entry into this small dark cave seems fraught with danger—certainly more perilous than staying put and searching (endlessly) for a more sensible-looking exit.

The fly's only hope is that a compassionate Wittgensteinian philosopher should happen along, and convince it that its only salvation lies in a lot of trust, courage and a temporary loss of sanity. To regain its freedom, the fly has to be persuaded to go crazy. From the outside, 'Whosoever would save his life shall lose it' is the literal and obvious truth. From the inside, it is just as self-evidently dangerous and perverted twaddle. From where our trapped fly is sitting (or buzzing), it makes perfect sense to tell Wittgenstein to buzz off, and if necessary to take out an injunction to stop him peddling his pernicious nonsense, and getting under the feet of thousands of good-citizen flies like itself who are trying to grapple with life-and-death issues. Or, to put it more formally:

> A belief is a system in which all acts of observation and judgment are made solely from within, and in which all other considerations are subordinated to the maintenance of the system itself. When an outside observer is in a position to see that such a system contains an incorrect belief, and also that no proof of its incorrectness can be given in the terms of the system itself, then he is in a position to say that the system has become a trap. In such a situation the outside observer will see those within as being dogmatic, while those on the inside will see the observer as someone who refuses to accept what is 'obviously so'. And, in fact, both will be right.[126]

A therapist is someone who is outside a trap in which the client experiences himself as 'bad'; who is able to see simultaneously both the absurdity and the tragedy of the predicament; and who is able to embrace simultaneously her perception, her sorrow, and the apparent hopelessness of the client's predicament. A mystic is someone who, however temporarily, is outside the trap of her own Self System, and is able to see simultaneously both the absurdity and the tragedy of the human condition, and to embrace simultaneously her own sense of liberation, her love for those still trapped, and her impossible desire for all beings to be where she is: upstream of their own self-made nets of misunderstanding. No wonder the Buddha is said to wear a sweet sad half-smile.

SEVENTEEN

Myths to Live By

Nearly every generation since the Renaissance has touted itself as 'modern', as 'the new age', as having arrived at the moment of enlightenment when the quaint superstitions and myths of the past are finally being swept into the dustbin of history. As is the case in every society, the myths and rites that form our minds, emotions and actions remain largely invisible and unconscious. One of the best ways to discover the living myth of any society is to examine what everyone accepts uncritically as the way things really are....The consensus reality *is* the myth, but it remains as invisible to the majority as water is to a fish.

Sam Keen [127]

Every society, as Sam Keen says, accepts as true, as valid guides to action, a whole raft of beliefs and assumptions that from 'the outside' can be seen as highly questionable. We can see so clearly—in history, in other cultures—the power of thought to shape lives and communities. And what we see often looks, with the wisdom of hindsight, absurd. They fought and died for causes that now seem trivial or bizarre. They clung to realities that we confidently dismiss as superstitions. How could anyone have been so foolish as to believe that dancing could have saved the crops? That you had better sail in circles, for fear of dropping off the edge? That your king was a God, whose every whim was a divine inspiration? That the sex of a child was determined by the direction of the wind at the moment of conception? How quaint of the Zande tribe to believe that they could cure epilepsy by eating the burnt skull of a red bush monkey!

Contemporary Myths of Health and Death

But if we follow the trail that these weird and wonderful beliefs mark out, it begins to get disconcertingly close to our own back door. Thousands of people today hold unproven beliefs about health and health care. Alternative medicine is booming, and nobody knows, for the vast majority of it, how to tell the good from the bad and the indifferent. In recent years, AIDS sufferers have been persuaded to pound themselves on the chest (to stimulate the thymus gland), expose their genitals to sunlight, squirt ozone gas into their rectums and inject themselves with hydrogen peroxide—not to mention forking out large sums of money for drugs like AZT, from the supposedly reputable pharmaceutical conglomerates, only to find that proper clinical trials subsequently show them to be ineffective.[128] Millions of us fall prey every mealtime to at least some of the quasi-scientific hocus-pocus of the various dietary and food product lobbies.

Some of our health myths are more central, and more invisible, than others. The World Health Organisation, for example, defines 'health' as 'a state of complete physical, mental and social well-being; not *merely* [emphasis added] the absence of disease or infection'—thus making almost all of us, almost all of the time, more or less 'unhealthy'. Old age, by this definition, is necessarily transformed into a medical problem; you cannot be elderly, and beginning to break down or seize up, without also being 'ill'. Such a grandiose conception of health turns it into a matter of permanent 'concern', a life-long 'quest', even, that threatens to turn us all into hypochondriacs, and divert our energies away from practical or social action into an endless and fruitless search for personal 'well-being'.[129]

Within such a myth there is no room for good old-fashioned fortitude, for honouring one's scars and putting up with the bad times. What Ivan Illich has referred to as 'the art of suffering' has no meaning within this mythology; the age-old practice of simply *bearing with* adversity can only be construed as fatalism or masochism.[130] When every form of personal discomfort can be embraced within such a broad conception of illness, the only way to see it is as a medical-technical problem to be solved. Grief? Here's a tablet to calm you down. Unhappy with your figure? Here's a pill to make you thin. Old? Sorry: we haven't quite cracked that one yet; give us another few years. The more lissome, happy youth is touted as the epitome of health, the more we are bound to see disfigurement, sadness, even eccentricity as afflictions. We end up in the absurd position of governments characterizing 'health care' in terms of the number of sick people who are 'treated' every year.

Most cultures develop a mythology of death and dying, and ours is no exception. If ageing is seen as the enemy, then death has to be the final defeat, a personal tragedy mocking the little one has achieved in life, and a failure of medical technology. Dylan Thomas's 'Do not go gentle into that good night; rage, rage against the dying of the light' is much quoted, and old people (I am refusing deliberately to use any of our common euphemisms for 'old') who have had enough and are ready to die are treated as an embarrassment by family doctors who have no professional framework within which to comprehend the idea of peaceful surrender. 'Don't be silly', they say brightly. 'Let's give you something to cheer you up'. Dead bodies are spirited away, prettified, and if possible hidden from the children who might be 'upset' by seeing Granny's carcase. Death is no longer a visible fact of life, a fact *in* life: young people are sent off to friends for a few days, and are deprived of the chance to get used to the reality—the sight, the feelings and the rituals—of death, thus ensuring that when their turn finally comes they will be bound to be scared, as they must be of anything unprecedented.

Having no grasp of statistical distributions, our mythology of death assumes that we must all be entitled to the average span, so that anything less than that is 'premature'; not just a sadness but a cruel violation of a fundamental human 'right'. This ensures that when people die young, as a few of us still must, the tragedy is compounded by a bitter sense of injustice, and the increasingly compulsive, litigious search for someone to blame, and to punish. The rare parent of a daughter murdered by a terrorists' bomb who refuses to buy this belief, and chooses simply to grieve, and not to be vengeful, is treated by the media as practically a saint.

In a pluralistic society, myths collide. A widow stands by the graveside of her soldier husband in calm and dignified restraint. Half of the viewers of the early evening news think 'How wonderful; how strong; how brave'. The other half see her as repressed and bottled up, misguidedly controlling her urge to throw herself wailing on her dead man's coffin. 'The Irish (or the Arabs, or the Poles) know how to 'do death' better than we uptight Anglo-Saxons' they believe. Kindly members of each contingent will try to foist their own liturgy of grief onto the bereaved, sure in their own minds of what is 'for the best'.

Myths of Maturity

The Myth of Health is a close cousin to the Myth of Maturity, which encourages us to see 'growing up' as being essentially a matter of 'growing away from'. Maturity is defined as 'autonomy', and therefore dependency is seen as immaturity. People who have never travelled abroad, or who are still, as adults, living with their parents in the same street that they grew up in, are seen as handicapped. Self-sufficiency is the watchword and 'neediness' a childish state to be outgrown as fast as possible. Education is the essential means whereby one 'betters oneself'—that is, is encouraged to see the culture of one's parents as impoverished—and a regional accent had better be quickly expunged during one's first term at university.

In other societies, a person's sense of identity has been firmly embedded in the physical and social soil of their culture. To define oneself as a perfectly portable set of individual attributes, skills and possessions, with such a shallow root system in the world of one's childhood that one could pick oneself up and be repotted in Manhattan or Melbourne or the Mull of Kintyre with guaranteed success, even to *want* to do so, would have seemed at best bizarre, and probably unthinkable.

The English ecologist Edward Goldsmith tells of talking to an Italian acquaintance in Tuscany who had never been away from his village. 'Why not give yourself a break?' suggested Goldsmith, 'Take yourself off to the seaside—go to Viareggio for a few days.' The Italian looked at him in bewilderment. 'But why?' he replied. 'I don't *know* anybody there.'[131] And not knowing anybody in Viareggio meant that he would not know *himself* in Viareggio. His identity could not just be packed up in a suitcase, as Goldsmith's could be. The idea that having long roots in a particular physical and social milieu is a pathological condition, which we contract when small, and remedy by growing up, is a myth peculiar in history to the certain sub-cultures of the modern Western world.

Myths of Nature

The myths that shape our relationship with Nature have begun to receive some attention in recent years from the school of 'deep ecology'.[132] When a species discovers an abundant new habitat or resource, the initial tendencies to assume that the resource is infinite, and that the waste its use creates is negligible, are understandable. They are, in the early stages of exploitation, reasonable working assumptions. But inevitably there comes a gradual turnabout: the resource begins to be in shorter supply, or more difficult to exploit (partly because it is running out, and partly because the abundance will have triggered a population explosion); and the waste begins to create a significant problem of pollution. By the time this happens, the idea that nature can be treated as a combination of inexhaustible supermarket and bottomless toilet has become part of the unconscious mythology of the culture. It becomes a 'truth' that is so embedded in the practices of the culture, and so embodied in the way people view the world, and their relation to it, that it is invisible and unquestionable.

The 'green history of the world' can be viewed as a catalogue, not so much of kings, queens, wars and conquests, as of the failure, time and again, of societies to escape from their mythologies of plenty in time to adapt to scarcity.[133] Those who have invested most in the culture of plenty will have embodied its mythology most deeply, and will not know how to live if they are not to exploit and consume *ad lib*. Their identity is literally and vitally threatened by a reduction in consumption or 'standard of living'. As these people are often in positions of considerable financial and/or political power, they are well placed to ensure that the mythology of plenty, and its consequence, the culture of consumption, persist well beyond their Use By Date, and thus jeopardize not just a particular lifestyle, but the continuing viability of the 'eco-niche' itself. These people are compelled by the beliefs that have colonized them to make sure that whatever is done is too little too late.

New eco-myths are springing up, either to buttress or to challenge the increasingly visible orthodoxy. One prevalent New Age misreading of James Lovelock's Gaia hypothesis is comforting: we are Gaia's children, and however naughty we are—however much we contrive to wreck the nursery with our potent mixture of naivety and greed—

Our forgiving Mother Nature will make everything all right.[134] She is so clever, her powers of self-repair so vast, that we have nothing to fear. The other, less reassuring but more accurate, reading of the theory suggests that Gaia is a rather more selfish mother. She can certainly put right aspects of her own constitution that we humans have disturbed; but if needs be she will have no compunction about terminating the unsuccessful experiment of *homo sapiens.*

If we trace these green controversies back to their source, we can begin to see that they too are reflections of our assumed psychology—what we will put up with; what power we have, or think we have, as individuals and communities to affect our governance; what we need; what *counts* as necessity. There is an epidemic of the mental disorder 'ecosis' in the world, a serious condition in which the perception of a person's relationship with the physical, and especially the natural, world is severely limited and distorted. The major symptoms of this disease are the delusions that nature is a kind of film set, a context that has no essential interconnection with the unfolding drama of the patient's life—that he or she is in the world but not of it—and that all one's needs for material and comfort are vital ones which nature can fulfil endlessly without significant cost or damage.

A person in the grip of this delusional state is unable to compute the true cost of a beefburger, or to see the connection between the proposed reservoir which will flood a favourite beauty-spot, and the obsessional cleanliness which demands constant piped water for washing machines, showers and toilets. Sufferers may manifest a kind of manic denial, and brittle cheerfulness, which collapses into confusion and depression in the face of any first-hand experience of death, incurable illness or genuine human (as opposed to material) tragedy. A serene death is contraindicated, and the prognosis for the patent's environment is increasingly gloomy.

Myths of Wealth and Time

One whole nest of myths of industrialized society concerns wealth, work, leisure and time. Only in the light of a society that does—or did—not share this apparatus of bank accounts, pension plans, career prospects and annual holidays can we make our own mythology visible. Linguist Helena Norberg-Hodge has beautifully described such a culture: Ladakh in northern India.[135] Up until 18 years ago, Ladakhi society was as it had been for hundreds of years. The simple economy revolved centrally around the yak, a hardy animal that gave work, milk, meat, leather and wool, in return for access to the high scrubby pastures of the Himalayan foothills. People worked hard, and had abundant time and inclination for socializing—storytelling, celebrations, and playing with the children. In those days a wedding could last for a fortnight.

One of the first fingers of Westernization to infiltrate this stable, poor, happy society, was the Jersey cow. Jersey cows give an average of 30 litres of milk a day, as compared with the yak's three. What could make more sense, then, than to import some Jerseys, whose surplus milk could be turned into butter and cheese to sell? The first problem to emerge, as the idea caught on, was the loss of— and therefore increased competition for—pasture. Jersey cows can only graze at 10–11,000 feet, compared to the yak's 16,000, so as the yaks started to go out of fashion, much of the land that had previously been a resource now began to become useless. What is more, the competition for cow pasture, and for fodder during the winter months, became so intense that food for the cows became more expensive than even the staple human diet.

But this was not the most devastating effect on Ladakhi society. Far from being innocent sources of a little extra wealth, these imported ruminants turned out to be Trojan horses, smuggling into Ladakh a Western mythology. Helena Norberg-Hodge began to notice something paradoxical, as a result of the introduction of these cows (along with other relatively low-technology wealth-creating, labour-saving practices). People started to have less time: less time to gossip, to help each other, to mark the constant round of births, marriages and deaths. Weddings shrunk from two weeks to a day or less. Changes that were designed to give people more time, more leisure, were having exactly the contrary effect.

The explanation, of course, lay in the change in *attitudes* that the cows and the rotavators brought with them. Instead of seeing their goal as being to produce 'sufficient', and time as being plentiful, they began to think in terms of producing 'surplus'; of 'wealth' as being that which enabled them to enjoy 'leisure'; of 'work' as something separate from 'leisure', a disagreeable activity whose only merit or meaning was to produce 'wealth'; and of 'time' as a commodity that was in short supply. Where previously work and leisure were not distinguished—they were just naturally dissolved in the round of daily life—now they were separated out and contrasted. 'Work' became the price one paid for 'leisure', and each demanded an allocation of this scarce commodity 'time'. Ladakhis began to become, in other words, like us.

It will probably, and sadly, be only a matter of time before Ladakh succumbs to the full-blown mythology of work that has insinuated itself into the fabric of 'Western' society. Men will come, mainly, to work for money. They will go to 'offices' or 'factories' which they do not own and will be paid to make things they do not need or cannot afford. Men's work and women's work will become polarized: women's work will be seen as of lower status—because it is not valued in monetary terms—and men will spend less time with their sons and daughters. The work that makes the most money (and is therefore the 'best' work) will be clean, sedentary work. Work that makes you physically tired, dirty or sweaty will be avoided.

'Education' will become the means whereby parents will encourage their children to escape from the world of poorly paid dirty work into the world of well-paid, clean paper work. Both men and the few women in this clean work will have to dress like undertakers to show how clean they are, and also to show that they are taking this clean work very seriously. The 'best' work will require them to 'sacrifice wide-ranging curiosity and fascination with the world at large, and become departmental in their thinking':[136] i.e. to specialize. And they will come to see themselves as technicians (or technical experts) in the money-making, money-processing business, unconcerned, while wearing their suit or their overalls, in their working persona, with issues of broader morality or even simple kinship.

Myths of Relationship

In 'primitive' cultures such as the earlier Ladakh, where each person's identity is diffused into their society, kindliness and affection are broadly distributed. The mythology of relationship in our Western societies, on the other hand, requires us to concentrate and ration our love, putting all our eggs, and our egos, into only a tiny number of baskets. Each of these 'special' relationships, designed by evolution to carry only so much emotional weight, is liable, as we well know, to buckle under the burden of expectation. Everywhere you look there are beliefs and injunctions that constrain the natural range and flow of relationships, transmuting the fundamental need for connectedness into a mine-field of disappointment and frustration. For example:

'Sexual attraction is a reliable and solid basis for a life-long partnership.'

'The purpose of being in a relationship is to pursue my own self-development (and the job of my partner—you—is always to support this quest).'

'The purpose of being in a relationship is to have someone to look after me (because I can't make it on my own). Your job is to make any sacrifice I ask, if I believe it is necessary to protect me from harm or distress.'

'The consequence of being in a relationship is that I will be happy. If I am not happy, something is wrong with the relationship (and probably with you). To be happy, I shall have to change you, or if all else fails, exchange you.'

'If you hit me, it shows you love me. (If you didn't care, you wouldn't bother.)'

'If you were sensitive and/or caring, you would know how I am feeling without my having to tell you. If you don't respond, you must be insensitive or uncaring. (So why should I worry about you?)'

'Closeness means entrapment, being engulfed or smothered—so I must keep my distance even from you, whom I love. I may even have to hurt you, or leave you, in order to avoid being trapped.'

'If I do what you want, you will love me. But you only love what I do, not what I am. If you don't respond, I am a failure. If you do, I am a fraud. Why is your love so unsatisfying?'

'Whatever I do that upsets you is done inadvertently. You cannot be angry with me; I "didn't mean it". Whatever you do that upsets me is done knowingly. Why are you trying to upset me?'[137]

Myths of Feeling

The modern Western mythology gives a curious status to feelings and emotions. We construe our own feelings as internal events caused by external ones. 'Stop doing that; it's really irritating.' 'It makes me very happy to see you so well.' 'She's really upset because he's left her.' The environment plucks the chord of anger or grief or jealousy, and we quiver. This view implicitly denies (by leaving them out of the picture that is painted by vernacular language) three aspects of emotionality. One is the way in which emotions are often aroused not by external happenings but by other emotions. Feelings tend to breed. We react to some of them as if they were intrinsically upsetting, to others as if they were pleasurable; and in that reaction is contained the seed, and the need, of another feeling. It is hard just to be fearful, without also reacting, with another emotion, to the fear. Sometimes we end up feeling ashamed of being angry about feeling guilty about acting selfishly....We do not claim any responsibility for this helter-skelter of action and reaction; we see it as just the way things are.

The second is the denial of any authorship of the original emotion. She pushed in ahead of me in the queue: I got angry. He looked sheepish and lost: I felt guilty for having shouted at him. She died: I grieved. No question mark, no option, no sense of choice intervenes; no idea that there may be something to do with the way I personally (or we collectively) look at the world that forms a vital bridge between the event and the feeling; that it is not the event but the way I construe it that matters. (The counter-myth, of course, is that I am completely responsible for whatever I feel, so deserve no sympathy for my loneliness or confusion. 'You're your own worst enemy, man, know what I mean?')

The third is the extent to which emotions are displays for public consumption, as much as episodes of private experience. Having (or perhaps 'doing') a feeling is an action as well as a reaction, often designed to communicate and to get some kind of result. Anger, obviously, is a tool for getting one's way and righting perceived wrongs. But a display of guilt, for example, may well be a way of warding off someone else's anger. If you continue to shout at me in the face of my *self*-condemnation, it is you who begins to look out of order. Guilt buys off your disapproval. After all, what kind of a person would I be if I had borrowed your car without permission, smashed it up, and *not* felt/shown my guilt?

The Myth of How to Be Happy

From this rats' nest of emotional misapprehensions arises the myth that, if bad feelings are directly caused by outside events, the way to be happy is by fixing the world in place so that it does not go awry and upset me. The freedom we have to be happy is either to ignore or 'manage' our feelings, or to get out there and rush around nailing things down: job, mortgage, insurance, relationships, enlightenment....Feeling bad is a *problem* that can almost always be fixed, at least in principle, and if not, can be best damped down with denial, distractions or drugs. The default strategy is always to *do* something. If that doesn't work, cultivate ignorance and stupidity.

What does this mythology—central to people's tacit philosophy of life—leave out? It leaves out, as we have seen, the possibility of giving suffering any meaning other than 'painful misfortune responsible for my loss of happiness'. It denies by exclusion any role for suffering, any dignity, any value. God can only be seen as vengeful or negligent in such a worldview. People are fond of quoting these days the prayer 'Lord, give me the courage to change those things I can change, the serenity to accept those things I cannot, and the wisdom to tell the difference'. Our dominant mythology of feelings has a place for courage, for banging one's head against a brick wall, even, but not much to say about the other two.

And this lopsided philosophy of life also leaves out insight—meditation, contemplation, reflection, stillness. 'Don't just sit there, do something.' The idea of the *value* of 'just sitting there' does not compute. If my happiness depends only on circumstances, there is no point to self-knowledge. It would be as much use as meditating while the sink is overflowing, or the house burning down. The possibility that suffering arises, even in part, because the heart is on fire, that 'plumbing the *psyche*' could be a meaningful or useful activity, does not make sense. Those who sit still are losers, dreamers and fatalists. What else could they be?

Any mythology that wishes to protect itself from discovery—from being revealed, that is, as simply one possible view to which there are alternatives, each with a different portfolio of pros and cons—should include within itself an antipathy to reflection, because reflection is the only tool of enquiry that is suitable for unearthing mythologies. Neither action in the world, nor cultivated unconsciousness, nor even simple forbearance, will touch the problem of false belief, because they all start *downstream* of perception; while the trouble with false beliefs is that they do their subversive work *upstream* of perception, in the dark reaches of the river before consciousness. We shall return to reflection as the essential myth-busters' tool in Chapter 21.

4

Unconsciousness
Regained

EIGHTEEN

Myths of the Mind

Who is there, that hath not opinions implanted in him by edu-cation...which must not be questioned, but are here looked on with reverence as the standards of right and wrong, truth and falsehood; where perhaps these so sacred opinions were but the oracle of the nursery, or the traditional grave talk of those who pretend to inform our childhood, who received them from hand to hand without ever examining them? This is the fate of our tender age, which being thus seasoned early, it grows by con-tinuation of time, as it were, into the very constitution of the mind, which afterwards very difficultly receives a different tincture....By these and perhaps other means, opinions come to be settled and fixed in men's minds, which, whether true or false, there remain in reputation as substantial material truths, and so are seldom questioned or examined by those who enter-tain them; and if they happen to be false, as in most men the greater part must necessarily be, they put a man quite out of the way in the whole course of his studies; and though in his reading and enquiries he flatter himself that his design is to inform his understanding in the real knowledge of truth, yet in effect it tends and reaches to nothing but the confirming of his already received opinions...men take up prejudice to truth without being aware of it, and afterwards generally feed on only those things that suit with and increase the vicious humour.

John Locke[138]

The myths we discussed in the last chapter distort our relationships with our environment, our labour and each other. But perhaps even more crucial are the myths that pervert our relationship with our-selves. Much of Parts II and III of this book were devoted to showing how and why the most central of these 'psycho-myths' arose. In this chapter I want to summarize those discussions, and put them into a more general context, before going on, in the last few chapters, to consider the ways in which the mind could be de-mythologized.

Metaphors for Mind

Ever since the idea of understanding, in the sense of having *explanations* for things, was promoted by our evolving culture from a minority interest (confined mainly to the philosophers and shamans) to an individual personal need, the mind has been offering images, metaphors and stories about itself to fill the vacuum that its essentially unconscious nature creates.

In Plato's famous image, for example, the mind was presented as an aviary with a variety of compartments, some of them containing birds of a single type, others housing several species.[139] A piece of knowledge in the mind was depicted as one of these birds, and the process of recall was represented by a hunt for the right bird. You 'forgot' when the right bird failed to fly within your grasp; you 'mis-recalled' when you grabbed the wrong bird by mistake. The trouble with images of this kind is that all the interesting work of deciding which bird is 'wanted' in a particular situation, choosing the compartment to search, and deciding whether a bird-in-the-hand was actually the right one or not...all this is simply not accounted for. The question is begged by assuming a human actor—the bird-fancier—whose intelligence and motivations are needed to make the model work. There is a relatively passive storehouse, and then there is the 'custodian', a self-like element who/which remains as mysterious as the 'you' or 'me' we are trying to understand.

This basic *structural* image of the mind predominated from the time of the classical Greeks right through the Renaissance, though it occurs in different forms at different times and in different cultures. St Augustine in the fourth century, for instance, likened the mind to the stomach. 'Memory is, as it were, the belly of the mind, and joy and sadness are like bitter and sweet food, which, when committed to the memory, pass into the belly, where they may be stowed, but cannot taste.'[140] And many authors, up to Descartes himself, and beyond, used the image of mind as a temple, with different areas or 'vestibules' being given over to different functions and faculties.

The second great metaphor of the mind, more closely associated with Descartes, but in common currency for at least three centuries previously, was of a machine. Ramon Lull, a celebrated thirteenth-century Spanish mystic, was also the inventor of ingenious robots and mannequins which mimicked human actions, and also feats of memory and logic. These machines were the forerunners of the billion dollar enterprise known today as 'artificial intelligence', the attempt to understand the human mind by building machines whose performance, if not their actual construction, is increasingly indistinguishable from that of a real human being. As these simulations are mostly achieved these days with the aid of computers, it is hardly surprising that the computer itself should have emerged as the late twentieth-century's predominant 'machine' metaphor of mind.

It is significant that up until very recently, this computer model of mind has been developed exclusively to explain those aspects of human intelligence that are conscious, rational and mainly verbal. The Cartesian agenda, which defines logic, language and reason as the most central, and definitely the most interesting, things about us, was accepted without question; and therefore these were the aspects of our performance that merited explanation. The fact that the mind was *embodied*, and that it was the body-brain-mind system as a whole that possessed intelligence, was entirely ignored. And in addition, though these models became very much more sophisticated than Ramon's robots, they still, without exception, needed a *real* human mind to get them going, to program them, and to help them out when they got stuck.[141]

In both these two families of images, the continued separation of the store from the storeman, the computer from the programmer, enabled 'consciousness' to retain its unquestioned status as the seat of power and the window of observation. Consciousness was not seen as a manifestation of the workings of an intrinsically active and intelligent system, but as 'the ghost in the machine', without which the machine could only cope with dull routines. Looking at human psychology through such distorting spectacles, it is no wonder that philosophers for 2000 years have kept themselves busy trying to figure out what the relationship between body, brain, mind and consciousness could possibly be.

This myth, as I have been at pains to point out, is not just limited and partial; it is so *wrong* that it enables all sorts of mistakes to germinate in the mind, which then send us off on wild goose chases and make us miserable, and it also screens from us much wisdom and serenity that is our essential birthright. By telling us 'the unconscious' either does not exist, or, if it does, it is some sort of psychological cess-pit that may need attention if it starts to smell too badly, but otherwise can be safely ignored, we are expelled, if not from Paradise, then from a world in which mystery and faith are the source of mundane miracles.

The third general metaphor for the mind is enjoying renewed popularity at the present time; indeed, the 'brain-mind' talk that I have used in this book is an example of it. This model sees the mind as a vast network of associations, like a tangled fishing net—or, in more 'self-organizing' versions, like the spontaneously active octopus colony, with which I introduced the idea back in Chapter 4. The British empiricist philosophers of the eighteenth century were the first to develop this image through their discussions of 'the association of ideas'. But it was not until the 1940s, as we have seen, that the Canadian neuropsychologist Donald Hebb developed a network model that was explicitly intended to do away with the mysterious 'ghost in the machine' of the self.

Part of the enormous current appeal of these 'neural network' models is that they re-embed the 'mind' in its natural biological context, they re-connect it with the rest of the body and its needs and capabilities, and they reinstate, as a central feature of the mind, the fact that its most important learning and development come about through *experience*, not through words. But perhaps the biggest advantage of these biological images, which is the one I have been trying to spell out in this book, is that they have encouraged people to re-connect, as part of a unified approach to the person, the conscious with the unconscious. And it also permits us to reclaim the notion of the 'unconscious' from those who have given it a predominantly pathological meaning. The Freudian unconscious is, as I have been trying to demonstrate, just one small, tactical, relatively recent *part* of the unconscious. To use the idea of the unconscious just to explain pathology (or even creativity, à la Jung) is rather like buying a tiger in order to catch mice. It may do the job, but it is built for bigger things.

The Myth of Self

We have considered in some detail the fundamental myth of self-hood: the idea that each of us is an individual pillar of mobile meat, with a mind of its own, making its way through an environment that it is *in* but not *of*. 'I, a stranger and afraid/In a world I never made': that sort of thing.[142] In so far as this myth presents us to ourselves as *separate* from our surroundings, it misrepresents our fundamentally ecological nature. In so far as the myth tells us we are *persistent*, that we stay essentially the same as we edge our way along the rope-bridge of time from birth to death, it weighs us down with an increasing burden of past-impressions that we are supposed to honour and obey, however unequal they are to the needs of each unprecedented moment. In so far as the myth gives us each an individual sense of *authorship*, it places inside our heads a kind of whimsical operator, a chauffeur of the body-mind, who can drive without being under the influence of anything whatsoever: the unconscious unity of world-body-mind are denied. From these root fallacies spring many of our troubles.[143]

The sciences of biology and cognition give the lie to each of these three 'legs' on which is placed the myth of self. In the early chapters of this book I showed how evolutionary biology, and the emerging science of 'systems theory', have sawn off the leg of separateness. We, like all life-forms, can only exist because we are *not* separate. For the body-brain-mind system to be, it has to be thoroughly and continually penetrated, in multiple ways, by the larger eco-system of which it is, in truth, just one local manifestation.

Likewise psychological research has buried once-and-for-all the myth of memory as a potentially accurate and objective record of the past. In some of the most famous demonstrations, the English psychologist Sir Frederick Bartlett showed in 1932 how stories are systematically reshaped by memory so as to make them conform more neatly to conventional expectations.[144] While more recent studies of eye-witness testimony show how easy it is to change what is apparently remembered just by changing the kind of question that is asked. People shown a film of a car accident were asked to judge the speed of one of the cars at the moment of impact. Those who were asked 'What speed was the car going when it *hit* the other?' recalled the speed as significantly lower than those for whom the question was 'What speed was the car going when it *crashed into* the other?'[145]

In fact, the situations in which we are simply trying to remember as 'objectively' as possible are rather rare. More normally we are trying to use memory as a way of convincing, entertaining or pacifying someone else—or ourselves.[146] Everyday remembering is typified much more by the fisherman's tale of 'the one that got away', the politician's self-serving 'memoirs', or the entertaining account of an incident at work, than it is by the witness stand or the psychological experiment. Sometimes these biassings or misrepresentings are conscious and deliberate; more often we think we are being accurate, unaware that the interests of the Self System are being slipped in as emphases and grace-notes. The sense of persistence, the second leg of the self, can only be maintained by the fraudulent misrepresentation of memory as a valid record of a real past. The minute we admit that *remembering* is a present activity, motivated by an ephemeral conjunction of current concerns, the stool of 'self' becomes even more unstable.

Perhaps the most crucial conceit of the Self is that it exercises independent authorship: it makes choices and takes decisions that are in some sense 'free', and that it does so within the rational theatre of consciousness. 'I sat down and thought about it, and after a lot of deliberation (or 'de-liberation') I decided on the best way forward, planned my course of action, and set it in motion.' 'I' here has a lot of executive power, and takes most of the credit. Who or what 'cogitated', 'chose', 'planned', 'implemented' and 'carried out'? *I* did. And if you want 'I' can show you my working—'I' keeps its rough notes—its memories of its thought-processes—and 'I' can tell you (accurately, if not exhaustively) why and how 'I' did what 'I' did.

But science and a bit of personal reflection cast doubt on this 'common sense' picture. We saw earlier that the accounts that people give in good faith for their actions are sometimes incompatible with what an observer sees. We offer plausible *post hoc* justifications for what we did: despite what we *think*, we often do not describe accurately how our actions came about.[147] Ambrose Bierce, the nineteenth-century American newspaper columnist, challenged the myth in his wickedly provocative book *The Devil's Dictionary*[148] with his definition of the verb 'to decide' as 'to succumb to the preponderance of one set of influences over another'. The problem is that we can pretend to claim conscious credit for our decisions only if we persist in denying the existence, or even the possibility, of *unconscious* influences. Once we see consciousness as an intermittent and unreliable print-out from the invisible biological system that underlies it, we can no longer claim the credit with such confidence.

In the next chapter we shall look at new scientific evidence for these unconscious forces. But they are, of course, not a new discovery, simply a re-cognition of what has long been known. Thomas Hobbes, for example:

> A wooden top that is lashed by the boys, and runs about sometimes to one wall, sometimes to another, sometimes spinning, sometimes hitting men on the shins, if it were sensible of its own motion, would think it proceeded from its own will, unless it felt what lashed it. And is a man any wiser, when he runs to one place for a benefice, to another for a bargain, and troubles the world with writing errors and requiring answers, because he thinks he doth it without any cause other than his own will, and seeth not what are the lashings that cause his will?[149]

And the philosopher Daniel Dennett invites us to ponder on a moment of ordinary introspection.

> Are decisions voluntary? Or are they things that happen to us? From some fleeting vantage points they seem to be the preeminently voluntary moves in our lives, the instants at which we exercise our agency to the fullest. But those same decisions can also be seen to be strangely out of our control. We have to wait to see how we are going to decide something, and when we do decide, our decision bubbles up to consciousness from we know not where. We do not witness it being *made*, we witness its *arrival*. This can then lead to the strange idea that Central Headquarters is not where we, as conscious introspectors, are; it is somewhere deeper within us, and inaccessible to us. E.M. Forster famously asked 'How can I tell what I think until I see what I say?'—the words of an outsider, it seems, waiting for a bulletin from the interior.[150]

But if we are waiting for a decision to present itself to us, where does the illusion of 'control' come from? How can we (sometimes at least) know what it is that we are going to do, if it is not the con-

scious knower who is *determining* what will happen? Ambrose Bierce
again offers us a clue in his definition of an *intention*:

> The mind's sense of the prevalence of one set of influences
> over another set: an effect whose cause is the imminence,
> immediate or remote, of the performance of the act intended
> by the person incurring the intention. (When figured out and
> accurately apprehended, this will be found one of the most
> penetrating and far-reaching definitions in the whole dictio-
> nary.)

Bierce's comment on his own definition is right: this alternative view
of intention strikes at the heart of our contemporary mythology of
Self. (He is also right in suggesting that it takes a bit of figuring out.)
We believe that the 'I' that *witnesses* the intention—the Narrator
making sense of what bubbles up into consciousness—is also the 'I'
that is responsible for formulating the intention, and carrying it out.
But what if it were the flow of activation through the unconscious
brain-mind network that were 'responsible' for formulating plans,
capable of doing so 'on its own', without any help from the Self
System, or from consciousness? And what if, at some intermediate
point in this shifting, tacit process, a bulletin were issued to consciousness of how things were going, *and of what the eventual outcome might be*: a summary of the way things were going 'down
below', and an interim *prediction* of the general course of action that
might finally be decided upon? (Based on its experience of its own
channels and patterns, the brain-mind is able to make educated
guesses about where its flow of energy is heading; and some of these
guesses [especially if they are related, however remotely, to a sense
of threat or need] attract an intense enough knot of activation to
emerge as a bubble of 'thought', or a sense of readiness or anticipation, in consciousness.)

How is a mind that has incorporated a view of itself as essentially
conscious, as an iceberg that is all tip and no underwater bulk, to
construe these apprehensions and intimations? It cannot interpret
them as predictions, so it has instead to see them as *controls*; as the
actual source of the intention, which then determines the act, rather
than as a tentative hypothesis about what might happen at some
point in the future. Our myth of consciousness puts us in the position of a person sitting by the side of a stream, idly watching all

sorts of things float past her. After a while she notices a regularity: whenever a cork goes by, a little later a bottle follows. In order to amuse herself, our observer invents a game in which she pretends not to notice the corks, and then every-so-often, out of the blue as it were, calls out 'Bottle!'—and sure enough, each time she does so, a bottle floats into view. After a while, she gets so good at the game that she is able to 'see' the cork—the signal—without any conscious recognition at all; so much so that she 'forgets' about the corks and falls prey to her own illusion. Now she is convinced of the executive power of her conscious mind, of its autonomy and author-ity, and begins to identify herself—who she really is—with this illusory sense of control. 'Look! I can *decide* "bottle"!'

'Decisions' are the fruits of a world-body-brain-mind system which may be talked about, roughly, as if it had 'parts' which 'inter-acted', but which in fact is a filigree of interwoven processes of such delicacy that they could not be ripped apart in reality, in the way that language shatters them conceptually, without radically altering or destroying the form that the system creates. Above the surface, a tree seems to stand alone; below the surface the distinction between roots and earth, between where 'tree' stops and 'ground' begins, is impossible to maintain. A sense of one's own unconsciousness, of the underground power source, is also a sense of this unbrokenness.

Yet our Mythology of Persons insists that this seamless web of interactions and mutual influences *can* be broken; and it therefore demands an answer to the question of 'Who did it?', 'Who's in charge around here?' Either it is the 'Me' to which I have hitched my own identity (and therefore destiny); or it is the 'Not Me', the out-side, the 'environment'. In the one case 'I' am free; in the other, determined. Having made this flawed metaphysical move, I am now bound to rig my perceptions and my priorities to defend it. I treat as unimportant those actions and influences over which 'I' can by no stretch of the imagination claim dominion. The growing of finger-nails is of less interest than the planting of daffodils: the latter 'I' can pretend to make choices (about how to arrange them, what vari-eties to buy); the former is too regular and predictable for me to be able to play the game of 'I did it!' at all. And in the areas of my so-called 'volition', I shamelessly (and of course unconsciously) select and titivate the evidence to paint my successful predictions as choices, and my failures as 'changes of mind'.

The Escape from Pure Reason

Rationality and sceptical thought are presented, in our mythology of mind, as being 'higher', more reliable, faculties than intuition and trust: they must be, for they are necessarily explicit, articulate, and conscious, while hunches and acts of faith more obviously float up through the dark waters of the unconscious. Yet the fact that reason's claim to preeminence is exposed as frequently fraudulent should not lead us to leap out of the frying-pan of bogus rationality into the fire of New Age whimsicality and impulsiveness. In its celebration of innocent forms of experience and fun, the New Age is providing a welcome antidote to the po-faced image of adulthood to which our reverence for grey-suited reason has led us. Reclaiming such simple pleasures as hugging, circle-dancing or story-telling from their unjust consignment to 'childhood' has to be healthy. Enjoying the same frisson of fear and excitement that children get from making themselves dizzy, and setting each other 'dares', in the revised form of a weekend 'encounter group' is likewise harmless fun provided you do not fall into the next illusion-in-waiting of seeing these as part of some great project for self-improvement.[151] If an encounter group is seen as a kind of psychological roller-coaster, for the bored or the brave to test their nerve, then no harm is likely to result.

The trouble with the New Age comes when it throws out the muesli with the plastic packet—denying the necessity for *good* thinking, *hard* thinking, in its rightful place; denying the real complexity of social and moral dilemmas—and opts instead for an uncritical acceptance of anything magical. Instead of seeing that the antidote to the self-importance of reason is playfulness, they become deadly serious instead about *bad* thinking, *woolly* thinking, doggedly mistaking beautiful symbols and legends for literal truth; earnestly defending the value of all kinds of unproven hocus-pocus. Horoscopes and tarot cards are taken as gospel (rather than as symbolic reminders of mystery and subtlety).

A conceptual free-for-all results which hopelessly muddles up different kinds of discourse that should properly be kept distinct. Sound science, such as James Lovelock's tentative Gaia hypothesis, gets intertwined with the history and the symbology of the Goddess; while entertaining allegories and conjectures that have the appearance, but only that, of being 'scientific', are instantly venerated, by those to whom they appeal, as profound and literal truths.[152] The question that *we* now have to tackle head-on is: which is 'the unconscious'—fact or fable; science or whimsy?

NINETEEN

Unconsciousness—
The Essential Mystery

There are hundreds of indications leading us to conclude that at every moment there is in us an infinity of perceptions, unaccompanied by awareness or reflection....The choice we make arises from these insensible stimuli, which, mingled with the actions of objects and our bodily interiors, make us find one direction of movement more comfortable than the other.

Leibniz [153]

Self-conscious man cannot use *conscious reason* to overcome his own impatience; for that he must surrender his conviction of the supreme importance of his own awareness and of the maturity of his reasoning; only if he can do that is he saved from humiliation....The pathology of the over-emphasis of self-consciousness has increasingly affected the entire Western community over three centuries, and lies deep in social and individual habits.

Lancelot Law Whyte

The Neglect of Mystery

Our contemporary mythology of mind leads us to give too much weight and power to 'consciousness', and to underestimate, and to be neglectful of, our unconscious side. By definition we cannot know that of which we are unconscious. But we have become unconscious of the essential fact that much of who we are *is* unconscious. The Cartesian spell blinds us to our own inscrutability. We have to live, like it or not, with the apprehension that our conscious life is surrounded and subserved by mystery; that the perceptions that we are aware of are flashes of lightning in a dark sky.

In chapters 15 and 16 I talked about two kinds of 'optional' unconsciousness: 'ignorance', which involves the deployment of various kinds of tactical inattention to prevent the emotional hot-spots of the brain-mind flaring up into consciousness; and 'stupidity', a more general coarsening and slowing of perception that allows experience to be laundered and starched before it is presented to consciousness. But underlying these discussions has been the presumption of a third form of unconsciousness, the 'mystery' at the centre of human experience, which we cannot ever penetrate, but which we can appreciate, we can be alive to. Paradoxically, as we roll back the frontiers of ignorance and stupidity (which, as I shall show in the next chapter, we are quite capable of doing if we choose), we find *both* increased clarity and precision of the mind, *and* a gathering sense of the irreducible, impenetrable mystery right at the centre of our world. We can get close enough to the source to see that our experience is gushing out of an underground spring, whose provenance it is not given to us to know.

De-pixilation

How can such a pixilated mind be reacquainted with its foundations? There are two basic routes, one through direct experience and the other via various kinds of arguments and demonstrations. The former route can lead to radical, even irreversible, changes in perception; the latter cannot effect such change directly. But the route of reason is nonetheless useful, if not essential. If the rational mind can be persuaded to entertain ideas of itself as resting on a base of mystery, then it might become interested, rather than fearful, in the possibility of investigating this 'hypothesis' directly. The second route can be a driveway that leads to the highway of the first. This chapter takes the scientific route, and reviews some of the accumulating evidence for a 'clever' unconscious. In the next chapter, I shall return to the question of direct, personal, experiential investigation.

Before we dive into the empirical pond of cognitive science, though, it is worth remembering that everyday life is littered with informal traces, the footprints, of the unconscious, if only we will notice them. *Slips of the tongue*, for example, show clearly how the censor sometimes fails in its duty, and permits into speech or action motives or thoughts that do us discredit. (I remember several years ago being delegated to show a rather boring visitor round my university department. After two and a half hours of listening to his rambling monologue, he finally took his leave and thanked me for my time. 'Oh,' I said brightly, 'No pleasure!'—a hybrid of 'My pleasure' and 'No problem' which managed to let slip my true feeling.) And in a somewhat similar vein there is *absentmindedness*, which reveals how we may continue to 'delegate' control of our actions to an unconscious 'automatic pilot', even when it is inappropriate. (Witness William James' famous story of going upstairs to his room to change for dinner—taking *all* his clothes off, getting into his pyjamas and climbing into bed.)

Similarly we are all familiar with the experience of *coming to*, and realizing that we have been performing a skilled action and registering and responding to all sorts of environmental cues, without any awareness or memory of what we have been doing. While the shifting ground of our *moods* often seems inexplicable and uncontrollable. (The Narrator can usually concoct a story to account for 'anger', but why we should have sudden periods of creative energy, or of 'the blues', may be beyond its powers of explanation.) In general we tend to ignore, dismiss or reinterpret the plethora of daily indications that Conscious HQ is not in control, and often does not know what is going on.

Science as Myth-Busting

In recent years it has been the scientific study of the mind which has drawn to our attention some of the most compelling evidence for the existence, the power and the range of unconscious processes. Though scientists are fallible, often insensible to their own mythology, prone to unwitting and even occasionally quite deliberate bias in their work, their enterprise is the honourable one of trying to observe the world in way that is *relatively* (for that is all it can ever be) free of personal hopes and fears. In our everyday thinking, we rig the evidence, and deny that we have done so. If we are afraid that the world has an edge, we may *think* we are sailing in a straight line, while imperceptibly, unwittingly, steering in an arc. By navigating thus we are able to believe that we have put the world-edge theory to the test, while actually having preserved ourselves from the risk of falling off.

Science, for all its tacking and jibing, may eventually live up to its promise of freeing us from these ingrained forms of self-deception. Through its intention to sail straight, it can and does improve on common sense, and while each generation of scientific 'breakthroughs' is seeping out into the culture to provide the next layer of mythology, the scientists are already working on *its* deconstruction and replacement. If a mind can ask an awkward question, a *scientific* mind can devise a way of seeing whether there is any truth in it—regardless of human need or belief. (This is both the value and the danger of science. It enables us 'to boldly go', like the Starship Enterprise, where the 'angled' fear to tread. But, by exactly the same token, its liberation from the [myth-ridden] world of human experience also loosens its sense of responsibility and morality. Creativity, as we know only too well, becomes unprincipled and unbridled, able to give birth to monsters.)

Thus the scientists are, along with the poets, the philosophers and the mystics, part of a loose collaboration, an un-wholly alliance, to keep society on its toes: to keep drawing to people's attention what it is that they have forgotten they believe; reminding them that their taken-for-granted views about what is sane, normal, obvious, natural, right and real are human constructions (to which there are therefore alternatives), not timeless and absolute truths.[154] Sometimes, in a temporary fit of grandiosity (succumbing to one of the pervasive myths about science itself), these people offer their researches and their theories as if they *were* 'reality'. They become mesmerized by the Sirens' song of Ultimate Truth, and Unified Theories of Everything, forgetting that the best they can do is offer a view that works perhaps just a little better, and which recaptures a part of the inscrutable whole that the previously dominant myth had excluded. (This is why science always seems to be sailing into the wind, making slow progress forward only through an endless series of compensations and overcorrections.)

Cognitive Science

The psychological unconscious documented by latter-day scientific psychology is quite different from what Sigmund Freud and his psychoanalytic colleagues had in mind in *fin de siècle* Vienna. Their unconscious was hot and wet; it seethed with lust and anger; it was hallucinatory, primitive and irrational. The unconscious of contemporary psychology is kinder and gentler than that and more reality-bound and rational, even if it is not entirely cold and dry.[155]

The cognitive scientists' special responsibility, we might say, is the unearthing and proving (in the sense of 'testing') of psychomythology, and the construction of interesting alternatives. Recently they have been able to demonstrate the extent to which unconscious processes play a vital and major part in every moment, however humdrum, of our waking, as well as our sleeping, lives. Some of their research findings concern the workings of minds and brains that we think of as 'normal'; others have focused on some startling phenomena that appear when the brain-mind system is malfunctioning in some way.

Neurological and Clinical Evidence

In recent years a number of clinical patients have been found to have neuropsychological disorders that, while distressing or debilitating for the patient, pose intriguing questions about the unconscious. Most famous now are the patients suffering from the so-called 'blind-sight' syndrome.[156] These patients have sustained brain damage that has left them totally blind in at least part of their visual field. That is, they report having no experience whatsoever of any visual event falling within the 'blind' area. To help in the patients' rehabilitation, neurologists commonly attempt to map accurately the extent and the borders of the blind area. This is done by getting the patient to sit facing into a large hollow hemisphere, the inside surface of which is painted black and studded with pea-bulbs which can be turned on one at a time. The patient fixes his gaze on a point straight ahead, and the neurologist asks him to report any spot of light that he detects.

'Blind-sight' patients behave just like any other blind person in this situation. They make no response when a light is flashed within the blind area, and accurately report and point to any light that falls outside it. But one day, after she had flashed a light within the blind region (and predictably received no response) a neurologist asked one of these patients an absurd question. 'I know that, as far as you are concerned, there was no light', she said, 'but humour me...if there *had* been a light, where might it have been?' The patient, presumably in a good mood, went along with this game—and pointed with perfect accuracy at the position of the spot of light which he had not 'seen'. Subsequent tests confirmed this extraordinary result. The patients' 'guesses' as to the positions of the (to them) imaginary lights were more-or-less spot on. And their ability is not just restricted to simple stimuli like bare points of light. Tony Marcel at Cambridge filmed these patients as they obligingly reached for objects that they could not 'see', and found that while they were in the act of reaching their hands automatically adjusted to the right size and shape of the 'invisible' object.

A disorder with the clumsy name of *prosopagnosia* results in patients losing their ability to recognize even very familiar faces, such as those of their families and friends, and celebrities of the day. They show no overt sign of recognition when they meet or are shown photographs of these people. Yet, if you monitor non-verbal reactions like the size of the eye-pupils or the conductance of the skin, you find that these patients *are* unconsciously discriminating between people they know and those they do not. The 'body' knows who is familiar and who isn't; the conscious mind does not.

Loss of memory, or *amnesia*, also gives evidence of unconscious cognition. If an amnesic patient is given a list of words to read and remember, and then asked a few minutes later to try to recall them, their puzzled response will be 'Words? What words?' However, if you give them the first two or three letters of words that were on the list, and ask them, not to recall, but just to think of a word that starts with those letters, they will come up with the word that was on the list, rather than an *a priori* more common word that wasn't.[157] Seeing the words has clearly left some priming in the brain which biases the way the activation goes when the 'association' test arrives; but it has not left a trace that is accessible to consciousness.

In '*hemiplegia with anosagnosia*', a person loses the ability to control the actions on one side of the body—yet in some ways seems extraordinarily unaware of what has happened to them. Tony Marcel has asked such patients to give a rating out of ten to their ability to perform a variety of actions like catching a beach-ball (for which the co-ordinated use of two hands is essential). They typically grossly overestimate how well they can do it, giving themselves ratings of 8 or 9 out of 10. Their conscious report of their own skill seems impervious to the sad fact of their disability. However if you ask them questions of a more indirect kind, you can tap into a level of self-knowledge that is more accurate. For example, if instead of asking the patient directly to rate their own ability, you say 'If I was in the same state as you, how well would I be able to catch the ball?', they will give *you* 1 or 2 out of 10—and happily explain, if asked, that this would be because 'you would need both your hands'. Or, intriguingly, if instead of asking the question in a normal 'doctorly' tone, you adopt a conspiratorial air, and whisper in an almost childish voice 'Is your arm ever naughty?', the patient will join in the 'game', and will confide that, yes, her arm *is* frequently very naughty indeed.[158]

One of the strangest of clinical effects is that which occurs in patients who, largely in order to prevent the spread of epilepsy, underwent surgery which effectively disconnected the two halves (or 'hemispheres') of the brain from each other. These so-called 'split brain' patients have become widely reported, and it was the early research on their plight that sparked the fashionable (and grossly exaggerated) association of the 'left-brain' with everything that is 'bad' about rational, logical intelligence, and the 'right-brain' with all that is exciting—creativity, intuition, imagination...you name it, if the New Age likes it, you can bet it has been located on the right.

These patients show some remarkable reactions, occasioned by the breakdown of communication between the two brain-halves. It is true that, in right-handed people, the language facility is much more fluent and abstract in the left than the right hemisphere. So if a right-handed split-brain patient is asked to fixate her eyes on a central spot on a screen, and a composite picture is flashed too briefly for the eyes to move, the left-hand half of the picture will be 'seen' only by the right hemisphere, and vice versa. Thus if the left half of the picture shows a snow-filled meadow, while the right half shows a bird's claw, the 'linguistic' side of the brain gets to know only about the bird, and the 'non-linguistic' side, only about the snow. If you ask the patients to select from an array of other pictures the one that 'goes with' the picture they have just been presented, the left hand (which is controlled by the right hemisphere) reaches out for a picture of a shovel, while the right hand (controlled by the left hemisphere) selects the picture of a chicken.

The left hemisphere, the verbal one, thus sees the claw, and it also sees the two hands selecting different pictures—but it has no knowledge of the snow-scene that prompted the selection of the shovel by the left hand. So if you ask the patient to explain his choices, he says something like 'Oh, that's easy. You see, the chicken claw goes with the chicken, *and you need a shovel to clean out the chicken shed*'. The Narrator in the left hemisphere gets to work, and confidently concocts a story which provides a *plausible* explanation of what happened, based on the information it has access to, but it is not an *accurate* explanation, precisely because it does not have access to all the salient facts, and does not consider that it does not have all the information. The left-brain assumes that what arrives in *its* consciousness is what there is, and thus mistakes its on-the-spot confabulation for the literal truth. This behaviour of the split brain dramatizes and makes visible what is happening in the intact brain all the time. It is not just a clinical curiosity, but a parable that reveals the relationship between the conscious tip, and the unconscious bulk, of the cerebral iceberg.

Normal Perception

In the population at large—people without (clinically diagnosed) brain damage—the study of unconscious perception has taken two forms. One we have discussed already: the idea stemming from von Helmholtz in the last century that normal perception quite generally represents the 'conclusions of unconscious inferences'. If we need explicit demonstrations of this, psychology has stockpiled many, in the form of visual illusions. The cleverness of these illusions resides in the fact that they manage to trick the unconscious processes of the brain-mind into making 'inferences' that are reasonable, but in this particular case turn out to be wrong.

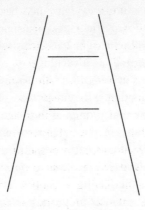

The Ponzo Illusion.

For example, the brain sees two straight lines on a page converging towards each other at the top, and unconsciously interprets them as two parallel lines disappearing into the distance—a conclusion that is, in everyday life, indeed often correct. Having made this assumption, *other* aspects of the drawing are interpreted, or even distorted, so as to conform to this 'theory'; so that if two short horizontal bars are placed between the lines, one nearer the top than the other, the higher is interpreted as 'further away' than the lower, and is automatically expanded a little by the brain (before presenting the finished conjecture to consciousness) to 'compensate' for the 'fact' that it is further way than the other. This is a useful compensation that we rely on all the time: as people walk away from us, they do not shrink in size 'perceptually' nearly as fast as the size of their image on the retina. We 'know' that the person is not getting smaller, and this knowledge gets embedded in conscious perception as a 'size correction'.

If we are aware of our own everyday perceptual mistakes and hesitations, we do not need any technical experiments to convince us of the point. I 'hear' my voice being called across a crowded room—only to discover that someone shouted 'Bye!', not 'Guy'. I sip the cup of 'tea' my wife has kindly brought me—and it tastes very peculiar, until I realize that it is actually coffee (and, having adjusted my 'set', it now tastes familiar and delicious). I sit in the stationary train and watch the platform pull away from me. I am angry with you for 'ignoring' me—until I hear you have just had some bad news, when the anger suddenly transmutes into concern. The evidence for the fact that I live in a world woven out of the 'conclusions of my unconscious inferences' is, if I will only notice it, overwhelming.

The other line of research on unconscious seeing is more controversial—'subliminal perception'. Here the see-er is not only unaware of her own unconscious assumptions: she is in danger of having her needs and actions manipulated by events that occur on the outskirts of awareness, and so avoid going through the checkpoint of consciousness—or so we think. We fear that we are especially vulnerable to (the occasional) influences that, because they have not been consciously appraised, we will be powerless to resist.

In the late 1950s a marketing executive claimed that he could dramatically raise the sales of popcorn, or Coca Cola, in a New Jersey cinema by flashing the appropriate exhortations onto the movie screen too briefly for people to see consciously. The public were outraged and terrified that this was the beginning of a technology that would 'break into the deepest and most private parts of the human mind and leave all sorts of scratch marks'.[159] However the good and bad news, as a result of much well-controlled research, is that subliminal attempts to persuade people to act in ways that they would not otherwise have done, are remarkably unsuccessful. This is bad news as well as good because it seems to apply also to 'self-help' subliminal audiotapes which claim to offer an effortless way to improve your memory or your self-esteem, or to learn a foreign language, while you are asleep.[160]

Implicit Memory

There are now many demonstrations of the existence in 'normal people' of the memory-without-consciousness phenomenon that I described above in amnesics. Behaviour or feeling gives evidence of remembering, while conscious experience does not. A common everyday example of this so-called 'implicit memory' occurs when watching old films on television. You start viewing under the impression that you have not seen this particular movie before. However, after a little while, still without 'remembering' that you have seen it, you start to be able to predict the next turn of the plot, or even an actor's words, with remarkable prescience. It is only a little later that the suspicion, and finally the realization, that you have seen it before, crystallizes. First the experience manifests in terms of how the brain-mind *behaves*, and only later as an actual memory. This phenomenon, incidentally offers a simple explanation for the *deja vu* experience: a genuinely first-time viewer who (for some unaccountable reason) is unsurprised by the action—who makes some (unconscious) lucky bets about what will happen next, may mistakenly attribute this ability to genuine familiarity, and so 'feel' that the events she is witnessing have happened before.[161]

Hypnosis

Ernest Hilgard, a long-time researcher on the curious phenomenon of hypnosis, has produced convincing reports of a strange hypnotic effect which he calls 'the hidden observer'.[162] Hilgard tells of a classroom demonstration of hypnosis during which a volunteer was hypnotized and told he would be temporarily deaf. While 'deaf', the volunteer did not flinch at loud sounds like gunshots and blocks being banged together. One student asked whether 'some part' of the subject might be aware of sounds, since his ears were presumably still functioning. The instructor then whispered softly to the hypnotized student:

> As you know, there are parts of our nervous system that carry on activities that occur out of awareness, like circulating the blood....There may be intellectual processes also of which we are unaware, such as those that find expression in dreams. Although you are hypnotically deaf, perhaps there is some part of you that is hearing my voice and processing the information. If there is, I should like the index finger of your right hand to rise as a signal that this is the case.

To the instructor's dismay, the finger rose. Immediately afterwards the hypnotized student spontaneously said that he felt his index finger rise *but had no idea why it had done so*....The instructor then released the volunteer from hypnotic deafness and asked what he thought had happened. 'I remember', said the volunteer, 'your telling me that I would be deaf at the count of three, and would have my hearing restored when you placed your hand on my shoulder. Then everything was quiet for a while. It was a little boring just sitting here, so I busied myself with a statistical problem I was working on. I was still doing that when suddenly I felt my finger lift.'[163]

Hilgard has confirmed the existence of this 'hidden observer' in many studies. One phenomenon that can be reliably induced is 'hypnotic analgesia': the use of a hypnotic suggestion to block the experience of pain. In one study, a young woman in such a state was able to hold her hand in a bucket of icy water without experiencing any discomfort. But while she verbally reported no pain, and appeared relaxed and calm, when her other hand was 'asked' to fill out a questionnaire rating the pain, 'it' reported an increased, essentially 'normal' level of distress.[164] The pain *is* being registered, at some level; but the presentation of this 'pain' as a conscious (and aversive) experience is being blocked. Somehow the brain-minds of hypnotically suggestible people are able to place a blanket of inhibitory activity over the top of the area that is being excited by the painful stimulus, and this blanket is sufficiently thick to keep the activation from building up to the concentration that is required by conscious awareness.[165]

Anaesthesia

There are some striking reports of people being able to respond to information received while under deep general anaesthesia. The received wisdom of the operating theatre is that the patient is completely 'out', and this sometimes leads to the surgical team making facetious or ribald comments at the patient's expense. But it seems that someone, somewhere may be wide awake and watching what is going on. In one study, patients were undergoing a form of surgery that often had, as a post-operative complication, the inability to urinate freely. While still under the anaesthetic, one of the surgeons spoke to each patient by name and said:

The operation has gone well and we will soon be finishing. You will be flat on your back for the next couple of days. When you are waiting it would be a good idea if you relax the muscles of the pelvic area. This will help you urinate so you won't need a catheter.

The results were striking. Not a single one of the patients given this suggestion needed catheterization during their recovery, while of a control group who did not get the suggestion, more than half needed the catheter.[166]

In another test, a different group of clinicians played a tape to anaesthetized patients which suggested to them that when someone came to interview them after the operation, 'it is very important that you pull on your ear so I can know you have heard this'. During the post-operative interview (during which no mention of the tape or the message was made) more than 80 per cent of those who had heard the message pulled their ears—most of them did it repeatedly.[167]

Learning

Recent experiments by Pawel Lewicki and colleagues at the University of Tulsa in the USA provide some of the most striking evidence for the complexity of unconscious processes in learning. As we saw earlier on in this book, the brain-mind is built to pick out from the mass of stimulation it is receiving patterns that crop up recurrently, and to 'remember' these patterns, not as verbal rules and generalizations, but as functional changes in the way the network works. The vast majority of these patterns do not pass through the gateway of consciousness as they arrive, so that whatever-it-is that one has learnt is not, as a rule, printed out explicitly. People can be shown, for example, to use all kinds of physical clues about other people in making intuitive judgments about their character—red hair indicates a fiery temper; rounded shoulders show a lack of self-confidence, and so on—but they are very often quite unaware of having made these dubious 'inferences', and do not even know that they 'believe' them.

In his laboratory tests, Lewicki showed his subjects a grid of numbers, and they had to indicate as quickly as possible whether the grid contained a particular specified target, which might appear in any position.[168] Unbeknownst to the subject, the displays contained some subtle correlations between the position of the target number, and the actual numbers that were used to fill in the rest of the grid. If there was a 4 and a 7 next to each other, for instance, then the target would be found in the middle of the top row. When such a correlation was present, subjects gradually became quicker at detecting the target, even though, when questioned afterwards, they had absolutely no conscious knowledge of the pattern that they were using to help them. Even when the people tested are used to the wiles of psychologists (if they are colleagues on the faculty of the psychology department, for example), and even when they are explicitly asked to try to detect the background pattern, they are unable to do so—and even strongly deny (because they cannot grasp it consciously) that there is such a pattern.

Even more startling, unconscious learning seems to leave the content of consciousness unaltered. In another of their studies, Lewicki and his co-workers elicited from subjects their ideas about the relationship between facial features (having a beard, say) and personality characteristics (being unconventional, or weak-willed, or whatever). They were then shown series of photographs which contained correlations between personality and physiognomy that were different from, or unrelated to, the ones they had expressed. It was found that people picked up and made use of these correlations at the nonconscious level, and that this learning had absolutely no effect whatsoever on the beliefs and prejudices they *consciously* espoused. The unconscious brain-mind continues to go about its pattern-finding business regardless of the particular patterns that happen to have got themselves previously enshrined in consciousness; and consciousness holds to its opinions even though contrary information has been picked up, and is being used effectively, unconsciously.

After describing his lengthy series of studies, Lewicki concludes (if you will excuse a bit of psychologist's jargon):

> Most of the 'real work', both in the acquisition of cognitive procedures and skills and in the execution of cognitive operations, such as encoding and interpretation of stimuli, is being done at a level to which our consciousness has no access. Moreover, even if the access to that level existed, it could not be used in any way, because the...sophistication of that level and its necessary speed of processing exceed considerably what can even be approached by our consciously controlled thinking. The 'responsibilities' of this inaccessible level of our cognition are not limited to 'housekeeping operations'...they are directly involved in (all) the...high-level cognitive operations traditionally associated with conscious controlled thinking.

Brain Activity

The final way of investigating the unconscious workings of the brain is to measure its electrical activity directly. By attaching electrodes to the scalp, it is possible to record the variations in the patterns, the locations and the amounts of activity that accompany different kinds of processing. Benjamin Libet and colleagues have wired people up in this way, and then asked them to perform a simple voluntary act, such as bending the fingers of one hand.[169] They are also asked to note the position of a moving spot at the precise instant at which they first become aware of the intention to bend the fingers, or the imminence of the movement. Libet was able to predict when the act would take place, on the basis of the electrical brain-waves, about half a second before the person themselves was conscious of their intention. Here we have physiological confirmation of Ambrose Bierce's definition of 'intention' as apprehending the imminence of an action. Behind the scenes the blind brain-mind is determining what action to take, and when to initiate it. And as it sends out messages to the muscles to move, so it also initiates processes that may end up as a conscious *prediction* of the act that is already on its way. Consciousness, however, ignorant of its own foundations, takes this prediction, and re-interprets it as control.

There is much more evidence, both scientific and everyday, which shows that consciousness is much more marginal to our psychology, and arrives on the scene much later, than its own inflated picture of itself would have us believe. It does much less of the work than it claims to, and consequently takes much more of the credit than it has a right to. By disowning what Henry James referred to as 'the deep well of unconscious cerebration', consciousness is condemned to sit in the middle of the road, like Toad of Toad Hall, shouting 'Parp! Parp!', and vigorously twisting backwards and forwards a steering-wheel that is connected to...nothing.

TWENTY

The Reconsecration of Unconsciousness

Listen, Shariputra, form is emptiness, emptiness is form, form does not differ from emptiness, emptiness does not differ from form....All things—all forms—are marked with emptiness. They are neither produced nor destroyed.

The Heart Sutra

Form is the wave and emptiness is the water. So 'form is emptiness, emptiness is form' is like 'wave is water, water is wave'....A wave on the ocean has a beginning and an end, a birth and a death. But Avalokitesvara tells us that the wave is empty. The wave is full of water, but it is empty of a separate self. A wave is a form which has been made possible thanks to the existence of wind and water. If a wave only sees its form, with its beginning and end, it will be afraid of birth and death. But if the wave sees that it is water, identifies itself with the water, then it will be emancipated from birth and death. Each wave is born and is going to die, but the water is free from birth and death.

Thich Nhat Hanh[170]

Each moment of experience arises, and if all we are aware of is consciousness itself, this moment can have no basis, no history, other than the preceding conscious moment. We must see each wave as the progeny of the wave before, and not of the instantaneous union of many unseen currents and swells, each of which is part of an indescribable oceanic system, and each of which has a history and a momentum of its own. Our sense of each wave as it breaks is entirely different, depending on whether we see it as self-existent, or as a manifestation of this incredible filigree of underlying forces—the 'implicate order', as David Bohm called it.[171] If we see only waves, being born, interacting, collaborating, fighting, breaking, dying, we live in one cosmology. If we see the sea as a whole, and the waves as transient forms that are adopted by, but are not—can never be—separate from the whole, then we live in quite another world. To live in the second world, it is not necessary to understand the ocean. You do not have to be an expert in fluid mechanics, oceanography or marine biology. To have a theory about how the sea 'works' is not required. You only have to know deeply what the sea *is*; to have a sense of the invisible, impersonal, ancient power below the surface of the waves. This is sufficient.

In the last chapter I reviewed some of the evidence for the ubiquity of unconscious mental processes and forces. But to *agree* with this old-new understanding of mind does not of itself cause an immediate perceptual flip into a qualitatively different worldview (any more than *understanding* that 'procrastination is the thief of time' will automatically stop you putting things off). Knowing *about* the importance of the unconscious can make one interested in a more direct kind of encounter—it can open us up to a new existential question—but intellectual knowledge is only the travel brochure, not the holiday. If scientific observation can 're-mind' consciousness of the dark waters on which it floats, it takes a moment of mystical insight to give one an immediate, awe-ful experience of the fathomless drop over which the conscious mind is suspended. The identification of the person with consciousness is one of the assumptions that sits at the centre of the Self System. When perception is downstream of that assumption, the mind is bound to ignore its dark roots. But if it were possible, even for an instant, to leap-frog *upstream* of this particular dualism, we would then reclaim our biological birthright of mystery—and also of belonging.

The Quality of Mystical Experience

Religious or mystical experience arises from a subtle but significant shift in the workings of the brain. When the Self System is 'taken out of the loop' the brain-mind automatically reverts to a way of functioning in which the conscious experience it creates *is* mystical experience. In order to show how this happens, it is necessary to remind ourselves of what the common qualities of these experiences are. Though reports are often fumbling—indeed, ineffability is one of the hallmarks of religious experience—and though the language chosen depends heavily on the writer's framework of culture and belief, nevertheless there are some common features that shine through these attempts to comprehend and express the essence of what has occurred. I shall start with some relatively modern accounts, as their language is more transparent to us.

Consider first this little gem of a poem by W.B. Yeats, taken from his longer series of verses entitled 'Vacillation', written in about 1933.

My fiftieth year had come and gone,
I sat, a solitary man,
In a crowded London shop,
An open book and empty cup
On the marble table-top.

While on the shop and street I gazed
My body of a sudden *blazed*;
And twenty minutes more or less
It seemed, so great my happiness,
That I was blessèd and could bless.[172]

First, mystical experiences often arise out of the blue—sitting in a London cafe or, as we shall see in a minute, on a commuter train. There seems to be no conscious preparation for an experience of tremendous significance. Secondly, such experiences are often limited in time: from a minute or so up to an hour or two is common. Thirdly there is joy, ecstasy, happiness, which seems to arise without cause, as an undeserved blessing, yet which suffuses whatever ordinary sights or activities happen to be going on. Fourthly, there is equally the sense of being gifted with a kind of holiness and wisdom. Not only was Yeats blessèd; he 'could bless'. And lastly, there is a sense of unusual bodily energy and perceptual intensity, often captured, as here, with a metaphor of fire, or sometimes light.

The next account is all the more poignant for the unprepossessing nature of its setting: a crowded suburban train on a dank night. Here the anonymous author tells us of the joy and the energy, but he puts at the centre of his reminiscence another key feature of the mystical experience: a passionate, selfless inclusive love for and kinship with his fellow human beings.

> Vauxhall station on a murky November Saturday evening is not the setting one would choose for a revelation of God!....The third-class compartment was full. I cannot remember any particular thought processes which may have led up to the great moment....For a few seconds only (I suppose) the whole compartment was filled with light....I felt caught up into some tremendous sense of being within a loving, triumphant and shining purpose. I never felt more humble. I never felt more exalted. A most curious but overwhelming sense possessed me and filled me with ecstasy. I felt that all was well for mankind....All men were shining and glorious beings who in the end would enter incredible joy...
>
> This happened over fifty years ago, but even now I can see myself in the corner of that dingy third-class compartment, with the feeble lights of inverted gas mantles overhead and the Vauxhall station outside with milk cans standing there. In a few moments the glory had departed—all but one curious lingering feeling. I loved everybody in that compartment. It sound silly now, and indeed I blush to write it, but at that moment I think I would have died for any one of the people in that compartment. I seemed to sense the golden worth in them all.[173]

The Psychology of Mysticism

Contemporary accounts are often revealing for their attempts to gloss the mystical experience in psychological terms. Many of the traditional descriptions drew instead on a religious vocabulary that invoked a transcendent 'reality', or the grace of God. The experience was interpreted as a revelation of Truth, a seeing into the 'real' nature of things, as if a curtain has been pulled aside. While this language is just as valid as a more inner, psychological one, and indeed is frequently more evocative, more poetic, it is less helpful when it comes to understanding mysticism as a phenomenon of mind. The next quotation, for example, draws both on the language of divine revelation, and on an imagery of inner states, in the effort to convey something of the experience. But above all there is the sense of knowing, and not knowing what it is one knows; of glimpsing something that is both profound and indelibly mysterious.

> ...it was as if suddenly a door had been opened in the mind.... I glimpsed what I can only call the Kingdom of Heaven. For a moment all time seemed to stand still. It was as if I was looking down into a great hall, but unlike an earthly hall it defies description. It was like an intuition of infinity...there were the answers to the mysteries of human life and of the existence of the universe. And if I could not understand those mysteries, at least I could know that there is something beyond....Then the door was closed quietly and the vision slipped away like a dream.[174]

William James himself also draws simultaneously on the languages of religion and psychology in making sense of his own mystical experiences. And he takes us one step further, by making the crucial suggestion that what gives access to these experiences is not the sudden possession of (or perhaps *by*) a Higher Power, but the suspension of some of the normal, everyday habits of perceiving and knowing.

> I have on a number of occasions felt that I enjoyed a period of intimate communion with the divine. These meetings came unasked and unexpected, and seemed to consist merely in the temporary obliteration of the conventionalities which usually surround and cover my life....What I felt on these occasions was a temporary loss of my own identity...[175]

It is a matter not of 'addition' but 'subtraction', and in particular, of subtracting from the perceptual process the sense of self. Where the Self System had been habitually adulterating experience with its own desires and phobias, now, suddenly, it is not.

In *The Varieties of Religious Experience*, James quotes a reflection by one J.A. Symonds, which takes a further step on the psychological path. He is aware not of a suspension of normal rules in an all-or-nothing fashion, but of an involuntary process in time, in which different *layers* of the Self System progressively dissolve away, until all the 'content', the attributes and characteristics of the self, are gone, and only the basic form is left. And that too is on the verge of disappearing...

> Always, I think, when my muscles were at rest, I felt the approach of the mood....It consisted in a gradual but swiftly progressive obliteration of space, time, sensation, and the multitudinous factors of experience which seem to qualify what we are pleased to call our Self. In proportion as these conditions of ordinary consciousness were subtracted, the sense of an underlying or essential consciousness acquired intensity. At last nothing remained but a pure, absolute, abstract Self. The universe became without form and void of content. But Self persisted, formidable in its vivid keenness, feeling the most poignant doubt about reality, ready, as it seemed, to find existence break as breaks a bubble round about it. And what then? The apprehension of a coming dissolution, the grim conviction that this state was the last state of the conscious Self, the sense that I had followed the last thread of being to the verge of the abyss...[176]

Self Suspended

The idea that these 'altered states of consciousness' arise from a shift of inner perspective is naturally accommodated within the view of mind that I have been developing in this book. The Self System is not biologically given; nor is a single 'monolithic' entity. It is an accretion of acquired beliefs which, though not actually 'true'—i.e. do not point to anything 'real'—nevertheless have the ability to change the way its host, the brain-mind system, functions, and especially the way in which it fabricates experience. It is thus entirely possible that, if parts of this Self System were to be short-circuited—if they were, for some reason, to be isolated from the rest of the active network—their influence would cease, and the quality of experience would automatically change. And the nature of this qualitative shift would depend absolutely on which bits of the Self System had been disconnected.

If it is the Narrator, the indefatigable commentator and critic, which is out of the loop, then its incessant chattering stops, and the mind feels fresher, calmer, more immediate. Instead of living in a conscious world that is riddled with half-heard inferences and judgments, one becomes aware of an inner peace and simplicity. If in addition the ganglion of self-centred needs is switched off, the mind not only becomes less choppy, less agitated; other more deep-rooted swells and tides may re-emerge with great clarity. Buried priorities resurface—the value of love, intimacy and belonging are re-membered—and the movements of the brain-mind come instantly to reflect these resurgent motivations. The world looks different; one behaves differently.

Helpfulness and generosity are comprised within our portfolio of basic priorities, and the brain-mind is built to perform subtle computations which include them. Kindliness is not an option; it in our nature to be kind, because the other members of our species are our kin. This does not mean that generosity always 'wins' in the internal horse-trading which the brain-mind is so good at. It means that it is always there, in the room, when courses of action are being discussed. But when the Self System is on, the voice of compassion may be drowned out by the clamour of personal needs. Thus the recognition of clear, selfless, undemanding love is *bound* to be one aspect of a mystical experience in which the whine of Self-centredness has mercifully died away.

Without the defensiveness, and the *un*enlightened self-interest, of the Self System, the brain-mind is free to register those 'threats' to the equanimity of the organism that are posed by the suffering or hardship of others. The suffering of the world does not have to be attenuated by self-protective devices.

My joy is like spring, so warm it makes
Flowers bloom in all walks of life.
My pain is like a river of tears, so full it
Fills up the four oceans.
Please call me by my true names,
So I can hear all my cries and my laughs at once,
So I can see that my joy and pain are one.
Please call me by my true names,
So I can wake up,
And so the door of my heart can be left open...[177]

231

One of the fundamental features of the whole human body-brain-mind system, you remember, is that it *is* a system: we are fundamentally ecological, only able to exist because we are constantly open to the public. If we were not penetrated to the core by air and energy and vegetation, we would not *be*. Yet one of the founding assumptions of the Self System is of separateness and (at least partial) autonomy. While Self is on, we seem to ourselves more independent than we truly, biologically, are. So, of course, when the Self is taken out of the equation, we are re-enabled to sense our mutuality, our *inter*dependence, our ecology. Thus the mystical experience is one in which the nagging sense of *longing* is replaced with an inviolable sense of *belonging*. 'The World is Our Mother'—a Native American refrain—is no longer a poetic image; it is known, without any shadow of a doubt, to be the literal, scientific truth.

Losing Your Inhibitions

All these facets of the mystical experience follow effortlessly from the model of the brain-mind which I have been developing. But what about the mystic's experience of *intensity*, the release of 'energy' that manifests itself as a surge of power and presence in both physical and mental domains? Why does the body 'blaze', and perception glow with an incandescent luminosity? The answer to this is found in the way that the Self System exercises its influence over the rest of the brain-mind. Remember that, because its 'needs' and 'threats' are non-biological, they tend to be represented as chronic priming of the relevant parts of the network. In order to set yourself to detect what is relevant to these needs, you have to keep sending a 'trickle charge' of the brain's limited pool of current to these areas; and therefore the more of these areas there are, the greater the fraction of this central pool that is going to be tied up. The more ways you have contracted of losing face, the less 'free energy' the brain has for noticing and representing what is actually going on.

Remember also that the Self System is threatened by the appearance *in consciousness* of certain prohibited experiences—irrational anger, guilt, loneliness, certain forms of wild thought or impulse, fear itself. Because it is *conscious* awareness of these states that is dangerous, the threat can be allayed by inhibiting the relevant areas:

raising their conscious thresholds high enough to prevent the accident occurring. But 'inhibition' is another form of the same energy,
the same cerebral current, that subserves excitation, and it therefore
further depletes the same limited reservoir. So the need for long-term
censorship of consciousness places an added demand on the central
resources of the brain mind. Where one of the hot-spots is both
attracting attention and also repelling consciousness, excitation and
inhibition may get locked into a positive feedback spiral that drains
the central batteries very considerably.

So the net effect of all these efforts to expurgate consciousness of
specific threats is that there may not be much activity left over to
underwrite efficient action and perception. You are so busy trying
not to notice the things that make you anxious that you literally do
not see the speeding car as you step off the kerb, or hear the tension
in your child's voice, or notice the edge of the table as you go to put
down the crystal vase. Perception gets dull and action gets clumsy
because they are starved of the necessary resources.

Turn off the Self System, and all this charge, which may have
been tied up for years, suddenly becomes free again. What happens?
Exactly what happened on 'VE Day', 13 May 1945, all over Britain,
when Germany's surrender was announced, and the Second World
War was over in Europe—an almighty party. Dancing in the foun-
tains in Trafalgar Square. Making love in Hyde Park. Celebration on
a grand scale. When the Self System is disconnected, and its solemn
vigilance is no longer required, the organism goes on the razzle. It
may well overflow with tears of joy, or tremble to its roots with a
belly-laugh of cosmic proportions. It too may mark its liberation by
embracing strangers or dancing in the streets.

A playfulness, a light non-aggressive sense of humour, is often
associated with the mystical states, which is to be expected. The only
things that are 'serious' are those that threaten the survival of whatever one is identified with. The more such threats there are embedded in experience, like landmines, the more carefully, seriously, you
have to walk. And conversely, the more assumptions one is
'upstream' of—the more one can see them for what they are—the
more one can skip lightly around them, or poke gentle fun at them
when they growl and posture. In a mystical state it is not that the
Self has disappeared. You still know who you are, and what you prefer. But the sting goes out of its antics. It may still prance around,
but without its ability to embarrass, control or hurt. The mystic can

see her own, and other people's, pretensions and evasions for what they are. And yet, while seeing them, can see also the beauty in people who are 'downstream' of their beliefs, forced to contort themselves in strange, even self-destructive ways, because they are still *in* their traps, not yet knowing them *as* traps, and not yet alive to the possibility of freedom.

And along with lightness comes flow: a feeling that life is unfolding with unprecedented ease and rightness. Returned to its balanced state, the brain-mind can at last get on with what it was designed for, and remains exquisitely good at: weighing up the options, and deciding what is the best thing to do next. Sometimes this happens quickly. Sometimes there may be a lengthy pause while the invisible machinery whirrs. Sometimes mistakes are made. Sometimes brilliant solutions appear from nowhere. But when the brain-mind is released from the constant interference, obfuscation and deprivation of resources that the Self System produces, it works with poise and grace: now pouncing, now resting; now broad and receptive, now focused and intent.[178]

Where Does God Come In?

The sense of *will*, of internalized control, of the personal executive behind the eyes, is one of the central features that we attribute to the self; so when the Self System is switched off, experience is bound to feel passive, out-of-control, as if one's thoughts and feelings were being 'run' not from the Field Headquarters of consciousness, but from somewhere else entirely. William James noted this as one of the cardinal aspects of the mystical experience: one 'feels as if his own will is in abeyance, and indeed sometimes as if he were grasped and held by a superior power'.[179]

'The first cut is the deepest', as the song says; and the first deep cut of dualism is that which severs 'self' from 'other'. Suppose then that this cut remains, active in the brain-mind, at the same time as the sense of internal, conscious control dies away. The source of action and experience is now no longer the self that I had always thought myself to be; and if it does not come from self, then it must come from 'other'. For the schizophrenic, 'other' may be an alien force controlling her thoughts. For the religious believer, this impersonal 'other' can only be God. 'Not my will but thine, O Lord'. For the secular mystic, there may be only a psychological framework within which to make sense of this extraordinary shift of power, and then what is felt may be the welling-up of experience from a pure mystery that is not transcendent but internal: one's own most impenetrable core. The only concepts that begin to be big enough and deep enough to capture this transformation are God, and the Unconscious—and even the latter, though profane, now demands a capital letter.

Whether one intuits God or Mystery behind the loss of personalized identity, one must marvel at the way it all keeps going on, without the individual contributions that I had held to be so essential. One could imagine an entertainer spinning plates on top of sticks, running backwards and forwards adding new plates while returning to wobbly ones to give them an extra spin, getting carried away until he collapses in an exhausted heap—only, to his amazement, to find that the whole show keeps going *without* his frantic efforts.

Mysticism as Encountering the Unconscious

No matter how deeply I go into myself my God is dark, and like a webbing made of a hundred roots, that drink in silence.
Rainer Maria Rilke[180]

Heaven opens inward, chasms yawn,
Vast images in glittering dawn
Half-shewn, are broken and withdrawn...
Alfred Lord Tennyson[181]

Many people have written of mysticism in terms of mystery and the Unconscious. William James talks of 'insight into depths of truth unplumbed by the discursive intellect.' Brother Henry refers, rather more elegantly, to the 'deep well of unconscious cerebration'. And Jung was emphatic about the relationship between mysticism and the Unconscious, which he describes as: 'simply the medium from which religious experience seems to flow. As to what the further cause of such experience may be, the answer to that lies beyond the range of human knowledge'.[182] But the richest source of writings that explicitly link religious experience to the unconscious and 'unknowing' is the apophatic tradition within Christian mysticism. Let me offer a few illustrations from this tradition, many of which meld the language of God and the language of Mystery in the most beautiful ways.[183]

The acknowledged 'father' of the apophatics was a legendary sixth-century Syrian who wrote under the name of Dionysius the Areopagite (sometimes called 'Pseudo-Denys'), who is reputed to have said: 'The most godly knowledge of God is that which is known by unknowing.' For him, the mystic is one who 'remains entirely in the impalpable and the invisible, belonging completely to him who is above all things, for he no longer belongs to anyone whether to himself or to another, but having renounced all knowledge, is united to the Unknowable in a better way, and knowing nothing, knows with a knowledge surpassing the intellect.' And God is 'the dazzling obscurity which outshines all brilliance with the intensity of its darkness'.[184]

One of the best-known representatives of this tradition is Meister Eckhart, the fourteenth-century German mystical philosopher. Eckhart makes a powerful distinction between God and 'the Godhead', equating God with the manifest, the visible and sensible forms of the Universe, and the Godhead with the unmanifest, the unknown *source* from which all the 'works of God' spring.

> When I existed in the core, the soil, the river, the source of the Godhead, no one asked me where I was going or what I was doing. There was no one there to ask me, but the moment I emerged, the world of creatures began to shout....There is only unity in the Godhead and there is nothing to talk about. God acts. The Godhead does not. It has nothing to do, and there is nothing going on in it. It never is on the lookout for something to do. The difference between God and the Godhead is the difference between action and non-action....The Godhead is poor, naked and empty as though it were not; it has not, wills not, wants not, gets not.
>
> There is something, transcending the soul's created nature, not accessible to creatures, non-existent as we term existence; no angel has it, for his is a clear nature, and clear and defined things have no concern with this....It is one; rather unnamed

than named, rather unknown than known. If you could naught yourself in an instant, less than an instant, I should say, all that this is in itself would belong to you. But while you have any mind for yourself at all you know no more of God than my mouth does of colour or my eye of taste.

So not only is the essence, the ultimate source of things, to be found behind or beyond the world of thoughts, actions and perceptions; preoccupation with this world is a hindrance on the road to an encounter with the Godhead. Any form of knowing, however subtle, constitutes a diversion.

The anonymous author of the fourteenth-century mystical text *The Cloud of Unknowing*, whose title wonderfully captures the mystical spirit, uses 'God' in a different sense. But he (or she) too tells us that we have to walk into the dark if we are to catch a glimpse of the Mystery of Mysteries.

By 'darkness' I mean 'a lack of knowing'—just as anything you do not know or may have forgotten may be said to be 'dark' to you, for you cannot see it with your inward eye. For this reason it is called a 'cloud', not of the sky of course, but of 'unknowing', a cloud of unknowing between you and your God....We are apt to think we are very far from God because of this cloud of unknowing between us and him, but surely it would be more correct to say that we are much farther from him if there is no cloud...

John of Ruysbroeck, in his mystical work *The Spiritual Marriage*, uses similar imagery to evoke his own experience.

At times the inward man performs his introspection simply...and here he meets God without intermediary. And from out of the Divine Unity there shines into him a simple light; and this light shows him darkness and nakedness and nothingness.

To have an immediate experience of God, he says, a person

must have lost himself in a Waylessness and in a Darkness, in which all contemplative men wander in fruition and wherein they can never again find themselves in a creaturely way....We expire into the eternal namelessness in which we are lost.

John Tauler, another fourteenth-century monk, tries to explain in his *Sermons* what is meant by 'The Kingdom of God is within you'. Where exactly?

> This Kingdom is seated properly in the innermost recesses of the spirit. When the powers of the senses and the powers of the reason are gathered up into the very centre of the man's being—the unseen depths of his spirit, wherein lies the image of God—and thus he flings himself into the divine abyss...

And three centuries later, also in Germany, we have Jakob Boehme, one of the greatest of Christian mystical writers, saying that 'the hidden man is God's own being'. He describes as clearly as anyone the core of mystical experience as a welling up from some ineffable source within.

> In my inward man I saw it well, as in a great deep; for I saw right through as into a chaos where everything lay wrapped, but I could not unfold it. Yet from time to time it opened itself within me like a growing plant.

Buddhism

Echoes of this inward discovery of the divine unconscious can be found in every mystical tradition. Let me conclude this chapter with just a few quotations from Buddhism. One of the best-known expositors of Zen Buddhism was the late D.T. Suzuki, who published in 1949 a small book on the life and teachings of Hui-Neng, the seventh-century Chinese 'Sixth Patriarch' of Zen. Hui-Neng's *Platform Sutras* much influenced the development of Zen in both China and, later, in Japan. Suzuki interprets these writings explicitly in terms of the Unconscious. In fact, 'according to Hui-Neng, the concept of the Unconscious is the foundation of Zen Buddhism'.[185]

O friends, if there are among you some who are still in the stage of learners, let them turn their illumination upon the source of consciousness whenever thoughts are awakened in their minds. When the awakened mind is dead, the conscious illumination vanishes by itself—this is the Unconscious.

And, in a deliberate reference to the Christian formula:

The Unconscious is to let 'thy will be done', and not to assert my own. All the doings and happenings, including thoughts and feelings, which I have or which come to me are of the divine will.

When questioned about the Unconscious and its relationship to the more conscious, deliberate faculties on mind, Hui-Neng sounds as if he were quoting Eckhart:

When one is forgetful of both memory and intelligence, one is in correspondence with it.

For Hui-Neng, the Unconscious is found upstream of all belief, all dualism, all identity. It is the place where, in his most famous phrase, 'from the first, not one thing is'. We might leave it to another renowned Zen Master, Huang-po, to explain why the search for the source of experience, the Unconscious—the 'Void'—seems even more dangerous than an expedition to find the source of the Nile:

Men are afraid to forget their minds, fearing to fall through the Void with nothing to stay their fall. They do not know that the Void is not really void, but the realm of the real Dharma.[186]

Elsewhere Suzuki offers this translation of a verse by the Chinese sage Chao-pien, which captures both the sudden grandeur, and the mundane reality, of this encounter with the Unconscious.

Empty of thought I sat quietly at my office-desk,
My fountain-mind at rest, as calm as water—
A thunder-roll, the doors of the mind bursting open,
And, look, there sits the old man in all his homeliness.

And the ancient Chinese religion of Taoism, which, with Indian Buddhism, formed the other parent of what was to emerge as Zen, contributed its own view of the Tao as the mysterious source:

The Tao is like an empty vessel
That yet may be drawn from
Without ever needing to be filled.
It is boundless; the very progenitor of all things in the world...
It is like a deep pool that never dries.

Tao Te Ching

TWENTY ONE

The Restoration of Sanity

Sekito once asked his disciple Yakusan, 'What are you doing here?' 'I'm not doing anything,' answered the latter. 'If so, you are idling your time away.' 'Is not idling the time away doing something?' was Yakusan's response. Sekito still pursued him. 'You say you are not doing anything; who then is this one who is doing nothing?' Yakusan replied, 'Even the wisest know it not.'[187]

Whether in my ordinary life or in my search for its hidden significance, I am most alive, closest to the source and meaning of my existence, when I am open to my immediate experience, receptive to what it can teach me and vulnerable to its power to change my being. In this moment, when I am sure of nothing, I am yet most deeply confident of the possibility of understanding. My actions spring most truly from myself, yet I have no idea beforehand what I will manifest. Like water welling up from a spring, I am new every moment, appearing miraculously from some source hidden deep within the ground of my being.

Robin Skynner[188]

The mystics describe a state of grace in which certain habitual assumptions are removed from perception, and in which the brain-mind reverts to a more natural *modus operandi*, one in which basic priorities are intuited more clearly, and 'right action' computed more easily. One of the dualisms that may be given up in this state is that which divorces consciousness from its unconscious bedrock, and leads us to place an unhealthy amount of weight on evidence that happens to become conscious. Cognitive scientists are telling us that the mystics' direct sense of an unknowable surround to consciousness is in fact an intimation of the basic function of the brain-mind.

Mystery, clarity, wisdom and compassion are fundamental character-istics of the biological system that we human beings happen to con-sist of; characteristics that have been overwritten or obscured by the habitual activity of the Self System.

The urgent question, then, is: how is this natural birthright to be regained? Is it even conceivable that a brain-mind, so thoroughly colonized by a swarm of conditioned needs and fears, could find a way out of its predicament? That it is *possible* to regain it is attested to by all the religious traditions of the world. But is it just a matter of waiting patiently for the 'grace of God' to touch us, for the Holy Spirit to descend into our hearts; or are there things we can *do*, and if so, what?

Psychotherapy

One of the newer myths of the Western world would suggest, at this point, that we find ourselves a competent psychotherapist. Yet we need to be a little cautious about accepting this idea. Therapy can be an invaluable aid to healing the debilitating hurts of the mind, yet, in dealing with the Self System *as a whole* it may not provide the best, or the only, way to proceed.

'Optimal well-being', in this mythology of healing, has come to be seen as what you get when the long schedule of structural repairs to the soul is finally completed. Those who believe in a continuum that runs from therapy to spirituality, from healing to *nirvana*, tend to see 'enlightenment' as the crock of gold at the end of the therapeutic rainbow. If you get over your shyness, clear up the stuff with your mother, work on your fear of death, and meditate long enough on the insubstantiality of the self—when all your neuroses large and small have been resolved or dissolved—*then* everlasting bliss will be your just reward. The ubiquitous language, within this framework, is of 'personal', and later on, as the errors and wounds that are being 'worked on' get deeper, 'spiritual' *growth*. When this myth of the human journey as one of progressive healing is accepted as the only valid or possible one, it comes to look as if liberation lies exclusively in the gradual dismantling of the Self System. In this view the 'self', the 'ego', is painted as the villain of the piece, the archetypal grem-lin, and only when it is finally cast out can 'the peace of God, which passeth all understanding' be attained.

But this mythology of psychological cleansing and repair is not the only option available. In evolutionary and biological terms, the collection of capacities that have grown together into the Self System is seen as having had (and still having) an honourable part to play in the story of human development. Each of these capabilities arose for good reasons, and still has a positive place in the scheme of things. It is not the Self itself that is at fault, but only its *status* within the overall economy of the brain-mind. It is a vital evolutionary servant that has developed, for understandable reasons, delusions of grandeur, and has usurped the functions of the brain-mind as a whole. To rectify the situation, therefore, it is not necessary (or even 'healthy') to banish the Pretender from the court of the brain completely, but only to restore it to its rightful place.

To have the facility to think of oneself in the 'third person' *as* an abiding object with identity and location, to be able to see yourself as others see you, is a helpful convention to subscribe to—only provided you do not fall into the trap of thinking that this internal object is who and what you really *are*. To be able to keep a running tally of one's more general preferences and dispositions, to have to hand a summary-sheet of oneself that can be used in conversation to ease collaboration and, occasionally, to facilitate deception is likewise useful. Only when this review is mistakenly seen as mandatory do things get out of balance. The Narrator's tales provide a useful 'centre of gravity', provided they are not taken as referring to any underlying reality. The narrow beam of consciousness reflects one mode of mind that has its evolutionary purpose. It is when the other modes are forgotten that this creates further home-made problems and limitations. All of these are resources that we would be hard put to do without. It is only when they seem to add up to a solid demanding whole, a resident Dictator which does not *contribute* to the internal energetic workings of the brain-mind, but attempts to preempt and override them, that things start to go awry.

So what is needed is not a magic to make the Self disappear, but an understanding of how it can be, to use the Freudian word again, 'decathected': deprived of the charge that fuels its prima-donna panics and demands, and returned to its status as a tightly knit group of team-players. The Self is neither our Messiah nor our Nemesis, but a cluster of company employees who are collectively suffering from delusions of grandeur. We are not at liberty to give them the sack:

we have too much need of their talents. And in any case, because the Self System is not a single entity, but a loose affiliation of hundreds of interlocked habits and beliefs, trying to deal with these constituents one by one is *never* going to deliver 'enlightenment'. The Self is a Hydra, a many-headed beast, whose heads grow again as fast as they are cut off. As the myth of Hercules reminds us, if we wish to finish the job we have to find a different way of de-powering this fabulous monster of the mind.

Temporary Losses of Self-Consciousness

An alternative strategy for liberation is deliberately to create circumstances in which the Self System is put temporarily Out of Order. Almost everyone is familiar with moments or periods of grace, when life seemed full of ease, naturalness and flow—only to come 'back to reality', sometimes with a nasty jolt, and find it once again sticky and fraught. Often heightened states of excitement, crisis or absorption will do it. At times of intense demand or concentration it is as if the operative part of the brain-mind network is using up such a high proportion of the total allowable 'energy' that there is simply not enough left over to keep underwriting the activities of the Self. (When the internal party becomes sufficiently wild, even the guards and the lookouts abandon their posts to join in the fun.) This may be one of the reasons why the self-conscious young find release in surfing, dancing or fighting. For a while the demands on the whole system reach such levels of intensity that any subsystem that is not absolutely required has to be shut down, with a resultant release of ease, flow and even joy.[189]

The 'high' of sex or of battle (like the high of heroin, which achieves a similar effect in a more direct, chemical way) can become addictive, an almost blessed interlude in a life that is generally pervaded with dis-ease. But precisely because the Self System is simply suspended, nothing can happen in such a state that alters the way it functions normally. As soon as the agony or the ecstasy is passed, the intensity of physical or mental demand dies down, and there is nothing to stop the Self System kicking back in again. As Marcel Kinsbourne says:

Of all mental states, intense concentration is perhaps the least suitable for elucidating...*self*-consciousness. Not only is the concentrating subject unaware of all but the most intense stimuli extraneous to those concentrated on, he may even be unaware of himself as a concentrating agent. The focus of attention is so narrowed that self-consciousness itself is among the excluded facets of experience. The self is a construct. It is incorporated in experience only at those times when the focus of attention permits.[190]

So these states of induced absorption offer relief that is welcome, but necessarily short-lived; and the more delightful they are, the greater temptation to keep recreating them. But of course, as they becomes more familiar, so they gradually lose their power to absorb, to 'take you out of your self', and the more dangerous, bizarre or intense the situation has to become in order to work the trick. Hence 'sensation-seeking', as a way of stressing out the Self System, is bound to become ever more perverse, violent or self-destructive.

In rather a different context, the likelihood of semi-mystical or 'peak' experiences can be increased by stressing the system-as-a-whole with deprivation, rather than by flooding it with excitement. Religious and monastic orders have known for thousands of years that 'encounters with God' can be encouraged through physical hardship, loss of sleep, fasting and protracted devotional rigours such as repeated prostrations or long periods of kneeling in prayer. Again, as the pressure builds up on the whole body-brain-mind system, so its resources diminish and become ever more thinly spread, until, at an unpredictable moment, the inherent prioritizing capability of the brain-mind decides that it can no longer afford to keep supplying energy to the Self System, and its valuable fuel is redeployed. It is like the situation when there is a miners' strike, a long cold spell, and the electricity supply is stretched to its limits: sooner or later the lights in the high-street shop windows are going to go out. They become a luxury that the system-as-a-whole can no longer afford.

Such emergency measures taken by the internal economy enable people to have an experience of life without their Selves—a taste, a glimpse, a brief whiff of enlightenment. And their effect in the context of spiritual practice may well be to strengthen the resolve and the commitment of a yogi or a nun. But they can no more *establish—*

stabilize—the direct, unshakeable knowledge that 'the kingdom of God is within' than can a snort of cocaine or a marathon swim. Access to the full-length feature, the Big Picture of enlightenment, is by an entirely different route from the one that shows you the 'trailer'.

Shocks to the System

In between these extremes of flooding or stressing the system one might find the contrived crises, the shocks and *non sequiturs*, of the notorious Zen masters. In their absurd utterances and outrageous actions, we can see again and again the attempts to knock the student's brain-mind out of its familiar self-based ruts, like a pinball machine jogged onto 'Tilt'. In setting up these psychological emergencies, the teacher is hoping to capitalize on the same old alarm mechanism that human beings still share with the nervous kangaroo feeding in long grass. Something does not compute. Things have suddenly lurched outside the range of anticipated futures. Action is demanded, but the world is out of joint. 'Thirty blows with my staff if you call it a "staff"'; thirty blows if you say it is *not* a "staff". Quickly—speak! Speak!'

Will you stay trapped within the whirling mind-streams of the Self System, desperately trying to figure out what you are *supposed* to do? Or will you be ready enough, and the 'emergency' well-judged enough, to be able to flow out from the moment of arrest into a response—symbolic, witty, elliptical, direct—without (even if just for a moment) reactivating self-consciousness? The Zen master is not trying to *tell* you anything, for her stock-in-trade is a form of truth that cannot be bottled and sold. She is trying to trick you, kick you or seduce you into an altered state of consciousness, a selfless frame of mind.

The Zen master Gutei raised his finger whenever he was asked a question about Zen. A boy attendant began to imitate him in this way. When anyone asked the boy what his master had preached about, the boy would raise his finger. Gutei heard about the boy's mischief. He seized him and cut off his finger. The boy cried and ran away. Gutei called him. When the boy turned his head, Gutei raised his own finger. In that instant the boy was enlightened.[191]

Mindfulness

In an emergency the Self System can be disconnected; but one cannot live *in extremis*. What we need is a way of disconnecting the Self *without* having to go into a state in which normal functions have to be suspended—a state in which attention is so locked-on to the emergency that *other* calls cannot be heeded; and in which the resources of the body-brain-mind are being consumed at an expensive and wearing rate. A crisis can cause the brain-mind to 'park' the Self System while the emergency is sussed and sorted; but in this state of intense reorganization, awareness is all loaded into the part of the network that is dealing directly with the problem.

Is it possible to cultivate a way of *attending*, of deploying the activity of the brain-mind, in which the Self System is stripped of its power to control and direct resources, while at the same time keeping awareness loose, open and relaxed? Or, to put it another way, is it possible to cultivate a state of 'selfless self-awareness', without falling back into the more familiar state we call 'self-consciousness'? Is it possible to dispel the self-motivated, self-protective fog of 'stupidity', to allow perception once again to be bright and keen, without at the same time suffering all the unwanted anxieties and frustrations which this fog was 'designed' to save us from in the first place? The answer, of course, is: Yes and No.

In the state of self-awareness without self-consciousness, it is as if one were sitting right at the prow of an ocean liner as it ploughs its way into the night. Looking over the front of the ship, down at the boiling sea, one is aware of the intense activity at the point where the hull is cutting its way into the future; and one is also aware of oneself as the watcher, as a spectator at this continual process of birth, unfolding and passing away. Looking up and forward into the night, one can only fallibly anticipate what will come next. One can predict, but always in a context of potential surprise—the freak wave, the flotsam, the flashes of the moon on the occasional flying fish—each one looming up unannounced from the 'unconscious' of the night.

As you turn and look back, there behind you are the reassuringly visible and known structures and sounds of the liner, and the wake stretching back into the past: the familiar furrows, fairy-lights, dance-tunes and cooking smells of personality and memory. And up on the bridge, surrounded by electronic gadgetry and storm warnings, with responsibilities and schedules to meet, is the captain, full of intentions, with her attention predetermined and circumscribed. She will very likely miss the shaft of silver on the dolphin's back. Her world is full of information, but devoid of charm. She can be relieved, but not delighted.

When you swap the role of responsible pilot for awe-struck observer, you, at the prow, with a wide-open mind, can notice much more, revel in it, and learn about the sea and the dark. As you look down at the spume and into the night, you see, hear, smell, taste and feel—and you can, in the immediacy of perception, be aware of the seeing, the hearing, the smelling, the tasting and the feeling. This knack of awareness that is at once intense, open and reflexive has been widely identified as having beneficial consequences, and given a variety of different names by the different 'schools' of spiritual education. In several traditions it is called 'witnessing'. George Gurdjieff called it 'self-remembering'. J. Krishnamurti referred to it as 'choiceless awareness'. The Buddhist tradition, which has explored the 'technology of awareness' in perhaps the most extensive detail of all, has given it a name which is usually translated as 'mindfulness'.

On a ship at sea, the intensity of experience grabs you and drags you into the present. But mindfulness can be cultivated via gentle discipline, so that the same keen-edged quality of awareness can be brought to any situation. To balance the romance of the ocean with the mundane urban reality of a journey to work, imagine you are standing on the platform of an underground station, busily thinking about paradise or lunch. If you wait till the train is rushing along the platform before you register it, you may not even have enough time to note the destination displayed on the front. But if you tune in to the arrival of the train earlier, you may be surprised how much you can learn. Being 'mindful' means being receptive to the minimal stirrings of wind, smell, sound and light that herald the arrival of the train. Mindfulness is standing at the edge of the dark tunnel of your own unconscious, senses aquiver for the first faint intimation of the next experience, the impending train of thought.

Night School

Every great religion has discovered and taught ways to hone the edge of perception. From the whirling of a dervish to the chanting of a monk, from *vipassana* meditation to the Jesus prayer, there are esoteric practices galore that waken and sharpen the latent reflective powers of the mind. In *vipassana* practice, for example, the object is not to fix attention on anything, but, having reduced the amount of external stimulation to a bare minimum, to let the brain-mind then go where it will—but without losing that *presence* of mind which knows, in immediate and precise detail, what it is that is going on, as it happens. And this is very different from the usual mish-mash of backchat and edited high-lights which passes for normal consciousness. Mindfulness or witnessing is open, non-selective and non-defensive. It is passive and receptive, interested in whatever happens to surface next, rather than purposeful. Take the 'pre' off *pre*meditation, and there you have it.

And every culture has its exoteric traditions as well: the vernacular pursuits that also stimulate and refresh the brain-mind so that it can, in the words of the Christian prayer, 'see Thee more clearly, follow Thee more nearly, and love Thee more dearly', day by day. Whether it be fishing or knitting, walking in the woods or gazing at the fire, watching cricket or listening to one of the late Beethoven quartets, there is no shortage of opportunities to cultivate an inner quiet.

The Easing of Belief

In this state of alert receptiveness, several beneficial changes to the mind's *modus operandi* can take place. First, it becomes possible to 'catch' experience in a more and more 'raw' state—before some of the perennial assumptions of Self have been stirred in. Temporarily without purpose, the subtler nuances and shifts of the brain-mind can get through to conscious awareness: they can impinge, and captivate. And when the brain-mind is in this different mode—playful, interested, vigilant, but without being churned up and unbalanced by the normal cross-currents of hopes, fears and expectations—then it begins to reveal its own more abiding concerns and assumptions. One's vantage point of consciousness shifts 'upstream' of such assumptions, and in doing so they become not only *visible* but *equivocal*. When the belief is upstream of consciousness it is dissolved in the way that consciousness is formed. If the evidence disagrees with the belief—too bad for the evidence. But when the vantage point of conscious awareness comes prior to the activation of the belief, then it is the belief that is put to the test. By practising the art of catching experience early, behind-the-scenes beliefs can be made to reveal themselves; and standing revealed, it is they who must defend themselves against the evidence, now unrigged, of their misdemeanours.

Any belief that shows up downstream of the point of perception is less tightly, unquestionably, associated with my identity; and therefore any enquiry into its validity is less likely to be construed by the Self System as a personal attack. In an acute state of mindfulness, beliefs can stop being 'embodied' in the very way we think and see: they become 'espoused'. And though we may remain attached to them, a 'merely' espoused belief is vulnerable to change because it is no longer clandestine.

Thus mindfulness not only sharpens perception as we look outwards; it is the active ingredient in the work of inner reflection, and it creates the conditions in which the sudden mystical experience of liberty and light can occur. The former represents the rehabilitation of a gradual process or learning, or more accurately, unlearning, not unlike that which happens in therapy, but now present more as a daily attitude of mind than as a matter of urgent problem-solving. The latter represents a sudden leap of insight, large or small, earth-shattering or simply funny, which may even act as the starting-point, the focus, for a subsequent process of enquiry.

The Rehabilitation of Serenity

As the fog of stupidity is gradually, non-selectively dispelled, so the hot-spots of the mind—which the fog was designed to conceal—begin to re-emerge; and this is painful. People who expect mindfulness to take them down a gentle slide into peace have got another think coming. Once you give up the deliberate effort to make the mind go, or not go, where you (i.e. the Self System) want it to, the natural attraction of the danger zones, now less effectively blanketed with inhibition, regain their access to consciousness. The threats they represent are now re-equipped with the power to trigger a conscious emergency. Mindfulness re-establishes the original ability of consciousness to *feel*; to feel fully whatever counts as a threat or a need. Taking off the brake of inhibition means that the train of thought is now free to revisit the dark and discreditable.

So at the same time as mindfulness develops, so too must the ability to sit quietly and observe these mental energies and emergencies as they happen—neither taking them at face value, nor fighting them and trying to stuff them back into the unconscious, but being able to expand around them, to resist the temptation to tighten up and repress them, to keep the vantage point upstream of what is unpleasant or frightening so that clear observation can do its work. In Zen this is sometimes referred to as 'learning to keep your seat while the horse is bolting'. So one of the beneficial side-effects of mindfulness practice is to strengthen and exercise powers of resilience and forbearance which may have become rather disused and atrophied. Even sitting still, cross-legged, for 40 minutes gives you the opportunity to practise observing the sensations in the knees simply *as* sensations, and to discover to what extent it is the *judgement* of a sensation as 'painful' that triggers all the feelings of aversion and impulses of avoidance (the 'emergency'); and to what extent it is this lapsing into emergency mode which is itself responsible for a good deal of the perceived 'pain'.

In mindfulness the brain-mind reveals not only its acquired assumptions, its buried, pragmatic philosophy of life; it also begins to uncover those values and understandings that are embedded in the deeper evolutionary strata of the body-brain's constitution, but whose presence had been eclipsed by the bright lights and loud alarms of the Self System. Kindness and wisdom are not qualities that can be sought by a mind that is governed by the Self System; they are naturally revealed in a mind that is progressively disidentified with this system.

Mindfulness also enhances creativity. It makes the operation of the brain-mind network more flexible and less predictable. Instead of rushing onwards, the stream of consciousness becomes temporarily dammed; pools of activity can form and deepen, and in doing so they can 'back up', revealing structures that had been latent, and other options than those which had been taken by default. If attention is held and intensified in this way, it is likely that it will head off, when it finally does so, in a different direction from the first available channel which it would habitually have taken: hence the possibility of insight and creativity. Instead of choosing the direction of flow in a way that is 'impulsive', on the basis of the most obvious habits and considerations, the consequences and possibilities of *other* routes can be explored. What one *does* is more likely to incorporate the promptings of the quiet voices of abiding virtue, and not just the brash and bossy stipulations of the Self. Through developing mindfulness, the brain is thus enabled to develop the power and the habit of *reflectiveness*; a disposition which is increasingly independent of external conditions, and which equips it to make decisions, and follow lines of thought and action, that are more fully informed, more likely to satisfy a variety of needs—yours as well as mine—at the same time.

It is not that mindfulness allows a conscious intelligence to reach into the brain-mind and switch the points. There is, it must be clear by now, no such governor. The deliberate cultivation of mindfulness is a facility, a trick, which enables the brain-mind to be self-correcting, in just the same way that a natural medicine does not 'cure' the body, but encourages or stimulates the body to cure itself. Exercise does not build muscles: it stresses the body in a such a way that 'building muscles' is the inherent response which is evoked. Likewise the intention to be mindful happens to create a particular 'stress' in the mind, the inherent response to which is the sidelining of part or all of the Self System, and/or the discovery of new channels of thought.

The great paradox of mindfulness is that it both dispels unconsciousness, and reveals the Unconscious. Mindfulness undoes some of the damage that strategic stupidity and tactical ignorance have done to the quality of life. It makes life clearer and sharper. It makes suffering, both home-grown and endemic-to-life, more immediate, and challenges us to find the wisest way of dealing with each different kind. It enables us to re-experience our connectedness with both the biological and the social world. Yet at the same time as it dispels fog and punctures self-deception, it is bringing us closer and closer to the *essential* mystery, the inaccessibility to consciousness of much of who we are. We are trading a petty, self-preservative kind of unconsciousness for the vast, vital Mystery of Life. To the Self

System, this can only seem perverse, reckless, even insane. To the world-body-brain-mind-self system as a whole, this deal is nothing other than an opportunity to reclaim its scientific and spiritual truth.

Notes

Foreword

1 See Ken Wilber's *Quantum Questions*, Shambhala, Boulder, CO, 1984.

Chapter 1

2 This is contentious; but see Daniel Goleman's review of meditative techniques in *The Meditative Mind*, Aquarian, London, 1990.

Chapter 2

3 The intellectual soup of speculations about the origins of life is far richer, these days, than the primordial soup itself. Currently there is open season on the question of how living matter came into being. What I present here is just one version to set the stage for the discussions that will follow. However much this early story turns out to be flawed or incomplete, it is useful if only to remind ourselves of the extent to which mind has its roots in simple biochemistry—for mind itself would prefer to deny its humble origins, and to disown the physical family of which it remains an integral member.

4 Recent exploration of the deepest beds of the ocean have discovered hot vents, where the crust is thin, and where rich concentrations of organic molecules, and even a range of bacteria, survive at temperatures of 300 degrees Centigrade. It is possible that some forms, or some of the ingredients, for life could have first been synthesized here. And it has also been suggested that the Earth may have been provided with 'starter-packs' of amino acids that were brought here by meteorites. But I shall stick here to the broad outlines of the conventional 'soup' story.

5 A.G. Cairns-Smith, *Seven Clues to the Origin of Life*, Cambridge University Press, Cambridge, 1985.

6 Lynn Margulis and Dorian Sagan, *Microcosmos*, Summit Books, New York, 1986.

7 See Francisco Varela, Ewan Thompson and Eleanor Rosch, *The Embodied Mind*, MIT Press, Cambridge, MA, 1991.

8 Cairns-Smith, op. cit., p103. He also has given us a beautifully precise definition of the process of natural selection itself. '*If* you have things that are reproducing their kind; *if* there are sometimes random variations, nevertheless, in the offspring; *if* such variations can be inherited; *if* some such variations can sometimes confer an advantage on their owners; *if* there is competition between the reproducing entities—*if* there is an overproduction so that not all will be able to survive to produce offspring themselves—then these entities will get better at reproducing their kind. Nature acts as a selective breeder in these circumstances; the stock cannot help but improve.' (op. cit., p2)

9 Cairns-Smith, op. cit., p3.

10 Reported by Jeremy Cherfas in 'The Difficulties of Darwinism', *New Scientist*, 17 May 1984. For the original essay, see Stephen Jay Gould, *The Panda's Thumb*, W.W. Norton, New York, 1980.

11 This example comes from Cairns-Smith, op. cit., p59.

Chapter 3

12 Lancelot Law Whyte, *The Next Development in Man*, Cresset Press, Chicago, 1944. p16.

13 Sir Charles Sherrington, *Man on His Nature*, Cambridge University Press, Cambridge, 1963.

14 Sherrington, ibid., p77, 150.

15 Sherrington, ibid., p79.

16 A review of systems thinking, and its relation to social as well as scientific areas of understanding, is in preparation by Fritjof Capra.

17 See Rodolfo Llinas, '"Mindness" as a State of the Brain', in Colin Blakemore and Susan Greenfield (eds), *Mindwaves: Thoughts on Intelligence, Identity and Consciousness*, Basil Blackwell, Oxford, 1987.

18 Llinas, ibid.

19 For example by Daniel Dennett in *Consciousness Explained*, Viking, London, 1992.

20 The idea of mind as a distributed phenomenon is explored more fully in Varela et al, op. cit.; and in an even more radical (though less intelligible) way by Gregory Bateson in, for example, his *Mind and Nature*, Wildwood House, London, 1979. Bateson argues for the use of the word 'mind' as a feature not just of bodily systems but of social and cultural ones as well.

21 Candace Pert, quoted in Schumacher College lectures by Fritjof Capra, May 1992.

22 See Varela et al, op. cit.

Chapter 4

23 Patricia Churchland, *Neurophilosophy*, MIT Press, Cambridge, MA, 1986. pp406-7.

24 Donald O. Hebb, *The Organisation of Behaviour*, Wiley, New York, 1949.

25 'Any frequently repeated, particular stimulation will lead to the slow development of a 'cell assembly', a diffuse structure...capable of acting briefly as a closed system, delivering facilitation to other such systems....Each assembly action may be aroused by a preceding assembly, by a sensory event, or—more normally—by both....The assumption in brief is that a growth process accompanying synaptic activity makes the synapse more readily traversed....When an axon of cell A is near enough to excite a cell B and repeatedly or persistently takes part in firing it, some growth process or metabolic change takes place in one or both cells such that A's efficiency, as one of the cells firing B, increases.' Hebb, op. cit., pp xix and 60-62.

There are a variety of other 'rules' for deciding how patterns of facilitation and inhibition are to develop within such a network. Some of the 'neo-connectionists' have worked with 'Instruction Rules', in which the system is 'told', in some way, that a particular pattern of excitation across its tentacles is 'exemplary'. Or you might weight the amount of facilitation/inhibition assigned to a particular junction, depending on whether that 'tickle spot' was involved in an overall pattern of movement that was, in some way, 'successful', as measured, for example, by the disparity between a prediction and the observed event; or between an intention and an observation. See for instance Marcel Kinsbourne, 'Field Theory of Consciousness', in Anthony Marcel and Eduardo Bisiach (eds), *Consciousness in Contemporary Science*, Clarendon Press, Oxford, 1988.

26 Hebb, op. cit.

27 Varela et al, op. cit.

28 Edward de Bono's *The Mechanism of Mind* (Penguin, Harmondsworth, 1971) has one of his neat images to make this clear. Imagine you have a tray of jelly ('jello' in the US), representing the brain-mind network, and 'learning' involves dropping a teaspoonful of hot liquid onto it at various places which you then suck up with a sponge, leaving a shallow impression in the jelly. If you drop a second spoonful near the first one, the liquid will run down into the first depression and deepen it, rather than making a new hole of its own. Thus concepts are born.

29 Jerome S. Bruner and Leo Postman, 'On the Perception of Incongruity: A Paradigm', *Journal of Personality*, 1949, vol 18, 206-23.

Chapter 5

30 Herbert Simon, 'The Architecture of Complexity', *Proceedings of the American Philosophical Association*, 1962, vol 106, pp467-82.

31 See for example his contribution to Arthur Koestler and John Smithies (eds), *Beyond Reductionism* (Hutchinson, London, 1969). This fascinating collection of papers, based on a conference held at Alpbach in Austria in 1968, is one of the earlier attempts to explore the systems approach to biological organisms.

32 Historically, much effort has gone into trying to find out which subsystems inhabit which bits of the brain, anatomically. To this day, there are those who argue that 'planning' happens in the frontal lobes, for example, or that consciousness is associated with the temporal cortex, and memory with the hippocampus. I am not going to enter this theoretical minefield here. The discussion that follows concerns *functional* subsystems—which may not be clearly anatomically localized at all.

33 'Minitheories' is the term I prefer for these sub-routines, and which I have used elsewhere. Similar ideas have been called 'schemas' or 'schemata' by Sir Frederick Bartlett (in *Remembering*, Cambridge University Press, 1932), Jean Piaget (see for example *The Child's Construction of Reality*, Routledge and Kegan Paul, London, 1958), and many other more recent writers. Other allied terms are 'scripts', used by Roger Schank (*Tell Me a Story*, Scribner's, New York, 1991), and 'frames' by Marvin Minsky (*The Society of Mind*, Picador, London, 1988).

34 Kinsbourne, in Marcel and Bisiach (eds), op. cit., p229.

Chapter 6

35 Nicholas Humphrey, *The Inner Eye*, Faber and Faber, London, 1986.

36 See Helena Norberg-Hodge, *Ancient Futures: Learning from Ladakh*, Element Books, Shaftesbury, 1991.

37 See Richard Byrne and Andrew Whiten (eds), *Machiavellian Intelligence: Social Expertise and the Evolution of Intellect in Monkeys, Apes and Humans*, Clarendon Press, Oxford, 1988.

38 Frans de Waal, 'Chimpanzee Politics', in Byrne and Whiten, op. cit., pp122-3.

39 In general, an animal's *attention* often gives a good clue as to its *intention*. So I can become an apparent mind-reader by learning to predict what you are likely to do next, on the basis of the unintentional indications you are letting slip as to what you are currently finding interesting. Human babies are almost from the word go experts in attending, especially to the signals of other people's (their mother's) attention. They need to be, because

in order to begin to learn language, they have to be able to figure out what their mother is talking *about*, and this means, often, being able to look at her eyes and figure out along what line of *her* sight the object she is talking about must lie: quite a sophisticated geometrical construction. Research on this ability has been reported by Michael Scaife and Jerome Bruner, 'The capacity for joint visual attention in the infant', *Nature*, 1975, vol 253, pp265–6.

40 Nicholas Humphrey, *Consciousness Regained*, Oxford University Press, 1983, p28.

41 Humphrey, ibid., p4.

42 Oxford ethologist John Krebs describes the evolution of quite complex signalling systems between birds, for example, some of which seem odd until seen in their evolutionary context. 'If you watch a pair of fighting cocks engaged in battle, one may suddenly break off from the physical contest of pecking and chasing to preen or peck at the ground, actions that are as incongruous and out of context as would be a boxer combing his hair or eating a snack in the middle of a championship fight'. Such actions, Krebs argues, are evolved from the natural behavioural accompaniments to states of internal conflict, fear or interruption–which became, over the course of evolutionary time, ritualized, stereotyped and exaggerated, and were 'offered', so to speak, to potential allies or opponents as either accurate or deliberately misleading clues as to how you were likely to act. The fighting cock preening his feathers is more like Muhammad Ali dropping his guard and clowning in front of Joe Frazier; it is an encouragement to the opponent to underestimate his skill or commitment, and so make a false move. See John Krebs, 'The Evolution of Animal Signals', in Blakemore and Greenfield (eds), op. cit., p163.

43 Dunbar argues that there is still evidence in the modern world for 150 being about the right size for a workable human community. The smallest independent unit in most modern armies is the company, which numbers 130–150. Business 'companies' often need to restructure into a more formal hierarchy when they exceed the 150 mark. The Hutterites, North American religious fundamentalists, regard 150 as the maximum effective size for one of their farming communities, their reason being that, when a group grows beyond this level, they cannot maintain a harmonious (and crime-free) community by virtue of peer pressure alone, but have to introduce some form of penal and legal code. This section follows quite closely (though not completely) the argument in Dunbar's article 'Why Gossip is Good for You', *New Scientist*, 21 November 1992, pp28–31.

44 This point is made forcibly by Brother David Steindl-Rast in his dialogue with scientist Fritjof Capra, *Belonging to the Universe*, HarperSanFrancisco, 1991. For the newborn baby, the urge to belong, to be accepted, to become, as quickly as possible a fully paid-up member of the Social Club, is as strong, and as obvious, as the urge to suckle. He wants nothing more than

to be shown how to dance with his elder partners, and there is nothing more upsetting than to find his tentative trust in the predictability and reciprocity of these encounters shattered. A child of a deaf mother, for instance, can easily learn his mother's dance, though its rhythm is different from that of a hearing mother. But when his mother is depressed, she may fail to pick up the baby's cues, or to give out any clear signals of her own, and then the baby becomes agitated and, if the dance fails to reappear soon, the baby's well-being, and even his cognitive development, are put at risk. For a good review of this area of research, see Daniel Stern, *The Interpersonal World of the Child*, Basic Books, New York, 1985.

Chapter 7

45 L.S. Vygotsky, *Mind in Society: The Development of Higher Mental Processes* (edited by M. Cole et al), Harvard University Press, 1978.

46 This clever and plausible 'Just So Story' crops up in several of Daniel Dennett's writings. I first became aware of it in a book of his that must be a contender for the All-Time Best Title Award, *Elbow Room: On The Varieties of Free Will Worth Wanting*, Clarendon Press, Oxford, 1983.

47 Vygotsky, op. cit.

48 Andy Clark and Annette Karmiloff-Smith, 'The Cognizer's Innards: A Psychological and Philosophical Perspective on the Development of Thought', undated pre-publication paper. Also Annette Karmiloff-Smith, *Beyond Modularity*, Bradford/MIT Press, Cambridge, MA, 1992.

49 For a review of this 'relational' approach to semantics, see P.M. Churchland, *Matter and Consciousness*, MIT Press, Cambridge, MA, 1984.

50 De Bono, op. cit., p20.

51 Aldous Huxley, quoted by R.E. Kantor, 'The affective domain and beyond', *Journal for the Study of Consciousness*, 1970, vol 3, 20–42.

Chapter 8

52 Dennett, *Consciousness Explained*, op. cit.

53 The French writer Lacan has tried, albeit obscurely, to make this crucial point. One commentator, Stephen Frosh of the University of London, says: 'For Lacan the human subject is constructed in and through language. This does *not* imply that there is any preexistent subjectivity which learns to express itself in the words made available to it by the language, but rather that the initially "absent" subject becomes concrete only through its positioning in a meaning-system....We are constructed according to the possibilities offered to us by words...Lacan's principal project is to show us how

what appears to be our central reality, our "selfhood", is actually constructed (as) we become inserted into the symbolic order of culture. The process is in important ways one of alienation'. Stephen Frosh, *The Politics of Psychoanalysis*, Macmillan, Basingstoke, 1987. See also J. Lacan, 'The function and field of speech and language in psychoanalysis', in his *Ecrits: A Selection*, Tavistock, London, 1977.

54 If you have difficulty empathizing with the predicament, I recommend the books by the English spiritual teacher Douglas Harding: for example, *The Little Book of Life and Death*, Arkana, London, 1988; and *Head Off Stress*, Arkana, London, 1990.

55 For the link between scientific scholarship and patriarchal language, see Brian Easlea, *Fathering the Unthinkable*, Pluto Press, London, 1983.

56 Kurt Vonnegut, *Galapagos*, Jonathan Cape, London, 1985.

Chapter 9

57 The 'catch' of such times, it has been argued, is that the lucky species becomes, eventually, fat, lazy and overpopulated, genetically stagnant, disinclined to learn and wasteful of resources, so that its members, by their attitudes, both hasten the ending of the Good Times, and are unprepared when they arrive. The history of the world can be seen as a catalogue of departed species that Adapted Too Little, and Woke Up Too Late. The collapse of the Easter Island civilization is the standard cautionary tale. See Clive Ponting, *A Green History of the World*, Sinclair-Stevenson, London, 1991.

58 Marshall Sahlins, quoted by Nicholas Xenos, *Scarcity and Modernity*, Routledge, London, 1989, p2.

59 Quoted in Xenos, ibid., pp25–6.

60 Glynn Isaac, 'Aspects of Human Evolution', in D.S. Bendall (ed), *Evolution from Molecules to Men*, Cambridge University Press, 1983, p533.

61 See Michael Gazzaniga, *The Social Brain*, Basic Books, New York, 1985.

62 Unfortunately we seem hell-bent on systematically ignoring and squashing this basic reflective capacity in schools, and then developing such hectic adult lifestyles that it has no chance to recover.

63 Bhagwan Shree (later Osho) Rajneesh, lecture 'The Heart Sutra, Number 10', Shree Rajneesh Ashram, Pune, India, 1986.

64 Vonnegut, op. cit.

65 Colvinaux, 1980; quoted by Parker in Butterworth et al, *Evolution and Developmental Psychology*, Harvester, Brighton, 1985, p93.

66 For some of these stories, see Paul Watzlawick, *How Real is Real?*, Vintage Books, New York, 1977.

67 Much research interest has recently centred on the young child's developing ability to take the perspective of others in this way; and it has been strongly suggested that *autistic* children are deficient in precisely this ability. See Simon Baron-Cohen, 'Precursors to a theory of mind: understanding attention in others', in Andrew Whiten (ed), *Natural Theories of Mind*, Blackwell, Oxford, 1991.

68 Humphrey, *Consciousness Regained*, op. cit.

69 Marvin Minsky, *The Society of Mind*, Picador, London, 1988.

Chapter 10

70 Nicholas Freeling, *A City Solitary*, William Heinemann, London, 1985.

71 Quoted in Guy Claxton, *Wholly Human*, Routledge and Kegan Paul, London, 1981.

72 For example the controversy about the correlation of wisdom with ageing continues to rage unresolved: see R.J. Sternberg (ed), *Wisdom*, Cambridge University Press, 1990.

73 Xenos, op. cit.

74 Xenos, op. cit., p5.

75 Quoted by Xenos, ibid., p25.

76 I should point out that Apple changed its pricing policy in the early 1990s, making this parallel less exact now than it was a few years ago.

77 Quoted by Xenos, op. cit., pp23-4.

Chapter 11

78 Dennett, *Consciousness Explained*, op. cit.

79 G.R. Goethals and R.F. Reckman, 'The Perception of Consistency in Attitudes', *Journal of Experimental Social Psychology*, 1973, *9*, 491–501.

80 Bartlett, op. cit.

81 Michael Gazzaniga, *The Social Brain*, Basic Books, New York, 1985; and *Mind Matters*, Houghton Mifflin, Boston, 1988.

82 The most famous exponent of this social-familial approach being the British psychiatrist R.D. Laing, most notably in his *The Divided Self*, Penguin, Harmondsworth, 1965.

83 Gregory Bateson, one of the most profound thinkers about the relation between the brain and madness, used this example at a lecture at the Institute of Contemporary Arts in London not long before his death. See his *Mind and Nature*, Fontana, London, 1980.

84 Gazzaniga, *Mind Matters*, op. cit., p75.

85 Julian Jaynes, *The Origin of Consciousness in the Breakdown of the Bicameral Mind*, Houghton Mifflin, New York, 1976.

86 The existence of 'sub-personalities' is now widely accepted. See for example John Rowan, *Subpersonalities*, Routledge, London, 1988; and Hubert Hermans, Harry Kempen and Rens van Loon, 'The Dialogical Self', *American Psychologist*, 1992, vol 47, 23–33.

87 The term 'centre of narrative gravity' comes from that inveterate phrase-maker Daniel Dennett, in his *Consciousness Explained*, op. cit.

88 Jacob Needleman, 'Psychiatry and the Sacred', in John Welwood (ed), *Awakening the Heart*, Shambhala, Boulder, Colorado, 1983.

Chapter 12

89 Patricia S. Churchland, *Neurophilosophy*, Bradford/MIT Press, Cambridge, MA, 1986.

90 This has been called the 'all hands on deck' response by German psychologist Odmar Neumann. See his paper 'Some aspects of phenomenal consciousness and their possible functional correlates', presented at the Zentrum fur Interdisziplinare Forschung, Bielefeld, Germany, May 1990; quoted by Dennett in *Consciousness Explained*, op. cit.

91 Kinsbourne, 'Integrated Field Theory of Consciousness', op. cit.

92 Lancelot Law Whyte, *The Unconscious before Freud*, Basic Books, New York, 1960. For the curative action of fevers see also Richard Gerber, *Vibrational Medicine*, Bear & Co., Santa Fe, 1988, p83: '...it now appears that fevers can be good for an individual with a bacterial illness. It has been shown that the white blood cells, our immunologic defenders, eat and destroy bacteria more efficiently at higher body temperatures. (White blood cells have recently been found to release a substance called "leukocyte pyrogen" which *induces* high fevers)...[fevers] may be produced by the body as an adaptive strategy toward returning the system to a state of homeostatic balance and health.' (Thanks to Rosemary Staheyeff for drawing this to my attention.)

93 This is one of the key components of the 'stress reaction', as described by Hans Selye, *The Stress of Life*, McGraw-Hill, New York, 1956.

94 Susan Mineka, 'Selective associations in the origins and maintenance of phobic fears'. Paper delivered at the 25th International Congress of Psychology, Brussels, 1992.

95 Sam Keen, *Fire in the Belly*, Piatkus, London, 1992.

Chapter 13

96 Many authors recently have tried to identify 'the' fundamental emotions, out of which the complex shadings of human feeling could have been constructed, though it boils down in the end to a matter of definition. One such attempt, not dissimilar from the approach I am taking here, is offered by Keith Oatley and Philip Johnson-Laird, 'Towards a Cognitive Theory of Emotions', *Cognition and Emotion*, 1987, *1*, 29–50. See also a paper by Oatley, 'Reports from the Self: Assessing Emotions and Intentions', presented at the Annual Conference of the British Psychological Society, Bournemouth, April, 1990.

97 Dennett, *Consciousness Explained*, op. cit., p181.

98 See Jay Haley, *Uncommon Therapy*, W.W. Norton, New York, 1973.

99 On altruism in babies, see Jerome Bruner, 'The transactional self', in J. Bruner and H. Haste (eds), *Making Sense*, Methuen, London, 1987; or Daniel Stern, *The Interpersonal World of the Child*, op. cit.

100 James Hillman and Michael Ventura, in their *We've Had a Hundred Years of Psychotherapy and the World Is Getting Worse*, Harper-SanFrancisco, 1992 suggest that the prevalence of depression in the Western world is not a matter of individual psychopathology, but a cry of outrage from our ecological depths about the state of the world.

Chapter 14

101 Whyte, *The Unconscious Before Freud*, op. cit.

102 John Donne, *Devotions*, XVII.

103 Whyte, *The Unconscious Before Freud*, op. cit.

104 Kathleen Wilkes, '-, yishi, duh, um, and consciousness', in Marcel and Bisiach, op. cit.

105 Whyte, *The Unconscious Before Freud*, op. cit. The following quotations are borrowed for the most part from Whyte's masterly historical study.

106 Albert Einstein, *Ideas and Opinions*, Souvenir Press, London, 1973.

107 René Descartes, *Meditations*. See S. Haldane and G.T.R. Ross (eds), *The Philosophical Works of Descartes*, Cambridge University Press, 1967.

108 John Locke, *An Essay Concerning Human Understanding*, (ed. A.C. Fraser), Dover, New York, 1959.

109 Whyte, *The Unconscious Before Freud*, op. cit., p71.

110 Hillman and Ventura, op. cit.

111 C.G. Jung, *The Undiscovered Self*, Routledge and Kegan Paul, London, 1958, pp48–9.

112 James Hillman, *Insearch: Psychology and Religion*, Spring Publications, Dallas, Texas, 1967.

113 Quoted by Gazzaniga, *Mind Matters*, op. cit., p17.

Chapter 15

114 Andrew Matthews, 'Controlled and automatic aspects of emotional processing'. Paper presented to the 25th International Congress of Psychology, Brussels, June 1992.

115 Much of this research is summarized in Norman Dixon's *Preconscious Processing*, John Wiley, London, 1981.

116 This story of inhibition and deviation fits well with the story of the brain that I have been developing in this book. It also builds on a seminal article by British psychologist Vernon Hamilton, 'Information-processing Aspects of Denial: Some Tentative Formulations', in S. Breznitz (ed), *The Denial of Stress*, International Universities Press, New York, 1983.

117 To give a well-worked-out physiological example, there are two systems that regulate the uptake of sugar from the blood-stream by the cells: one of them promotes the import of sugar into the cells; the other promotes the export of sugar back into the blood. If there were only the uptake system, cells could extract too much sugar from the blood, causing a dangerous drop in the blood sugar level, resulting perhaps in a hypoglycaemic coma. In a healthy person, when there is a risk of this happening, the export system kicks in, swiftly restoring the blood sugar to a safe level. But in various forms of diabetes, one or other of these systems malfunctions, and the delicate control of this balance is lost.

118 Daniel Goleman says, 'early in evolution this brain alarm went off when a sabre-toothed tiger came into view. In modern times, a meeting with the accountants will do.' Goleman, *Vital Lies, Simple Truths,* Simon and Schuster, New York, 1985, p32.

119 David Livingstone, *Missionary Travels*, as quoted by Daniel Goleman, op. cit. The account of the system that turns on unconsciousness, and turns off pain, is largely based on Goleman's synthesis of the research findings.

Chapter 16

120 One of the reasons why Darwin's theory of natural selection has been underestimated by its critics is that it is so hard to grasp the power of a principle that works, in many cases, so imperceptibly slowly, a point forcefully made by Richard Dawkins in his books *The Selfish Gene* and *The Blind Watchmaker*, op. cit.

121 Richard Gregory is perhaps the best-known contemporary demonstrator of the 'theory laden-ness' of perception: see his book *The Intelligent Eye* (Weidenfeld and Nicholson, London, 1970).

122 This phenomenon is discussed in a paper by Brian Simpson, 'The Escalator Effect', *The Psychologist*, October 1992, pp462-3.

123 Goleman, op. cit.

124 This is how some pickpockets work. They jostle you, creating a 'harmless' short-term emergency—and while you are still sorting that one out, and your vigilance for other sensations is reduced, the accomplice is able to lift your wallet with a greater margin of error.

125 I have compiled this definition from the entries in *The Shorter Oxford Dictionary*, *Chambers Dictionary* and *The Penguin Dictionary*.

126 Gabriel Stolzenberg, 'Can an Inquiry into the Foundations of Mathematics Tell Us Anything Interesting about Mind?', in P. Watzlawick (ed), *The Invented Reality*, W.W. Norton, New York, 1984.

Chapter 17

127 Keen, op. cit., p33.

128 See 'Preying on the AIDS Patients', *Newsweek*, 1 June 1987; and 'The AIDS Underground', *Newsweek*, 7 August 1989.

129 James Hillman and Michael Ventura write passionately about the myth of endless self-improvement in their book *We've Had a Hundred Years of Psychotherapy and the World's Getting Worse*, op. cit.

130 Ivan Illich, *Medical Nemesis: The Expropriation of Health*, Penguin, Harmondsworth, 1977.

131 See Edward Goldsmith, *The Way: An Ecological Worldview*, Rider, London, 1992.

132 See Warwick Fox, *Towards a Transpersonal Ecology*, Shambhala, Boulder, CO, 1991; Arne Naess, *Ecology, Community and Lifestyle*, Cambridge University Press, 1989.

133 See Ponting, op. cit.

134 James Lovelock, *Gaia: A New Look at Life on Earth,* Oxford University Press, 1979.

135 Norberg-Hodge, op. cit.

136 Keen, op. cit. I have drawn on his analysis of the mythology of (male) work in this section.

137 Some of these explicit formulations of belief are adapted from Gestalt therapist Marty Fromm's 'Laundry List of Marital Mishaps' (privately circulated photocopy).

Chapter 18

138 J.L. Axtell, *The Educational Writings of John Locke,* Cambridge University Press, 1968.

139 See my book *Teaching to Learn* (Cassell, London, 1991) for a more detailed résumé of these models of mind. Also John Cohen, *The Lineaments of Mind* (W.H. Freeman, Oxford, 1980); and D.J. Herrmann and R. Chaffin, *Memory in Historical Perspective* (Springer-Verlag, New York, 1988).

140 Cited by Cohen, op. cit.

141 See for instance Hubert Dreyfus, *What Computers Can't Do,* Harper and Row, New York, 1979.

142 The lines are from A.E. Housman, *Last Poems* (1922), no.12.

143 This formulation of 'suffering' and its cause are obviously very close to that provided by the First and Second Noble Truths of Buddhism.

144 Bartlett, op. cit.

145 See Elizabeth Loftus, *Eyewitness Testimony,* Harvard University Press, 1979.

146 See Derek Edwards, Jonathan Potter and David Middleton, 'Towards a Discursive Psychology of Remembering', *The Psychologist,* October, 1992.

147 See R.E. Nisbett and L. Ross, *Human Inference: Strategies and Shortcomings of Social Judgment,* Prentice Hall, Englewood Cliffs, New Jersey, 1980.

148 Ambrose Bierce, *The Devil's Dictionary,* Dover, Toronto, 1958.

149 Quoted by Daniel Dennett in his *Elbow Room: On the Varieties of Free Will Worth Wanting,* op. cit.

150 Daniel Dennett, ibid.

151 See Hillman and Ventura, op. cit., again for their powerful attack on the idea of 'growth' as a guiding principle for living.

152 The fun, of course, is to be had in trying to tell the difference. A current case-in-point is provided by Rupert Sheldrake's 'myth' (or 'theory') of 'morphic resonance', which suggests that the planet is not just an organism in the Gaia sense, capable of regulating aspects of its own 'body', but is also capable of 'learning', so that what we have taken to be 'natural laws' are actually 'habits' picked up in the course of cosmological evolution. See Rupert Sheldrake, *A New Science of Life*, Grafton, London, 1987; and *The Presence of the Past*, Vintage, New York, 1989.

Chapter 19

153 G.W. Leibniz, *New Essays on Human Understanding*.

154 The responsibility of philosophers in this regard is elegantly described by Mary Midgley in her paper 'Philosophical Plumbing', in A. Phillips Griffiths (ed), *The Impulse to Philosophise*, Cambridge University Press, 1992. She also points out the kinship with the poets.

155 J.F. Kihlstrom, T.M. Barnhardt and D.J. Tataryn, 'The Psychological Unconscious: Found, Lost and Regained', *American Psychologist*, June, 1992.

156 For the most comprehensive account of these studies, see Lawrence Weiskrantz, *Blindsight*, Clarendon Press, Oxford, 1986.

157 See Lawrence Weiskrantz, 'Some Contributions of Neuropsychology to Vision and Memory to the Problem of Consciousness', in Marcel and Bisiach (eds), op. cit.

158 A.J. Marcel, 'Slippage in the Unity of Consciousness', in CIBA Foundation Symposium No 174, *Experimental and Theoretical Studies of Consciousness*, Wiley, Chichester, 1993.

159 A reaction at the time, quoted by E.F. Loftus and M.R. Klinger, 'Is the Unconscious Smart or Dumb?', *American Psychologist*, June 1992.

160 See A. Greenwald, E. Spangenberg, A. Pratkanis and J. Eskenazi, 'Double-blind tests of subliminal self-help audiotapes', *Psychological Science*, 2, 119–122, 1991.

161 This example is also noted by Anthony Greenwald in his paper 'New Look 3', *American Psychologist*, 1992, vol 47, No 6, 766–779.

162 Ernest Hilgard, *Divided Consciousness*, John Wiley, New York, 1977.

163 This report is quoted from Daniel Goleman, op. cit.

164 Quoted by Goleman, ibid.

165 This interpretation has been suggested by Helen Crawford, 'Attention and Disattention: Neurological Processes Correlated with Hypnotizability', paper presented to the 25th International Congress of Psychology, Brussels, July 1992.

166 W. Mainord, B. Rath and F. Barnett, 'Anaesthesia and Suggestion', paper presented to the American Psychological Association Annual Conference, August 1983; as reported by Goleman in *Vital Lies, Simple Truths*, op. cit.

167 H. Bennett, H. Davis and J. Giannini, 'Posthypnotic Suggestions during General Anaesthesia and Subsequent Dissociated Behaviour', paper presented to the Society for Clinical and Experimental Hypnosis, October, 1981; as reported by Goleman, ibid.

168 A review of these experiments is provided in Pawel Lewicki, Thomas Hill and Maria Czyzewska, 'Non-Conscious Acquisition of Information', *American Psychologist*, June 1992, Vol 47, No 6, 796–801.

169 B. Libet (1985), 'Unconscious cerebral initiative and the role of conscious will in voluntary action', *Behavioral and Brain Sciences*, 8, 529–566.

Chapter 20

170 Thich Nhat Hanh, *The Heart of Understanding*, Parallax Press, Berkeley, CA, 1988.

171 David Bohm, *Wholeness and the Implicate Order*, Routledge and Kegan Paul, London, 1980.

172 From *Yeats: Selected Poetry*, Pan, London, 1974.

173 Quoted in Cohen and Phipps, *The Common Experience*, Rider, London, 1980, pp10–11.

174 Quoted in Cohen and Phipps, ibid, p21.

175 William James, *The Varieties of Religious Experience*, Collins/Fontana, London, 1974, p70.

176 William James, ibid., p385.

177 Extracts from a poem called 'Please call me by my true names' by the Vietnamese Zen scholar and teacher Thick Nhat Hanh. From his book *Being Peace*, Parallax Press, Berkeley, CA, 1987.

178 For a discussion of the relationship between Self and Flow, see M. Csikszentmihalyi, *Optimal Experience*, Cambridge University Press, 1988.

179 William James, op. cit., p300.

180 Rainer Maria Rilke, quoted in Robert Bly, *Iron John*, Element Books, Shaftesbury, 1991, p134.

181 Alfred Lord Tennyson, 'The Two Voices'.

182 C.G. Jung, *Civilisation in Transition*, Collected Edition, Routledge and Kegan Paul, London, 1964, para. 565

183 The quotations in this section are drawn from a number of sources. Anne Bancroft, *The Luminous Vision*, Unwin Hyman, London, 1989; Cohen and Phipps, op. cit.; J. Ferguson, *An Encyclopedia of Mysticism*, Thames and Hudson, London, 1976; R.A. Gilbert, *The Elements of Mysticism*, Element Books, Shaftesbury, 1991.

184 This paradoxical imagery of the dark-that-is-light recurs throughout this tradition. See for instance the poetry of the eighteenth-century Welsh doctor Henry Vaughan:

There is in God, some say
A deep but dazzling darkness: as men here
Say it is late and dusky, because they
See not all clear.
O for that night! where I in him
Might live invisible and dim.

185 All quotations in this passage are taken from D.T. Suzuki, *The Zen Doctrine of No Mind*, Rider, London, 1949.

186 John Blofeld (ed), *The Zen Teachings of Huang Po*, Grove Press, New York, 1958.

Chapter 21

187 Suzuki, op. cit., p75.

188 Robin Skynner, 'Psychotherapy and Spiritual Tradition', in John Welwood (ed), *Awakening the Heart*, op. cit.

189 For a psychological account of the attractions of football 'hooliganism', see Elizabeth Rosser, Peter Marsh and Rom Harré, *The Rules of Disorder*, Routledge & Kegan Paul, London, 1978.

190 Marcel Kinsbourne, 'Integrated Field Theory of Consciousness', in Marcel and Bisiach (eds), op. cit., p246.

191 From Paul Reps, *Zen Flesh, Zen Bones*, Penguin, Harmondsworth, 1975.

Index